D1587552

THE PERSIAN EMPIRE

THE PERSIAN EMPIRE

EMPIRE
A HISTORY

LINDSAY ALLEN

THE BRITISH MUSEUM PRESS

© 2005 Lindsay Allen

Lindsay Allen has asserted the right to be identified
as the author of this work

First published in 2005 by The British Museum Press
A division of The British Museum Company Ltd
38 Russell Square, London WC1B 3QQ

www.britishmuseum.co.uk

A catalogue record for this book is available
from the British Library

ISBN-13: 978-0-7141-1154-4

ISBN-10: 0-7141-1154-6

Designed and typeset in Bembo
and Trajan by Harry Green

Maps by Technical Art Services

Printed in China by C&C Offset Printing Co., Ltd

ACHAEMENID DYNASTY
(*c.*559–330 BCE)

Cyrus II	*c.*559–530
Cambyses II	530–522
Bardiya	522
Darius I	522–486
Xerxes I	486–465
Artaxerxes I	465–424/3
Xerxes II	424/3
Darius II	423–405/4
Artaxerxes II	405/4–359
Artaxerxes III	359–338
Artaxerxes IV (Arses)	338–336
Darius III	336–331
Artaxerxes V	331

CONTENTS

INTRODUCTION

Unhappy Persia, that in former age
Hast been the seat of mighty conquerors,
That, in their prowess and their policies,
Have triumph'd over Afric and the bounds
Of Europe where the sun dares scarce appear
                    Christopher Marlowe, *Tamburlaine pt. 1*

'The Persian empire' is how we refer here to the rule of a dynasty from southern Iran, who politically united the territory of the ancient Near East for over two centuries between the mid sixth and the late third century BCE. The Persian 'Great King, King of Kings' himself saw his rule in terms of the many peoples who acknowledged his power and the far-flung resources at his disposal. The survival of this unity rested on communications, diplomacy, regional ambitions and, occasionally, the persuasiveness of a large army. The territory covered, from the coasts of Asia Minor and Libya to the deserts of Central Asia and the Indus river system, is a massive area to consider as a cultural or political whole; it includes all or part of a large number of modern nation states. To present the full diversity of this region in ancient times is impossible, on the basis of the data currently available, but this book is intended to provide an introduction to the history of the empire. The history of the rise and fall of Persian power originally reached modern western consciousness through Classical and Biblical traditions, a story that influenced laments such as that of Christopher Marlowe (written in the 1590s CE and cited above). This narrative follows the reigns of kings, from the emergence of the empire's founder Cyrus the Great to the intrusion of the invader, Alexander of Macedon, who destroyed the ruling power structure.

The specialized study of the culture and politics of the empire through evidence unearthed from within its bounds, whether a contemporary text or an archaeological artefact, has developed much more recently. An international academic community spanning the number of disciplines concerned with this subject continues to raise new questions, opinions and evidence. There is great potential in this exciting field for discovering new insights into the ancient world, as evidence emerges from the multiple languages and cultures that made up the empire. The following comments outline some of the conventional categories and definitions used as the building blocks for writing about the period.

TERMINOLOGY

'As the herald made his proclamation, it is said that Cyrus asked of those present who, among the Greeks, were these Lacedaemonians, and how many of them were there …?' (Herodotus, 1.153). The campaigning king Cyrus asks the questions relevant to both conquerors and historians everywhere. The language of Near Eastern scholarship includes a multitude of geographical and ethnic terms derived from various languages; used to orientate us in the ancient world, the usage and definition of these terms can also create confusion and disagreement (not least about the relevance of the traditional phrase 'Near East', for example, used for roughly the area called 'Middle East' in modern terms).

The first Persian empire is usually called the Achaemenid empire, in order to distinguish it from the later Parthian and Sasanian Persian empires (c.171 BCE–224 CE and 224–651 CE), which also originated in Iran and covered large tracts of the same territory. The name 'Achaemenid' (generally pronounced 'A-*kee*-mĕn-id', also occasionally seen spelled as 'Achaimenid' or in the form 'Achaemenian') comes from the dynastic ancestor claimed by the family of the ruling kings from c.520 BCE onwards; used as a general adjective, it commonly refers to things originating within the political and cultural milieu of the court and ruling system around the king. The word is in fact a simplified Greek version of the Old Persian word *Haxamanishiya*. Similarly, we tend to refer to Darius rather than *Dariyavaush*, Xerxes rather than *Xshayarsha* and Artaxerxes instead of *Artaxshaça*. The Greek versions continue to be used in European languages, since they are familiar from hundreds of years of Classical scholarship, compared to the two hundred years during which Old Persian has been known.

'Persia' derives ultimately from the Greek and Latin simplified transliteration of the original Persian 'Parsa' (*Persai* for the place, and *Perses* or *Persis* for a Persian). As a term referring specifically to southern Iran (in the area of the modern administrative province of Fars) it also surfaces first in Old Persian in 521–520 BCE, although it may appear in other languages as an ethnic or geographical title before then.[1] 'Mede' and 'Median' also came into European languages from Classical texts and Greek and Latin translations of the Bible. The Greek *mēdos* originates in the Persian word *mada*, which in royal inscriptions designates a separate ethnic group subject to the king; Greek and Biblical texts often identify Persians and Medes so closely as to treat them as the same, both because of their linguistic and geographical proximity and because of traditions which placed the origin of Persian power in Media.

'Persian' is also used by modern scholars for the first language of the Achaemenid kings, Old Persian (distinguishing it from the later forms, Middle or Pahlavi and Modern Persian). But the one ancient reference to the language in Old Persian in fact calls it *ariya* or Aryan. The word's negative, twentieth-century association with Nazism has little to do with its ancient usage to designate peoples using a mutually comprehensible Indo-Iranian language, who perhaps held an idea of shared kinship. *Ariya* in Old Persian is the ultimate origin of the modern name for the country and people of Iran. Writers about the ancient world use 'Iranian' as a geographical term (for the plateau stretching between the Zagros mountains and the Kopet Dagh, the modern border with Turkmenistan), a linguistic term (for the larger language group of which Old Persian was one strand), and, less clearly, as a generic term referring to material culture and traditions associated with the larger spread of Iranian-speaking populations both across the plateau and further east.

Other commonly used terms mix Greek understanding of Eastern geography with traditional regional names. For example, Mesopotamia is the Greek geographical word for the area encompassed by the river systems of the Tigris and Euphrates below the Taurus mountains. The area today constitutes the territory of modern Iraq and parts of Syria, Turkey and Iran. 'Mesopotamian' is used as a catch-all term for the civilizations and empires that developed in this area over the millennia. In the first millennium BCE, these included the Assyrian and Babylonian empires, whose names were derived from their respective traditional capitals. Assyria and Babylonia are used also as geographical and ethnic names for the north and south of Mesopotamia during the Achaemenid period and, in modern scholarship, as terms to designate persistent artistic or cultural features considered characteristic of those empires.

CHRONOLOGY AND ARCHAEOLOGY

The Persian or Achaemenid period is traditionally measured from *c.*550 to 330 BCE, a span defined by the first expansion of Persian-ruled territory under Cyrus II and the death of Darius III during the invasion of Alexander of Macedon. Although Alexander's crossing into Asia later became one historical measure of a new era, chronology within the Achaemenid period was based on Babylonian models, with years dated by royal reigns. These purely historical limits do not match concrete changes in material culture. For example, while Alexander may have minted new coins and destroyed cities on his invasion, leaving an immediate material impact, the styles of other types of object, such as vessels or seals, as far as it is possible to tell, changed only gradually. The Achaemenid period as a whole lies in the archaeological phase known as Iron Age IV. Within this structure, archaeological chronologies independent of strict historical dates may be worked out, using the development of ceramic styles and building layers.

'Achaemenid' is frequently used for building phases and pottery styles from sites across Iran, Turkey and the Caucasus. This usage has the advantage of balancing out an earlier lack of recognition of levels containing ceramics characteristic of the Achaemenid period, a recurrent problem which leaves us seriously lacking in archaeological data.[2] However, the definition of the term in an archaeological sense, beyond the walls of the royal palaces on which attention has traditionally been focused, remains difficult. In different regions, excavators consider different objects to be characteristic of the Achaemenid levels. In nearly all cases where 'Achaemenid' is used as an archaeological classification, it cannot be taken as referring only to a dating within strict historical limits.[3]

In regions with slightly different histories of scholarship, the terminology can change. Excavators in the Levant and Egypt favour the term 'Persian period', for example. In Egypt, this archaeological period is divided into two, the first and second Persian occupation (interrupted by sixty years of local rule by competing dynasties), producing peculiarly exclusive phases of material culture. Determining the criteria and structures for the comparison of archaeological data from different areas for the Achaemenid empire is a perpetually developing process. Most of the Achaemenid objects illustrated in this book can be assigned only generally to the fifth to fourth centuries BCE, with very little further precision, unless they are associated with a text of a particular king. Later or earlier dating can be proposed on the basis on stylistic judgements; but this subjective process can itself be inconclusive.

LANGUAGES AND TEXTS

The written texts that offer us accounts of events in the Persian empire make up a whole spectrum of authorship, function and transmission. At one end, we have immediate contemporary sources, which included inscriptions on stone (usually trilingual, written in cuneiform), imprinted texts on clay (mono- and sometimes bilingual in cuneiform) and ink-written texts on papyrus or leather (using the scripts for Aramaic, Egyptian Demotic or Greek). The multi-lingualism of the empire is reflected in the use of several languages in parallel. Royal inscriptions employ two authoritative and deep-rooted languages, Elamite and Akkadian, using wedge-shaped or cuneiform signs, which stand for letters, words or ideas, alongside one newly written language, Old Persian, in cuneiform signs adapted to symbolize syllables and words. Clay tablets were a long-established writing technology, imprinted when soft with cuneiform signs formed with a wedge stylus. The early Achaemenid administration used Elamite, a language from south-west Iran associated historically with the dynasties of the area.

Tablets from Babylonia continued to be written in Babylonian Akkadian, the written language rooted in the literary and scientific culture of Mesopotamia. Both kinds of clay tablets could be briefly annotated in ink in cursive scripts, usually in Aramaic, the Semitic language that had become widespread in imperial administration before Achaemenid rule, in the eighth to sixth centuries BCE.[4] The remaining traces of the probable large-scale use of Aramaic in the written culture of the Achaemenid empire are regrettably scanty as a result of the perishable materials used. Surviving evidence includes short inscriptions and a few collections of letters. Both these and fragments of contemporary Greek papyri are usually recovered only from the driest climates, in Egypt and parts of Central Asia.

These written sources are in some way immediately connected to a contemporary material context, by way of their location, form or find-spot. Three further groups of texts offering a view of Persian history defined by the interests of particular groups reach us through more indirect stages of creation and transmission. Greek texts by authors writing at the time were repeatedly recopied in different centres of learning from the third century BCE onwards, either as complete texts or as quoted fragments used by later writers. Hebrew and Aramaic accounts of the Jewish community's history in the empire were compiled, edited and translated (as the Torah and Pentateuch) from the Hellenistic period and are accessible in an edited form in the Old Testament. Finally, texts copied in the medieval period in Avestan Persian also contain accounts of ancient Persian courts and traditions. These religious texts are traditionally seen as preserving a long-memorized oral tradition about the origins of Zoroastrianism. Secure evidence is lacking for the date at which these were compiled, edited and written down. Containing archaic, sometimes impenetrable, language and ideas, they are part of the historical tradition of Iran and its historical communities; however, their direct relevance to the reconstruction of an ancient Persian past is often hard to establish.

None of these textual sources presents us with unambiguous, unmediated historical facts. The material in all is chosen and created through their function, or through the knowledge, interests and intentions of their authors. The texts are frequently redefined by the refractions of hundreds of years of interpretation, or merely by our own interests as modern readers. We might want to draw evidence for a wider diplomatic or economic situation from Babylonian business archives, or from tablets unearthed from two archives at Persepolis (the Persepolis Fortification Tablets and the Treasury Tablets) which carry terse administrative records, notations made for immediate reference or compiled accounts of transactions over a period of weeks or months. We also search for securely dated historical events in the databank of omens, the Astronomical Diaries, compiled on tablets by scholars who wanted to interpret the signs around them for the benefit of state or religious decisions.

These kinds of evidence are highly concentrated on their specialized purposes: such as keeping track of resources, transactions or interpreting cosmic signs. The historical information that we search for is embedded in these sources as a by-product of their function. Analysis of the context of these texts is necessary before they are mined for evidence and brought to bear on wider issues. Often this kind of study brings forth richer pictures of intellectual and cultural history than the single-minded pursuit of a historical narrative produces. The majority of private documents from Babylonia, for example, are most valuable as artefacts of social and economic history, enabling a detailed picture to be drawn of how (admittedly literate and well-off) individuals conducted aspects of their lives.

Longer Near Eastern texts such as the Babylonian Chronicle appear to offer us more recognizable narrative history, but stand in their own traditions, in this case the accumulation of a city's memory of events, which affected it. The Chronicle's focus is specific and is not usually concerned with the wider empire. Babylonian literary texts, such as the Dynastic Prophecy, which appears to refer to the Macedonian invasion, contain more of an imaginative context for historical events, rather than standing as independent correlation of them. Such prophecy texts as the Dynastic Prophecy, or parts of the book of Daniel, are a strong tradition in Near Eastern literature, and in particular permeate ideas about the past in the Achaemenid period. Again, while such literary texts may purport to predict such events as the coming of Darius or the invasion of Alexander, they reveal more about contemporary efforts to reshape the past into a comprehensible shape.

Our most garrulous informants who speak about the Persian empire as a political power wrote in Greek. Herodotus of Halicarnassus (a cosmopolitan Carian city that was within the empire) wrote his *Histories* (no later than the 430s BCE) about the history of the tumultuous relations between Persians and Greeks, culminating in the two Persian expeditions on the Greek mainland. The Cecil B. de Mille of ancient history, his work is comprehensive and hugely discursive, taking in the origins of the Scythian monarchy and the habits of Egyptian priests amongst other essential titbits (Herodotus promised an Assyrian history but, to the perplexity of future readers, did not produce it). At the same time, he focused with great precision on a vivid but highly satirical presentation of the Persian king and court. He can be read with equal measures of enjoyment, enlightenment and scepticism.[5]

Dramatic authors of the fifth and fourth centuries, including Aeschylus, Aristophanes and numerous other comic writers, exploited a similar, but sometimes less informed, vein of critical fascination with Persian power and culture. This definition of an alien culture changes somewhat in the works produced by Greeks who worked within the empire, most notably Xenophon and Ctesias of Cnidus (also a city in the satrapy of Caria), who both served different segments of the royal court. Ctesias' work is available only in fragments and summaries preserved by other writers (who also preserve pieces of several *Persika* works on Persian matters written in the fifth or fourth century). The creative, novelistic, even romantic tone of these authors' accounts of their adventures and their versions of Persian history is often the subject of stern comment by serious historians. But this colourful style of narrative suffuses nearly all treatments of Persian court history, including those in Hebrew and Avestan. While we may treat some of their reported facts with great care, the style of such stories represents truthfully the imaginative perspectives and preoccupations of the multi-ethnic society encircling the court and administration of the empire.[6] The dramatic and stylized content of the tales provided for their ancient audience exemplary entertainment based around elite ethics, rather than the tell-all facts of central government.

The same context applies to some of the material relating to Persia in the Old Testament. The books of Esther and Daniel (and the apocryphal Book of Judith) centre on the role of Jewish groups in past imperial systems, with the Persian court to the fore. The books of Ezra and Nehemiah include a comparable setting, but include models of administrative relations that also contain indirect parallels to contemporary letters.[7] The books expand on a picture of multiple interest groups of many ethnicities converging on the court. Although much of the Avestan material is purely religious in character, stories relating to the career of Zoroaster contain some parallels with the Greek, Aramaic and Hebrew stories. While all four language traditions influenced each other, the Zoroastrian tradition may represent the experience of another facet of the court population, engaging with the Achaemenid authority in a similar style. It is possible that Zoroastrian tales are related to largely lost historical traditions connected to the east of the empire, which unfortunately otherwise remains a blank page to modern historians. This void is a constant reminder of the massive gaps in our knowledge of the Achaemenid empire as it was experienced and perceived by the vast majority of its inhabitants. This guide, for now, offers an overview from the top of the pile dealing with the conquerors' 'prowess and policies'.

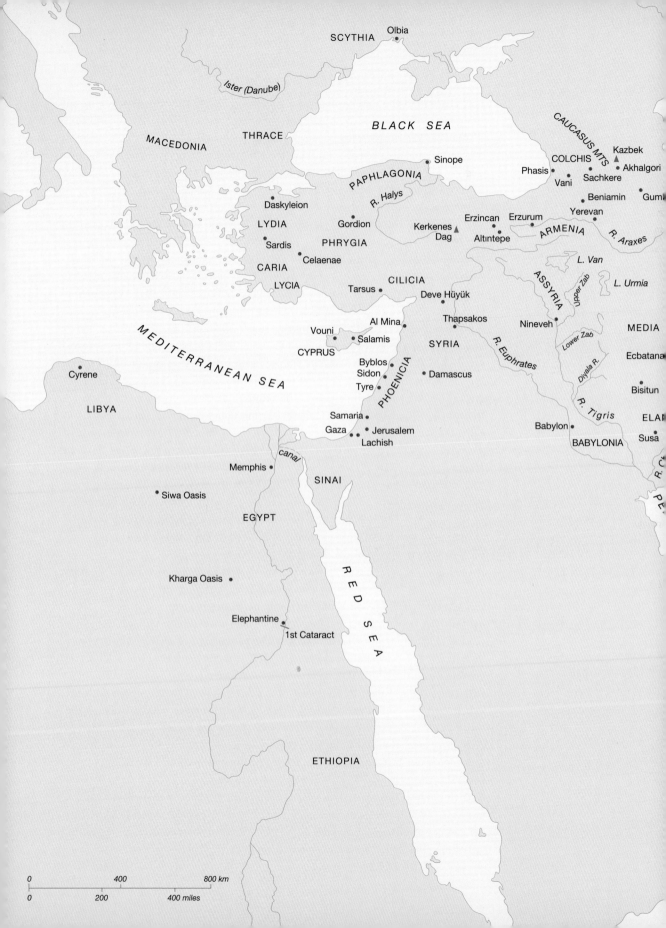

SCYTHIA

Olbia

Ister (Danube)

BLACK SEA

CAUCASUS MTS

Kazbek

THRACE

MACEDONIA

Sinope

PAPHLAGONIA

COLCHIS

Phasis

Vani

Sachkere

Akhalgori

Beniamin

Gumi

R. Halys

Daskyleion

Gordion

Kerkenes
Dag

Erzincan

Erzurum

Yerevan

LYDIA

Altıntepe

ARMENIA

R. Araxes

Sardis

PHRYGIA

L. Van

Celaenae

CARIA

ASSYRIA

L. Urmia

LYCIA

CILICIA

Tarsus

Deve Hüyük

Upper Zab

MEDIA

Vouni

Al Mina

Thapsakos

Nineveh

Ecbatana

Salamis

SYRIA

Lower Zab

CYPRUS

Diyala R.

Bisitun

Byblos

Sidon

PHOENICIA

Damascus

R. Euphrates

ELAM

Cyrene

Tyre

Babylon

Susa

LIBYA

Samaria

R. Tigris

Gaza

Jerusalem

BABYLONIA

R. C...

Lachish

canal

PE...

Memphis

SINAI

Siwa Oasis

EGYPT

Kharga Oasis

R
E
D

Elephantine

S
E
A

1st Cataract

ETHIOPIA

MEDITERRANEAN SEA

0   400   800 km

0   200   400 miles

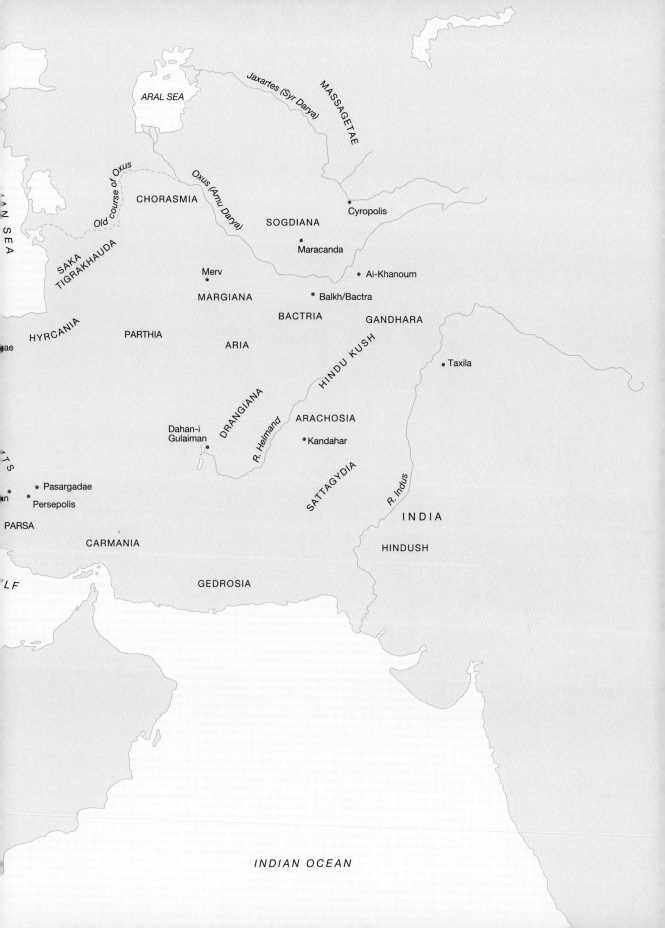

1 THE ROOTS OF PERSIAN RULE

> Cyrus … finding the nations in Asia also independent … started out with a little band of Persians and became the leader of the Medes by their full consent and of the Hyrcanians by theirs; he then conquered Syria, Assyria, Arabia, Cappadocia, both Phrygias, Lydia, Caria, Phoenicia and Babylonia … and many other nations of which one could not even tell the names … the tribes which he brought into subjection to himself were so many that it is a difficult matter even to travel to them all, in whatever direction one begins one's journey, whether towards the east or the west, towards the north or the south …
>
> Xenophon I.i.4–5[1]

1.1 Human-headed divine bull guardian (*lamassu*) from Khorsabad, a capital founded by the neo-Assyrian king Sargon II. Perhaps seen at the ruined entrances of neo-Assyrian palaces, these figures provided inspiration for two forms of winged guardian at Persepolis, and possibly Pasargadae.

The genesis of the Persian empire is anchored to the dynamic conquests of Cyrus the Great. According to contemporary and later sources, starting with territory ruled by the Medes, he managed to annex most of the territory between Asia Minor and the edges of the Central Asian steppe within forty years of the middle of the sixth century BCE. His was the founder's story that defined the origin of the Persian empire to later audiences. Yet portraits such as Xenophon's 'Education of Cyrus' (quoted above) are very far removed from the actual context for the rise and definition of Persian power. The well-travelled Athenian was aware of Cyrus overcoming older powers in the areas of Media, Babylon and (dimly) Assyria, but these rivalries were inevitably oversimplified and distorted – problems shared by the other Greek authors to tackle the history of early Persia: Herodotus and Ctesias.[2] Some of the complexity of the world of successive dynasties and interacting cultures that was transformed into the Persian empire is revealed instead in contemporary historical sources and archaeological evidence. These material remains and traditions of pre-Persian empires influenced how the later monarchy shaped itself. Other aspects of their imperialism and customs contrast with innovations and changes of the Achaemenid period. Some aspects of the origin of Cyrus and the Persian army he led are still unclear. But Cyrus' appropriation of older states in Mesopotamia, Anatolia and Elam fixed his place irrevocably in their histories.

ASSYRIA AND ITS NEIGHBOURS

For most of the first half of the second millennium BCE, the entire Fertile Crescent stretching from the Arab-Persian Gulf to the Levant coast, including south-east Anatolia and sometimes Egypt, was ruled by the Assyrian kings.[3] This monarchy had very deep roots in north Mesopotamia; the cities of Ashur, Nineveh, Erbil and

15

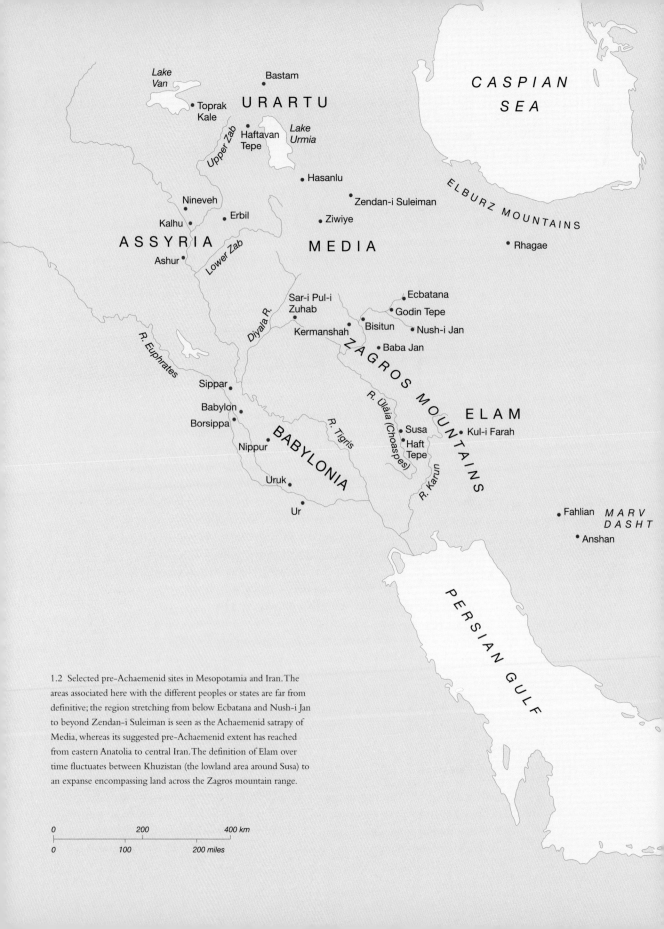

CASPIAN
SEA

*Lake
Van*

Bastam

URARTU

Toprak
Kale

Haftavan
Tepe

*Lake
Urmia*

Upper Zab

Hasanlu

ELBURZ MOUNTAINS

Zendan-i Suleiman

Nineveh

Erbil

MEDIA

Ziwiye

Rhagae

Kalhu

ASSYRIA

Ashur

Lower Zab

Ecbatana

Sar-i Pul-i
Zuhab

Godin Tepe

Diyala R.

Bisitun

Nush-i Jan

Kermanshah

Baba Jan

ZAGROS MOUNTAINS

R. Euphrates

Sippar

ELAM

Babylon

R. Tigris

R. Ulāia (Choaspes)

Susa

Kul-i Farah

Borsippa

Nippur

BABYLONIA

Haft
Tepe

R. Karun

Uruk

Fahlian

*MARV
DASHT*

Ur

Anshan

PERSIAN GULF

1.2 Selected pre-Achaemenid sites in Mesopotamia and Iran. The
areas associated here with the different peoples or states are far from
definitive; the region stretching from below Ecbatana and Nush-i Jan
to beyond Zendan-i Suleiman is seen as the Achaemenid satrapy of
Media, whereas its suggested pre-Achaemenid extent has reached
from eastern Anatolia to central Iran. The definition of Elam over
time fluctuates between Khuzistan (the lowland area around Susa) to
an expanse encompassing land across the Zagros mountain range.

0   200   400 km

0   100   200 miles

1.3 King Assurbanipal plunges a sword into a wounded lion in a scene from an episodic series of reliefs depicting a staged lion hunt. A similar image of king versus lion spread through Assyrian territory via the stamp of the royal seal on clay documents, an influential resource for later Achaemenid iconography.

Kalhu and the surrounding fertile plains had been their settled heartland since the middle of the second millennium. The neo-Assyrian period is a modern definition marking the phase starting in the late tenth century BCE, when the kings of Ashur re-established control over Upper Mesopotamia and in the following three centuries expanded their dominance to incorporate provinces across the Fertile Crescent. The Assyrians themselves had no historical boundary, seeing their king-list stretch back in an unbroken line, distinguished by a great continuity of literary, religious and artistic traditions associated with the royal court.

One of the last of the neo-Assyrian kings, Assurbanipal (668–*c.*630), made his knowledge of ancient science and literature a particular feature of his suitability for the kingship. His proud account of his own accomplishments, written as a propaganda document on a clay tablet, demonstrates how the Assyrians saw themselves as the heirs of two thousand or more years of intellectual culture from Babylonia and Sumer:

> I am versed in the craft of the sage Adapa; I studied the secret lore of the entire scribal craft, I know the celestial and terrestrial portents … I have read intricate tablets inscribed with obscure Sumerian or Akkadian, difficult to unravel, and examined sealed, obscure and confused inscriptions on stone from before the Flood.[4]

A multi-ethnic court of political advisers, scholars and artists from conquered and allied territories gathered in the cities of Assyria around the king. The general pop-

1.4 Assyrian diplomacy of last resort: an Elamite client king is installed by the victorious Assyrians (and 'welcomed' by the inhabitants). The exploitation of local factions was a key tool in international relations for both Assyrian and, later, Achaemenid rulers. However, the Achaemenids chose not to represent such specific international relations on their palace walls.

ulation benefited from the spoils of expansionist, exploratory campaigns led by the king to the four corners of the world, into the mountains of Anatolia, Armenia, Iran and the deserts of Arabia and Egypt. The wealth and order obtained by the king through these successful wars were expressed in the creation of royal palaces, occasionally founded within new or entirely renovated cites. From the second quarter of the tenth century BCE onwards, the Assyrian kings built or maintained a series of large palace complexes, partly built and decorated with monumental sculpted gypsum slabs and colossal figures. Generic or narrative scenes (and inscriptions) of campaigns, hunts and ritual covered interior walls in low, painted relief. The Assyrian kings used imagery and words in all scales and media to define and advertise their rule.[5]

The core of Assyrian power lay in the band of trade routes, cities and cultivated land spanning the Fertile Crescent. Great potential wealth and further power lay in exploiting neighbouring states through diplomacy and annexation. During the course of the ninth and particularly the eighth to sixth centuries, the territory directly ruled by the Assyrian king had been greatly expanded to include Syria, Cilicia, Phoenicia and Babylonia, with intermittent holds on Elam, Egypt and the very edge of the Iranian plateau. Campaigns on the very fringes in search of resources inevitably involved the Assyrians in diplomacy and conflict with the states and fiefdoms there. At the same time that the Assyrians were consolidating their position, a stable dynasty in power in Urartu to the north set about asserting and defending its own territorial claims, perhaps in reaction to their neighbour's activity. Southern bulwarks were built up on conquered land at the sites of Hasanlu, Haftavan Tepe and Izoglu. The people of Urartu, like other forming states, used some of the same tools as their powerful neighbours, the Assyrians, to shape their state: royal inscriptions on stone slabs (*stelae*) or rock-faces (for example, several on the cliff overlooking Lake Van) and stelae, iconography and rich furnishings, practical measures such as population deportation and city foundation.

1.5 Urartian sites have produced quantities of bronze-work. This cast furniture leg is from Toprakkale, eastern Turkey; it incorporates motifs also in use in Assyria, such as the winged disk. Lions' feet formed part of Assyrian royal furniture and, later, the Achaemenid royal throne.

The Assyrian kings tackled the perceived threat with a mixture of military and diplomatic expeditions, but the Urartian state seems to have dissolved gradually, perhaps with the assistance of invaders from the north rather than excessive interference from Assyrian armies, by the late seventh century BCE.[6]

Meanwhile, in the mountains further to the east, Assyrian royal inscriptions and administrative letters testify to a fractious relationship with another group of peoples. The land of the Medes, a people speaking an Iranian language, appears as the target of expeditions in search of tribute from the mid eighth century onwards. An inscription of Tiglath-pileser III (744–727), on a stele said to have come from the area of ancient Media, illustrates the resources that could be channelled back to Assyria as a result of compliance, recording 'horses, mules broken to the yoke, Bactrian camels, cattle and sheep'.[7] Some of the Median population had the opportunity to experience imperial power at close quarters when Esarhaddon (681–669) deported them wholesale to Assyria.[8]

Some accounts list names of settlement centres as sources of tribute, with no sign of a hierarchy of cities or rulers (who could in fact be in conflict with each other).[9] By the middle of the seventh century, the Assyrian rulers seem to have been targeting individual rulers and their families who held several cities in their power. Tablets dating to the reign of Esarhaddon preserving private queries addressed to the sun-god, seeking omens about the future to inform political decision-making by the king, disclose more detail than the ideological inscriptions.[10] A frequent focus of anxiety was the activity of one Kashtaritu of Karkashshi, who was allied with other rulers in the Zagros against Assyria.[11]

The Median king who is seen in alliance with the Babylonians in their attacks

1.6 Ancient Media stretched over mountainous territory in north-west Iran and eastern Turkey. Remains of the seventh century BCE were excavated here on the slopes of an extinct volcano, Zendan-i Suleiman, or the Prison of Solomon, in east Azerbaijan province, Iran.

The predominant periods of use of sites excavated so far do not coincide with the imperial golden age assigned to Media by later authors, after the fall of Assyria. The nature of the Median state is still a matter for debate.

on Assyrian centres from the years 630–612, is merely called the 'king of Ummandu' in the Babylonian chronicles which intermittently cover those years.[12] Their combined assault on the city of Nineveh in 612 devastated the city's defences and removed one of the last bastions of the Assyrian kings. The collapse of the Assyrian power structure, after successive attacks and a royal succession crisis, left the empire it had held together free for the taking by the conquerors. Most of the territory from Mesopotamia to the shore of the Mediterranean was taken over by the Babylonian king, Nabopolassar. The pharaohs of Egypt may have initially taken advantage of the crisis by sending armies into the Levant, while a swathe of mountainous territory, from the Elburz mountains to beyond the former kingdom of Urartu, seems to have fallen to the Medes.

It is this period of rule that is transformed in the Greek authors into a vision of an expanding empire, a kind of pioneer Iranian power which fed directly into Cyrus' empire-building. Herodotus attributes the formation of the Median state to an early civilizing leader called Deiokes, who united villages and instituted all the elements of monarchy (a palace, a guard, town defences at Ecbatana, royal protocol).[13] According to Herodotus' account, the dynasty that Deiokes founded began to subject other peoples, among them the Persians, until they controlled all the territory reaching to the Halys river in Anatolia. Most of the elements of Herodotus' story are difficult to corroborate, including the subjection of the Persians.[14] It seems that Median power grew significantly in later memory, as it became more of a reflection of the Persian empire. The details concerning this period surviving in Ctesias show a further stage along the same road.[15] The neo-Babylonian kings who inherited the lion's share of Assyrian provinces are reduced to mere (admittedly learned) deputies of the Medes, who in turn become luxury-loving magnates of the same cut as the decadent Assyrian kings before them.[16]

Nevertheless, these later accounts seem to be rooted in reports that preserved

recognizably authentic elements. Herodotus' dynastic names, Phraortes and Cyaxares and Astyages, are Greek versions of two royal names that occur elsewhere. Khshathrita 'of the family of Cyaxares', in the Bisitun inscription of King Darius I in 521 BCE was a title claimed by a local governor disputing Darius' kingship.[17] The name Khshathrita in turn seems to have been an authentic royal name in one of the powerful Median clans of the early seventh century; it is similar to the Kashtaritu, who so worried Esarhaddon.[18] Whatever the line of descent, the authors agree that the last Median king was Astyages, or Ishtumegu as he is known in the Babylonian texts, who encountered his successor Cyrus in court or battle.[19]

The archaeological remains offer a limited picture of the cultures in the Zagros and north-eastern plateau, one that appears remote from the later literary memory of all-powerful and wealthy Medes. Excavations have been limited and material is as yet insufficient to define to us an extensive and distinctive 'Median' culture; much effort is still spent in trying to detect Median elements in later Achaemenid art.[20] The reputed capital of the Medes, Ecbatana, has yet to reveal structures dated securely to the relevant period.[21] However, 60 km away, Nush-i Jan, one of the few monumental complexes dating to the seventh century, stands on a prominent hill or *tepe* overlooking a fertile plain near the present Gamas Ab, the river that runs on to Bisitun, where structures assigned to the Median period have also been excavated. Two storeys of a mud-brick façade, with storage magazines and guard rooms behind, are preserved, along with two separate cult buildings and a columned hall (fig. 1.8).[22]

To the west towards Kangavar, a decorated fortified building at Baba Jan, a site with multiple occupation layers, was in decline by the sixth century, the very period when later historians imagined the Medes revelling in the wealth of Assyria.[23] North-east of Kangavar is the site of Godin Tepe, near the route from Ecbatana to Bisitun and Babylon beyond.[24] There, the foundations of eighth-century bastions, magazines and a columned hall were excavated, parallel to the features at Nush-i Jan (fig. 1.9). The type of architecture at these sites is connected to earlier monumental structures in the Zagros area; such large and well-defined structures testify to well-organized manpower and a sustained effort to control strategic sites and resources. The type of political organization they supported and their relationship to any later unified Median power, though, remains enigmatic.[25]

BABYLON, ELAM AND PARS: SETTINGS FOR THE RISE OF CYRUS

In Babylonia, Nabopolassar (626–605) and his son Nebuchadnezzar (604–562) asserted control over the former Assyrian territory, with repeated military campaigns into the Levant. The cities of the region were restored and developed by Nebuchadnezzar into a renovated imperial heartland to rival Assyria.[26] In the capital Babylon, the city's tradition of independent kingship was enhanced with massive monumental building projects. The walls, bridge, *ziggurat* (a stepped pyramidal temple) and the Esagila, the sanctuary of the city-god Marduk, were restored and added to. Prestige decorations of rich, blue glazed brick adorned the processional

1.7 A chronicle written in Babylonian Akkadian cuneiform tersely records events occurring in every year, reign by reign. This tablet documents the progress of the assaults of the Medes and Babylonians on Assyrian cities. Nineveh fell to their combined forces in the summer of 612 BCE.

way leading from the Ishtar gate to the Esagila and the extensive palace complex to the north of the city (fig. 1.10). If the visual effect were not striking enough, the neo-Babylonian dynasty produced numerous building texts, advertising on stamped bricks, inscribed stelae and buried foundation cylinders their pious investment in the material and spiritual fabric of the city.

1.8 The mud-brick walls of Nush-i Jan, near the modern town of Jowkar in Kermanshah province, Iran are elevated 37 m above the plain. The fortress-like façade shields storage magazines, behind which stand two cult buildings (one with an altar) and a columned hall.
The complex was in use from c.800 to 600 BCE.

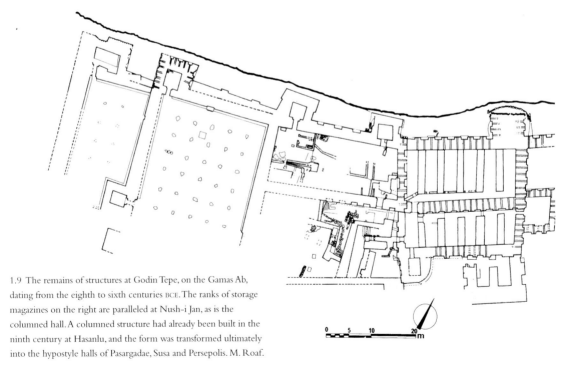

1.9 The remains of structures at Godin Tepe, on the Gamas Ab, dating from the eighth to sixth centuries BCE. The ranks of storage magazines on the right are paralleled at Nush-i Jan, as is the columned hall. A columned structure had already been built in the ninth century at Hasanlu, and the form was transformed ultimately into the hypostyle halls of Pasargadae, Susa and Persepolis. M. Roaf.

0   5   10   20
m

1.10 One of a troop of glazed brick lions that paced along the Processional Way towards the Ishtar Gate at Babylon. Part of a renovation dating to the reign of Nebuchadnezzar II (604–562), this urban adornment influenced palace décor at Susa three generations later.

After Nebuchadnezzar's forty-two-year reign, three of his successors failed to last long in the competition for the throne. Stability within the court was restored only under a new ruler with no connection to his royal predecessors, Nabonidus (555–539). A relative profusion of texts from his reign (triggered by his need to justify an irregular accession) expand on his role as virtuous builder and pious pursuer of divine favour (fig. 1.11).[27] In particular, he set to work to restore the temple of the moon-god Sin at Harran and, in support of repeated campaigns into Arabia, he built up a crucial base at Teima, an oasis on the caravan route. In his absence, his adult son Bel-shar-usur (also known as Belshazzar) undertook

1.11 Three columns of cuneiform covering a clay cylinder memorialize the restoration of the Sippar temple of Shamash under King Nabonidus. The barrel shape, which was characteristic of neo-Babylonian foundation inscriptions, was later appropriated by Cyrus II to assert his own authority in Babylon.

day-to-day government in Babylonia. But even before Nabonidus had secured the throne, it is likely that a king had come to power, in Elam to the east, who was to seize power in Babylon over fifteen years later.

Our estimates of the chronology of his reign see Cyrus, the founder of the Persian empire, becoming a king in 559.[28] He did not accede to the rule of Media or Babylonia. The title taken by him and at least one of his two known predecessors was 'king of Anshan', a title first used in the third millennium. Anshan (modern Tall-i Malyan) was an ancient capital of Elam, the area very roughly corresponding to the modern Iranian province of Khuzistan and the western part of Fars. The area had maintained a strong political and cultural identity while developing significant links with the neighbouring states to the west.[29] The relationship of this region with the rest of the Iranian plateau and Central Asia was also significant; by the late second millennium, an Iranian-speaking population (related linguistically and culturally to the Medes to the north) were living in the region. The process of their migration and the nature of their settlement there is still a matter for debate, but the resulting population included other ethnicities, including the resident Elamites.[30]

1.12 Tablets from Persepolis preserve impressions from a cylinder seal with the image of a victorious horseman, and the Elamite inscription 'Cyrus of Anshan, son of Teispes'. According to Cyrus II's own genealogy, this Cyrus (I) was his grandfather. The seal's style, language and inscription all establish a connection with the old kingdom of Elam. The use of this seal long after even Cyrus II's death, at a palace built under Darius I, may have been a conscious evocation of the dynasty's past.

In the mid seventh century, Elam came into serious conflict with Assyria, resulting in a destructive invasion.[31] In the disintegration resulting from the Assyrian victory, it appears that Anshan and the reaches of Elam in Fars became the political base of a new dynasty. This dynasty, apparently beginning with a King Teispes (in Elamite, Tishpish) presided over an increase in population in Fars during the seventh century.[32] The degree to which these rulers distinguished themselves as a separate Persian tribe is unclear at this period, but they became the genealogical foundation for Cyrus and his successors as kings of Persia.

Later traditions about Cyrus' early career connect him more firmly to the court of the Medes than his native milieu and seek to explain the origin of conflict between Anshan and the Medes in terms of divine prophecy and adventure. In the stories later retold by the authors Xenophon, Herodotus and Ctesias, the king's childhood and young adulthood follow folkloric patterns based on the idea of his royal destiny.[33] These were influenced by long-lived legendary tales about ancient kings of Mesopotamia and beyond, which circulated widely throughout the Near East.[34] Particular patterns of tales (often already firmly attached to one well-known character in both literature and oral tradition) became transferable story models from which the popular biographies of more recent figures could be formed.

One such typical tale was that of the rise to power of a conquering king or inspirational ruler from humble and anonymous origins, versions of which surrounded Cyrus. According to this story, a baby, usually borne in secret by a noble or a royal woman, was abandoned to die on a hillside or in a river. A poor worker, variously a shepherd or gardener, would by accident or design find and take pity on this baby, raising him virtuously as his own. The poor but talented youth by chance came to the attention of the king, sometimes after gaining a position in the palace, and through his virtue and skill rose to a prominent position. He was eventually elevated to the kingship after the previous monarch was killed or overcome in some way (through folly or rebellions).

A version of this story was attached to the third-millennium king Sargon of Agade. A long-lived and popular tradition, it was given a boost during the reign of the neo-Assyrian king Sargon II (721–705), for whom the legendary king's reputation was perhaps an ideological buttress to his own irregular succession. In the two folkloric versions of Cyrus' childhood, Herodotus' story most strongly asserts the inevitability of Cyrus' expansionist rule: he is the son of a Median princess, Mandane, and a noble Persian, Cambyses. His birth and boyhood in exile are surrounded with prophecies, his grandfather, the Median King Astyages, is a paranoid, impious and repressive ruler whose deeds invite his own downfall. A later variation of this story, written down in the early fourth century, gave Cyrus non-royal, peasant parents but described a career closer to the heart of power as raised by patronage to the position of cupbearer in the palace beside Astyages, a trajectory that mirrored the legendary life of Sargon of Agade. The richness of the tales surrounding Cyrus indicates a need to explain his extraordinary achievements in so vastly expanding the boundaries of Persian power. His legendary life also set the rise of Persian rule in close association with the decline of Media in a schematic succession of empires.

Contemporary chronicles reveal very little beyond the brutal facts of invasion and conquest. The Babylonian Chronicle restricts itself to a terse account of the final confrontation in the heartland of Media (fig. 1.13). According to the chronicle, in 550 BCE Astyages aggressively marched against Cyrus, but his army mutinied and surrendered him to the enemy, whereupon 'Cyrus marched to Ecbatana, the royal city. The silver, gold, goods, property … which he carried off as booty [from] Ecbatana he took to Anshan'.[35] Cyrus' behaviour follows the traditional pattern of the Near Eastern conqueror; the contemporary evidence does not suggest that Ecbatana immediately became a new rival capital to Anshan. His authority over the swathe of Median territory brought Cyrus into direct, abrasive relationships with neighbouring groups southeast of the Caspian, the Lydian kingdom in western Anatolia and, finally, Babylon.

Cyrus' conquests in the east are barely documented, whereas the defeat of the Lydian king Croesus (possibly linked to Astyages by marriage) is usually assumed to have happened in the 540s.[36] The conquest of Lydia, being closest to the Mediterranean world, received the

1.13 This chronicle tablet, often known as 'the Nabonidus Chronicle', covers the events of the reign of the last neo-Babylonian king. It is a vital primary source for chronology and the practical progress of Cyrus II's campaigns, but gaps and ambiguities in the text still leave some stages of his conquest unclear.

most attention from later Greek authors, who passed on divergent views of Croesus' fate.[37] Largely ignorant of the historic wealth and sophisticated city culture of the Assyrian and Babylonian kingdoms inherited by Cyrus, the Greeks attributed the Persian discovery of civilized and soft living to their takeover of the Lydian kingdom. The story was a fateful prelude to the later bruising encounters between the Greeks and the kings Darius I and Xerxes I, and was accordingly given prominence in Herodotus' epic account of the entire history of Greek–Persian relations. By 540, though, Cyrus' attention had clearly returned to the core of Babylonian power in Mesopotamia, although it is unclear how isolated Babylonia had become in the meantime (the status of Assyria and the western 'Beyond the River' province, which reached to the Levant, remained in question).

The conquest of Babylonia was pursued tactically with a punishing battle at Opis followed by the submission of Sippar:

> In the month Tishri [September to October] when Cyrus did battle at Opis on [the bank of] the Tigris against the army of Akkad, the people of Akkad retreated. He carried off the plunder [and] slaughtered the people. On the fourteenth day [6 October] Sippar was captured without battle. Nabonidus fled. On the sixteenth day [8 October] Ug/Gubaru, governor of Gutium, and the army of Cyrus without a battle entered Babylon.
>
> Afterwards, after Nabonidus retreated, he was captured in Babylon.[38]

Despite the apparently uncontested takeover of Babylon, it was twenty days before

1.14 'I, Cyrus, king of the world, great king … king of Babylon, king of Sumer and Akkad …' Unlike the Nabonidus Chronicle, the Cyrus Cylinder text is composed with an eye to giving a positive and predestined feel to the conquest of Babylon. Both the inscription's form, borrowed from Cyrus' defeated predecessors, and its content, use the city's past to suggest the legitimacy of the new monarchy.

Cyrus made his official entry into Babylon, with the conciliatory assurance of the continuity of cult in the Esagila.[39] The local notables were immediately placed under the supervision of Cyrus' deputy, Gobryas, who may have been quickly succeeded by his son. In the following year, Cyrus' heir, Cambyses, was installed as king of Babylon, perhaps in a temporary echo of the last independent neo-Babylonian government.[40] To advertise his conquest of Babylon to posterity, Cyrus took over a form recently used by the Babylonian king. A foundation inscription in the cylinder shape of preceding neo-Babylonian texts was unearthed in the excavation of Babylon in the nineteenth century and since its decipherment has been known as the Cyrus Cylinder (fig. 1.14).[41]

This sophisticated text is a concerted assault on the suitability of Nabonidus as king. He is alleged to have stopped the required offerings at the Esagila, made unsuitable religious reforms and neglected the gods of Babylonia, 'whose dwelling-places were in ruins'. The negative characterization of one's predecessor's care for ancestral cults was a common strategy (Xerxes I was to be used by Alexander in much the same way just over two hundred years later). The slighted city god Marduk is described as searching the lands for a more suitable monarch; naturally, his gaze alighted on Cyrus, whose conquest became an act of beneficent protection:

> The black-headed people [the Babylonians], whom he allowed his hands to overcome, he protected in justice and righteousness. Marduk, the great lord … looked with pleasure at his good deeds … He ordered him to go to Babylon … Like a friend and companion he went by his side … He saved Babylon from its oppression.[42]

The bloody battle at Opis fades into the background, as the inhabitants of Babylon joyfully welcome their liberator who assumed the traditional titles of 'king of the universe, mighty king, king of Babylon, king of Sumer and Akkad, king of the four quarters', alongside his Anshanite identity. According to the cylinder, Cyrus literally leaves no stone unturned to take on the role of the virtuous restorer of the traditional material environment. He restored the gods' shrines and returned statues that had been gathered into Babylon (as a protection against looting after battles) to their temples throughout the countryside. After stating that the city wall and gates were renewed, Cyrus borrows a further ideological tactic from his Babylonian predecessors, suggesting that his excavation in the city's foundations uncovered an ancient royal inscription. For the Babylonian kings, this kind of discovery of old layers and royal foundations was an affirmation of their continuing safeguard of the city. Cyrus' use however introduces a shrewd twist. His notable contact in the past, whose own inscriptions had influenced the style of the Cyrus Cylinder, is the Assyrian King Assurbanipal; he was a past restorer of the city, but also a foreign conqueror, not a native son.

The negative characterization of Nabonidus which was born in Cyrus' propaganda took root in tradition and was expanded in a poetic account of his fall usually called the 'Verse Account'.[43] The Babylonian's near-madness in impiously living away from his civilized homeland at Teima in the desert became a prototype of bad kingship, shadowing later deposed kings and influencing the Biblical presentation of Babylon. Nevertheless, the later accounts of Xenophon and Berossus still preserved alternative traditions that the takeover of Babylon had been violent. The end of Nabonidus' life described by Berossus, pensioned off to preside over the district of Carmania, parallels the genteel decline of both Croesus and Astyages in Cyrus' entourage described by Herodotus.[44] It is as though it was seen as beneficial for deposed kings to become submissive courtiers for their successors.

The conquest of Babylon opened up the provinces of Trans-Euphrates and the Mediterranean coast to Persian influence. Cyrus exploited the fractious history

1.15 From the fortified *takht* or platform on a high ridge, the site of Pasargadae sweeps down in an open landscape of scattered structures. Visible at the right by the road is the surviving façade of the latterly named 'Prison of Solomon', a mysterious tower building. The foundations of the central palace area lie in the middle distance, while over two kilometres away stands the solitary tomb of Cyrus.

existing between the powers of Mesopotamia and Levantine states such as Judah with a particularly beneficial public relations move. Influential segments of the Judaean elite had been deported and exiled to Babylonia following Nebuchadnez-zar's conquest of Jerusalem in 597 BCE. Cyrus' actions are known only through ret-rospective (and therefore edited) citations in the Biblical books of Isaiah and Ezra of his special concern for the community in Jerusalem. In allowing the return of the exiled group to their home city, and, reportedly, granting permission for the restoration of their temple, Cyrus gained not just decades but centuries of good press as the guarantor of the Jewish people's status within the empire.[45]

For the conquest of large swathes of the rest of the later empire, even Herodotus demurs from filling in the gap in our contemporary evidence, saying 'Cyrus him-self subdued all the peoples of Upper Asia without exception. I shall pass over most of these ...'[46] Nevertheless, Herodotus does place Cyrus' death in battle at the furthest reach of the empire, battling against the Massagetae across the Syr Darya (the Jaxartes river), suggesting that some tales of Cyrus' eastward exploration were current, if in an elaborated form, a century or more later.[47] Herodotus had possibly selected this variant of Cyrus' death as an early illustration of his theme that the Persians had a tendency to overreach themselves. In contrast, Xenophon elaborated on an alternative vision of Cyrus' peaceful demise, handing down wise words on the nature of government and the soul to his son and heir Cambyses.[48] Xenophon's expansive visualization of Cyrus' life saw him systematically introducing the organization of the empire into 'satrapies' (provinces or administrative districts) and bestowing a completed system of Persian court life on each capsule of government across his territory.[49]

The *Cyropaedia* is an illustration of both Xenophon's ideological aspiration to order and good government and the popular tendency to attribute all the elements of an empire to its compelling founder. The text in fact offers more material for the analysis of ideas about Persian history at the beginning of the fourth century, and the transformation of the vision of earlier kings in the eyes of their successors. For only indirect indications of policy decisions, evidence comes almost exclusively from administrative documents recording some continuity of administration personnel in conquered territory.[50] The two self-evident lasting foundations of Cyrus' reign were a stable succession to his son, and the creation of a monumental capital in Parsa, a project which was the first expression of a unique status for the region in the new Persian empire.

1.16 The central palace area at Pasargadae showing the main, monumental columned halls and, an equally important part of the royal setting, the reconstructed, fourfold garden plan in the centre. Gate R stands to the south-east (after Stronach).

Two bequests: Pasargadae and Cambyses

The creation of a monumental capital in Parsa was an entirely new kind of project, different from the historical city mining of Nebuchadnezzar and Nabonidus. Some evidence suggests that the land of Parsa was bound up in the identity of local Persian tribes, or that the site of Pasargadae was significant in the history of Cyrus' conquests. As far as we know, the dynasty from which Cyrus emerged had not expressed its power in such monumental construction before. It was planned on a grand and expansive scale; the surviving stone constructions are scattered across several kilometres through the middle of the fertile Dasht-i Morghab, a valley formed by the river Pulvar, flowing south-west towards the Marv Dasht plain (fig. 1.15).[51]

The site is roughly bounded by the tomb of Cyrus at its south-western end, and by the Tall-i Takht over 2 km away to the north-east, a fortified hill overlooking the rest of the complex. In the plain below the Tall-i Takht stand a number of surviving stone buildings, which were once spaced at intervals around a formally defined landscape, at the centre of which was an irrigated rectangular garden. The central area of formal cultivation has been reconstructed at up to 230 by 200 m on

the basis of excavated stone watercourses, corner sluices and the structures aligned
with them (fig. 1.16). The recent discovery of further watercourses beyond this arc
extends the range of possible cultivation towards the river. The largest columned
hall, known as Palace P, extended approximately 73 m within the northern border
of this garden. A central room contained thirty columns standing on precisely
carved, bichrome bases; similar, but smaller columns supported the two long
porticoes flanking this hall. The interior would have been brightened with painted
plaster coating the walls, upper wooden portions of the columns and possibly also
five rectangular mud-brick pillars that stood at either end of the hall. Large robed
figures stood in carved relief on the jambs of the portico doors.[52] The southern
portico, bordering the garden, was the longest, with a low stone bench lining its
entire length. A substantial limestone foundation at its central point has been interpreted as a throne base. The presence of a throne would turn this grand, shaded
structure framing the garden into a formal setting for the king and court society.

Two other much smaller structures were closely aligned with the garden plan;
known as Pavilions A and B, they consisted of small central columned halls flanked
by two porticoes running the length of the building. Their position and alignment

suggest that they functioned as gateways to the central garden. To the south-west of the central garden stood another large columned hall known as Palace S; only one interior limestone column remains standing, at over 13 m high. Only small fragments of the black stone column capitals in the forms of lion, horned lion and bull-heads survive. The palace's plan (covering an area of around 54 by 22 m) is aligned on the same axis as the pavilions and Palace P, its long north-eastern portico, again featuring a long stone bench, facing towards the area of the garden, its outer south-western portico enclosed and guarded by two corner towers. Here too, a simple decorative effect was produced by combining dark and light stone in the construction of the interior columns and portico.

Palace S had a simpler, more open interior, and its four doorways oriented at the centre of each wall give it an open character, perhaps acting as a location both for gathering and for passing through. Surviving in the doorways of this palace are fragmentary reliefs showing the feet and lower legs of humans and fantastic creatures stepping through.[53] The demons are similar to figures found in neo-Assyrian palaces; flat taloned eagle-feet belong to a lion-demon, hooves and a curly tail belong to a bull-man. Such creatures, who guarded the walls and dark corners of Assyrian rooms, may have been talismans against evil entering the building. On a door jamb of the south-western palace doorway, the feet of humans lead a bull or cow, an animal that could have been a gift or a sacrifice.

The most complete surviving relief sculpture at Pasargadae stands as part of the structure of a detached gateway another 200 m south-east of Palace S, known as Gate R (fig. 1.17). The isolated structure, standing at least 16 m high, was pierced at the middle of each wall with an entrance. Two rows of columns inside led between the two main doorways. The southern entrance was guarded with bull guardians like those later built into Xerxes' gate at Persepolis, while the northern door still holds its door jamb carved with a complete winged figure known as the Pasargadae genius.[54] This figure, winged like an Assyrian demon, crowned like a pharaoh and cloaked in an Elamite robe, remains enigmatic. A cuneiform inscription reading, 'I am Cyrus the Achaemenid', which once topped the door jamb has been in the past taken to identify the relief as representing the king himself. The royal attribute of the crown counts towards this conclusion, while the combination of this with the divine attribute of wings complicates the identity that the image was designed to project. The inscription itself was a generic one, added to several prominent points of the Pasargadae buildings after their construction, most likely in the reign of Darius I.[55] The position of the gateway building is the most striking illustration of the strung-out space of the Pasargadae complex, the patchwork of buildings and cultivation transforming the entire plain into an environment embodying the king's control over his people and his territory.

By the time of Alexander III's use of the site after his defeat of Darius III, the area of Pasargadae was known as a royal *paradeisos* or a lush, cultivated landscape. By the end of the Achaemenid period, the focus of the site's activity and identity may well have been the tomb of Cyrus, a gabled chamber built on top of a four-stepped pyramidal base to the south-east of the main cluster of buildings (fig.

1.18 The gabled top of the tomb of Cyrus stands up to 10 m high; in ancient times it was surrounded by a garden and was tended by a permanent priestly staff. The doorway (on the opposite side to this view) gapes open, and the chamber is empty save for the inscriptions and *mehrab* or prayer niche of the later Muslim shrine.

1.18).[56] Yet during the many years of the site's construction and the early years of its use, the Murghab plain must have been a residential and administrative centre – both functions for which limited evidence has been found. The fortified *takht* at the highest part of the site has been suggested as a possible site for the capital's treasury, but does not appear to have been any kind of citadel residence for the king. Below the *takht*, the so-called Zendan-i Suleiman may have been the focus of religious or ceremonial activity (fig. 5.14). The workings of Pasargadae as an imperial capital in everyday use have yet to be discovered but a recent geophysical survey has revealed the footprints of less monumental structures around Palaces S and P, and some further construction near the tomb of Cyrus. A further stone structure is one of a series of remains near the Zendan-i Suleiman. On the slope below the *takht* and within the walls, 3 m thick, of its outer fortifications are numerous small structures.

The style of construction at Pasargadae, as well as its plan, was distinctly different from the city and palace planning of Assyria and Babylonia. While the organization of space and the elaboration of pillared audience halls both echo existing building projects in western Iran, such as Godin Tepe and Hasanlu, the stone framework and monumentalization of the buildings reflect influences from further west. The use of toothed chisels in the shaping of stone, and the style of some column construction in particular, may be evidence for the participation of Ionian craftsmen in the construction of Pasargadae.[57] This manpower will have been accessible to Cyrus II after his conquest of Lydia. The inspiration behind the huge magnification and elaboration of the traditional columned hall built elsewhere in the Zagros may have come both from the semi-ruined palaces of northern Assyria and the early temples and sanctuaries of western Asia Minor, particularly that at Ephesus. With the later development of capitals at Susa and Persepolis, the style and setting of the palaces of Pasargadae remained almost unique in Parsa. The only parallel lies in the soil of the Marv Dasht plain, near the same river Pulvar to the south, where the incomplete foundations of a columned hall were found at Dasht-i Gohar in the 1970s.[58] The plan and column bases are similar to those of Palace S at Pasargadae, and apparently reflect an immediately subsequent phase of building. That this building was part of a more extensive development along the lines of Cyrus' capital to the north is suggested by its association with a stepped foundation that strikingly resembles the lower layers of the tomb of Cyrus. Left unfinished, the Takht-i Rustam, as it is called, has frequently been suggested as the intended burial place of Cambyses, Cyrus' son. While this intention is difficult to prove conclusively, these meagre foundations probably have some relationship to the later use of the cliffs of Naqsh-i Rustam and the platform of Persepolis as respectively the burial place and the ancestral capital of the kings of Persia. The development of the landscape all along the eastern edge of the vast Marv Dasht, encompassing a religious site to the north and a defensive gathering place to the south, may have been planned as a grandiose successor to the *paradeisos* at Pasargadae. While Cambyses may have been the plan's initiator, the business and brevity of his reign left the Marv Dasht to be transformed along radically new lines by his successors.

Cambyses' status as legitimate heir had been confirmed by his installation as king of Babylon during Cyrus' lifetime.[59] There is absolutely no sign of unrest on Cyrus' death, and Cambyses' accession is indicated with administrative smoothness in a sale contract dated August 530 in Babylon.[60] This stability contrasts with both the chaos that followed his eight-year reign and the violent terms in which his rule, and particularly the major project of his reign, the invasion of Egypt, were described in later tradition. Contemporary documents dated to Cambyses' reign testify only to calm recognition of his rule in Mesopotamia and his adherence to the necessary rituals of kingship further afield, in Egypt. Nevertheless, the reputation for violent insanity created for him in Greek sources was so powerful that a playwright of the sixteenth century, describing his lurid drama based on this source, explained bluntly that it would tell of Cambyses' 'many evil deeds, and his one good one'.[61]

The root of all subsequent troubles appears to lie in Egypt. Cyrus' expansion into the west had isolated Egypt's pharaoh, Amasis, by removing many of his local allies. Amasis conspired with a neighbouring Greek tyrant, Polycrates of Samos, to

1.19 Near to the foundations of an incomplete palace in the
Marv Dasht, two stepped base layers of masonry may have been
intended to support a tomb structure. The monument was
never completed, but the tombs of the Achaemenid dynasty
were later carved into the lowest end of the sloping cliff visible
in the middle distance.

assert their own power on the fringe of Persian territory. Evidently, Cambyses decided that the western frontier of his territory needed to be stabilized and, perhaps, that Egypt could be advantageously annexed by war or diplomacy.[62] Four years of Cambyses' reign passed before the major expedition was launched. This interval was necessary for the massive programme of ship-building and naval organization needed to prepare for any attempt on Egypt; Cambyses, by investing in the naval technology of Phoenicia, created the Persian navy.[63] Other preparations are obscured by the concentration of our main source, Herodotus, on Egypt, and the absence of other documents.

Amasis died in 526 and his son and successor Psammetichus III failed to hold out against the Persians in a battle at the Nile and then besieged at Memphis.[64] A contemporary reported, 'The Great King of all foreign lands, Cambyses, came to Egypt, and the foreigners of all foreign lands were with him. They made their dwellings therein, and he was the Great King of Egypt.'[65] Cambyses' successful conquest of Egypt is signalled by his incorporation in documentation recording the regular responsibilities of the Egyptian kings. His efforts to comply with the traditional requirements of a good king in Egypt are attested in the self-aggrandizing inscription of Udjahorresnet (above), the adviser who informed the new king of his responsibilities, and assisted him in composing his royal titulature. There is also some surviving documentation for Cambyses' patronage of cult practice in Memphis during his reign. In 324, the sacred Apis bull, linked to the god Ptah, died and was buried in the Memphis Serapeum; his monument, as recorded on both epitaph and sarcophagus, was respectfully 'dedicated by the king'.[66] Cambyses also reportedly visited the shrine of Ammon in the western desert. This journey and an expedition southwards to the fringes of Ethiopia may have had the diplomatic objectives of enabling meetings with embassies, but were probably reported as heroic, exploratory campaigns.[67]

Herodotus' account of Cambyses' campaigns in Egypt, on the other hand, is entirely shaped to convey, at first, ominous divine disproval, and then the inevitable, wholeheartedly vicious fulfilment of these omens by the Persian king. Cambyses did not (as the evidence shows) honour the Apis bull, but murdered him in a rage, whipped the priests and desecrated royal tombs.[68] The frontier campaigns were spun into a traumatic disaster for the Persian army. Most of Cambyses' reported evil actions are in fact impious perversions of good royal ideology. In an echo of Egyptian divinity and distant dynastic practice, the king was alleged to have married his sister but then killed her in a rage. The horror of these actions is particularly tailored to an Egyptian perspective. Herodotus' sources may have been influenced both by early resistance to Cambyses in the district of Sais and by the long-term blackening of Cambyses' reputation after the accession of Darius I.[69] Part of the latter trend, Cambyses' greatest alleged evil deed was committed not against his new subjects, but against his own flesh and blood far away in Persia. According to Herodotus, the king inexplicably sent an assassin to murder his brother and heir.[70] To this fratricide was linked political turmoil reaching right across the empire.

2 CONQUEST AND POLITICS

I am Darius the Great King, King of Kings, King in Persia,
king of countries, son of Hystaspes, grandson of Arsames,
an Achaemenian.   DBa

2.1 The burial places of
Cyrus II's sons, Cambyses
and Bardiya, are unknown.
In contrast, Darius I's tomb
(centre right) was the first
of a series cut into the cliff
at Naqsh-i Rustam (with
two more at Persepolis).

The tomb façade,
modelled on the
proportions of Darius'
private palace at Persepolis,
contained enough rock-cut
sarcophagi to house his
wives or closest family –
like dynastic houses in
death. The pit in which the
tower building known as the
Kaba'a-i Zardusht stands
(bottom left) gives an idea
of the ancient ground level.

The aftermath of Cambyses' successful invasion of Egypt was to be a dramatic transformation of the monarchy. The king never returned alive to Persia, but died mysteriously en route. At the same time or even before his death, someone who bore his brother's name, Bardiya, took the throne in Persia. Babylonian loan documents drawn up in western Iran and dated to April 522 BCE refer to the 'accession year of Barziya, king of Babylon, king of lands'.[1] But, less than a year later, this Bardiya was deposed and a Persian noble called Darius claimed the kingship. In response, several more leaders and pretenders rebelled, first in the provinces of Elam, Media, Persia and the area of Babylon, then Assyria, Egypt and the central eastern provinces of Margiana and Sattagydia.

Such serious division could have torn the empire apart from its core. But Darius and an allied group of Persian, Median and Armenian nobles and generals successfully led armies against these new 'kings'. Darius was able to prevail after nearly three years of conflict, and his thirty-six-year reign ultimately shaped a more durable monarchy. Through his relatively plentiful inscriptions (one of which is quoted above), his voice dominates our impressions of the Persian monarchy. But how did he come to power?

REINVENTING THE MONARCHY

The only contemporary account, inscribed on a windswept mountainside in western Iran called Bisitun, speaks only for Darius.[2] He claimed that this deep chaos in the heart of Persian territory in fact resulted from a sinister plot sparked by an evil deed of Cambyses. He alleged that Cambyses secretly killed his brother, Bardiya, and that the figure who became king in Persia just before Cambyses' death was an impostor called Gaumata. This first lie, he says, spread like a virus through the land, causing further rebellions. The true story may be even murkier, but it is difficult to recover from Darius' story, notable just as much for what he leaves out as for what he tells us.[3]

> Much else was done by me, that has not been inscribed in this inscription; for this reason it has not been inscribed, in case to those who shall hereafter read this inscription, what has been done by me will seem excessive and … false …
>
> DB IV, lines 47–50

This statement shows that the text was designed to be persuasive, rather than to narrate all the facts of the affair. Apart from Darius' story, we have Herodotus' much later retelling of the turmoil (where the king's brother *and* the impostor are both called 'Smerdis'); this is dependent in many points on the victorious king's account.[4] Emerging from the tales surrounding a well-established monarchy (two or more lifetimes after the events), it cannot independently confirm any facts. The historian's clever tapestry of tales only underlines Darius' untrustworthiness. What the new king's story at Bisitun does reveal, however, is an incredibly successful reinvention of the monarchy, aristocracy and their relationship with the multitudes inhabiting the territory they ruled. For a closer look at this transformation we must begin with the Iranian mountainside where Darius planted the seeds of his new dynasty.

2.2 Mount Bisitun, in the Zagros mountain range, photographed in 1934 from 550 ft from the plane of the Chicago Oriental Institute's archaeological expedition. The relief is situated 60 m above the road in the dark cleft visible in the centre.

2.3 An 1840s engraving from a drawing by Pascal Coste shows his colleague Eugène Flandin examining the trilingual inscription on the Bisitun cliff face. The group, and the later relief, by the river below show how this point was a focus of interest along the main road.

MOUNT BISITUN: DARIUS' STORY

The highway crossing the Zagros mountains, between Hamadan and Baghdad, is lined with the signs of territorial conflict of four millennia. Near the modern Iraqi border at Sar-i Pul-i Zuhab, one of several early rock reliefs on a pair of gate-like cliffs demonstrates the supremacy of the late-second-millennium king Anubanini over his defeated enemies.[5] Every few kilometres beyond, battered tanks displayed on plinths testify to a more recent conflict. In the Persian period, this route linked two crucial old centres, Ecbatana and Babylon; the road, in fact, was a hinge at the heart of the empire, between the rich land of Mesopotamia and the high Iranian plateau. Eighty kilometres from Kermanshah, Mount Bisitun rises abruptly above the plateau to nearly 3,400 m above sea level (fig. 2.2). Traces of its importance as a staging or watch post, place of worship and haven from the prehistoric period onwards cluster around the mountain and the spring, which collects at a cleft in the south-eastern face before running into the nearby Gamas Ab river. The name itself conjures the fabulous: Bisitun derives from the Old Persian name *Bagastana* meaning 'place of the gods'.

This face of Bisitun, with its existing divine, historic and strategic associations, was chosen for a great rock relief commemorating the new monarchy. In the aftermath of the tumultuous reaction to Darius' accession, the new king wanted to fix his story of events in the memory of the empire, using both its landscape and peoples as his messengers. The first element of the monument to be completed was the scene showing the life-size king towering over nine conquered kings, including Gaumata, who lies on his back under Darius' foot.[6] Parts of the composition echo the relief of Anubanini, to the west on the same road. Texts were added to this picture giving the identity of each figure; and then a widening spread

2.4 The sculpted relief summarizing Darius' victory over his rivals is about 3 m high and 5.5 m wide. The first text was added on the right, in Elamite, and a Babylonian version of the same text was inscribed on the projecting slope to the left. Finally, directly below the king and his captives, four columns of a text in Old Persian were added. The cutting of a Scythian captive into the first text at the right led to the addition of a new Elamite inscription below the Babylonian and an extra column of Old Persian. Water erosion through crevices within the cliff is eroding the Old Persian text.

of inscribed cuneiform in three languages covered the cliff below and to the sides of the relief. Of the three, both Elamite and Babylonian Akkadian were prestigious ancient languages adopted from two areas of the empire associated with much older monarchies than the newly powerful Persians. The relief must have been begun at the end of 521 BCE, shortly after Darius' victories, but in 519 further campaigning led to the addition of an extra column in Old Persian and a freshly inscribed Elamite version below the Babylonian.[7]

The different languages represented different traditions of language and records in the empire, but this new multilingual approach was not restricted to the cliff-face.

Darius the King says: By the favour of [the god] Ahuramazda this [is] the form of writing, which I have made, besides, in ariyan. Both on clay tablets and on parchment it has been placed ... And it was written down and was read aloud before me. Afterwards I have sent this form of writing everywhere into the countries. The people strove [to use it].

DB IV, lines 88–92

Darius mentions two writing materials: rectangular clay tablets impressed before baking with cuneiform (wedge-shaped) characters, and parchment, which could carry

2.5 'I have sent this inscription everywhere among the lands,' said Darius I. Copies of the Bisitun text have been found in Babylon, by the Processional Way, and in Elephantine, Egypt. This is one of several fragments of the Elephantine papyrus carrying an Aramaic version, recopied from an older original during the second half of the fifth century. Edited into this copy were lines taken from Darius I's tomb inscription at Naqsh-i Rustam. The roll's breadth and neatness suggest that this could be an officially made copy.

Aramaic (a language that had been in widespread administrative use since the neo-Assyrian period) written in ink. He also specifies a form of writing or set of characters exclusively for the 'ariyan' language, or Persian, suggesting that the last cuneiform text to be added was an innovation, a newly written language.[8] At Babylon, where the same road led, a version of this text was displayed on the processional way below the palace, along with a copy of the relief.[9] That the text, along with Darius' tomb inscription, was definitely translated into Aramaic is shown by a later, large scroll from the distant garrison of Elephantine in upper Egypt (fig. 2.5).[10] But one of the major routes of transmission was probably by oral story-telling. Every part of the inscription is introduced as the voice of the monarch: 'proclaims Darius, the king'. He appeals directly to those who read or heard his story to 'make [it] known to the people, do not conceal [it]!' (DB IV, line 54). The effects of this urge to communicate can be seen in Herodotus' version, written down nearly a century later.

In Darius' version of events, he was descended from a long line of eight kings in a genealogy which related him to the family of the empire-founder Cyrus II through a mutual ancestor called Teispes (which eight kings he referred to remains a mystery; his father Hystaspes, alive at the time of the rebellion, was not a king but a satrap) (DB I, lines 1–11). Teispes was the great-grandfather of Cyrus II, but, for good measure, Darius added a legendary progenitor called Achaemenes: '... Proclaims Darius the king: For this reason we are called Achaemenians, from long ago we have been noble. From long ago our family have been kings' (DB I, lines 8–11). This Achaemenes now gives his name to the entire dynasty in most modern scholarship. Inscriptions added to Cyrus' capital at Pasargadae, in which he called himself Achaemenid, enveloped the founder himself in this new long genealogy.[11] With this royal history shuffled into shape, Darius was the righteous successor and opponent of the false Bardiya.

Darius claimed that Bardiya (the impostor Gaumata) threatened those aware of the usurpation with death. In response, he and a band of nobles dared to venture into the heart of the palace, where they slew the impostor. According to Darius' account, the body of Bardiya–Gaumata was not put on public display, unlike other rebels (who were flayed and displayed at palace gates for 'all the people' to see).

Darius claims that no one alive knew of the usurpation by the priest, a 'magus'. His desire for public belief in this completely unverifiable story is huge:

> You, whosoever shall read this inscription hereafter, let what [has been] done by me convince you, lest you should esteem Falsehood … Proclaims Darius, the king: I will take Ahuramazda's anger upon myself that I did this truly, not falsely in one and the same year.
>
> DB IV, lines 41–5

Darius' protestations have not quite convinced modern historians, who largely suspect that Bardiya may well have been the real brother, the legitimate successor of Cambyses, and that his death was probably an act of regicide. Coincidentally, Herodotus' dramatized tale of the succession turns Darius into a cynical politician who finally wins the crown with a trick.[12] This entertaining version roughly follows Darius' sequence of events, leaving out the laborious military campaigns, embellishing it instead with extra incidental characters and court intrigue. Many of Herodotus' apparently anecdotal episodes are tales which undermine the idea of Darius' power through sidelong references, rather than the revelation of what we think of as historical fact.[13]

So Darius may not have been as natural a legitimate successor as he claimed. He asserted a link with the royal family through his patrilineal ancestors, but he also, according to Herodotus, took the practical step of marrying two daughters of Cyrus II, Atossa and Artystone, and Phaidyme, a woman who had apparently previously been married to Cambyses and Bardiya. The marriage alliances were a way of knitting himself into the fabric of the previous dynasty. The families of six named accomplices who appear both at the end of the Bisitun inscription and in Herodotus' version of events were vital allies, for whose support Darius promised long-term status benefits and privileges.[14]

Darius' lack of legitimacy would partly explain the extent of the subsequent rebellions. They may have included individuals in the ruling class who thought they had equal title to power. His enemies appealed to older royal rights; several of the rebel leaders apparently claimed descent from archaic kings such as Cyaxares or Nabonidus and won over to their side serious support. Darius' response combined his 'ancient' royal genealogy with a new Persian identity distinct from those Babylonian and Median imperial histories. This Persian identity included a new patron god, Ahuramazda, as bringer of divine approval and help to the king. Like Marduk in the Cyrus Cylinder, Ahuramazda 'bestowed the kingdom' on a man whose honesty and righteousness he discerned. Ahuramazda was one of a pantheon associated with Iranian religions and, later, the god of the Zoroastrian religion. As well as being named constantly in Darius' inscriptions, it is likely that the winged figure which appears hovering above the king in the Bisitun and Persepolis reliefs is intended to show Ahuramazda's divine alliance with him.

The king's god was cast in a form recalling older Mesopotamian imperialism; the same was done with his language, Persian. Darius' statement about making the inscription in 'ariyan', too, strongly suggests that cuneiform characters were adapted to record the Persian language for the very first time at Bisitun. Although

2.6 This headless inscribed
statue of Darius I clad in a
Persian robe was found cast
down near the palace gate at
Susa in 1972, probably its
second place of display after
its manufacture in Egypt.
The Persian king is translated
into Egyptian form, with a
back pillar, a hieroglyphic
text in addition to Akkadian
and Old Persian, and
Egyptian iconography.

the cuneiform of Old Persian was read in a very different way from the older signs of Akkadian, it made the new conquerors' language look as authoritative as the old.[15] The visual impact of royal inscriptions was perhaps more important than their legibility to a limited audience. Reports could be spread widely through speech and translations in other languages; casting them in cuneiform gave them a prestigious core.

Bisitun was Darius' first mark on the landscape recording his own achievements, but it was only the beginning. Soon, his desire to reshape history in the image of his new monarchy extended to the creation of two new royal capitals. First, he took in hand Susa, an old capital of Elam, where two rebellions had occurred. This royal statement from tablets in three languages found at the site makes reference to his victories:

> Darius the king says: I changed many bad things that had been done to good things. By the favour of Ahuramazda I dealt with the countries which fought against each other, where people were killing each other, so that their people do not kill each other any more, and I return everyone to his place … Darius the king says: By the favour of Ahuramazda, I completed many building projects which previously had been abandoned.
>
> DSe, lines 30–8

Darius' project at Susa reshaped parts of the old city mound into a massive platform supporting a new kind of palace complex combining Babylonian, Iranian and Elamite building traditions. The new palaces decorated in glazed brick represented a royal capital to rival Babylon visually, if not in size and population. In recently annexed Egypt, Darius invested in inscriptions and buildings that emphatically proclaimed his power, legitimacy and his Persian ethnicity (fig. 2.6). He claimed credit for ordering as well as finishing the construction of the first Suez canal, left incomplete by the Egyptian king Necho at the turn of the sixth century:

> I am a Persian. From Persia I seized Egypt, I ordered the digging of this canal from a river called Nile, which flows in Egypt, to the sea which begins in Persia. Afterwards this canal was dug just as I ordered, and ships passed through this canal from Egypt to Persia, as I wished.[16]

Opinions are divided as to how functional the canal was, but Darius' inscription highlights the importance of the idea of a direct connection between Persia and the empire's edge.[17] A statue made near Heliopolis in Egypt and captioned with the name of Darius strongly recalls traditions of Egyptian sculpture, but depicts a Persian royal figure with cartouches of the peoples of the empire on the supporting base.[18] The ethnic groups into which they are divided were also newly defined back in Persia, on the new monuments Darius began. On the fringe of the Marv Dasht plain, a raised stone hall and large columned audience hall were planned and raised during his reign. The stone hall, called the palace (or *tachara*) of Darius, contained newly formulated images of the monarch, carved on the door jambs as if stepping through the entrances. Across the plain at Naqsh-i Rustam, the king reappears again on a massive dynastic tomb carved in the cliff-side. Lifting his hand towards a fire altar and a winged disk, the king is supported by rows of his subjects, each distinctively dressed as a separate nation:

2.7 The largely unchanging format of the royal tomb façade, is illustrated here in a fourth-century tomb at Persepolis. The king's religious or worship scene is placed on top of a platform supported by a simplified, distinctively clothed selection of his subjects. The same symbolic platform appears supporting the enthroned king in two further buildings at Persepolis.

If now you shall wonder 'How many are the countries which King Darius held?' look at the sculptures [of those] who bear the throne, then shall you know, then shall it become known to you: a Persian man has delivered battle far indeed from Persia …

DNb, lines.42–7

For the first time, an emphasis on the multiple and distinct peoples of the territories under their rule suffused Persian ideology. In monumental art, the king and his subjects were always portrayed peacefully in their fixed hierarchy.[19] The thirty to thirty-two groups represented in the palace imagery are idealized; their differences are indicated only by changes in dress and weaponry. In the more diverse, privately commissioned images of cylinder and stamp seals, these contrasts in dress sometimes reappear in scenes of conflict, Persian against Ionian, Scythian against Persian (figs 2.8, 2.9).

Something like the stability to which Darius' inscriptions aspired may have prevailed over large swathes of the empire after the initial succession crisis; but it was a difficult ideal towards which the king took practical steps. Later tradition sees Darius as a regulator of both provincial finance and law.[20] Where contemporary documents survive, they testify to a close administrative involvement in local justice and Persian interests such as land holdings.[21] In the reigns of both Darius I and his son Xerxes I, historical texts narrate only their continuing military interventions in the western empire.

EXPANSION AND REVOLT

The last few lines of the Bisitun inscription hint at the expanding nature of Darius' original campaigns for stability. His expedition against the Scythians took him further away from the original succession conflicts in Persia, Media and Mesopotamia. Military activity on both the eastern and western fringes of Persian

2.8 An agate Achaemenid cylinder seal inscribed with 'Darius, the Great King' in three languages preserves an action scene of the type absent from the calm reliefs of Persepolis. Although the scene as a whole draws on Assyrian traditions of the royal lion hunt, the ingredients, equipment and composition are distinctively Achaemenid.

2.9 A robed Persian spearman overcomes foes in Iranian or Scythian clothes on this chalcedony cylinder seal from the Oxus Treasure. In this and other seal images of Achaemenid warfare, the unfortunates get it in the neck. A winged disk and divine figure protectively hover over the action, while defeated foes underfoot act as pedestals for the combats.

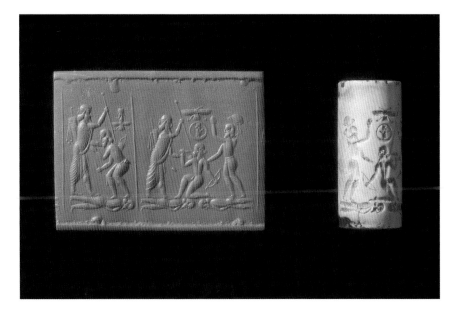

territory continued throughout his reign, but no more is recounted by inscriptions in the voice of the king. Some of this seems to have had the definite aim of further territorial conquest, for example Thrace and the Bosporan region, and north-west India or 'Hend'. But new peoples became allies or subjects in a variety of ways. After the installation of military garrisons, proportional tribute could be imposed. Alternatively, co-operative rulers in border regions might offer gifts in diplomatic recognition of Achaemenid power (for example early on in Samos, Cyrene and perhaps European Scythia). Neighbouring states and cities could achieve favoured status through a mere acknowledgement of the Persian king's status, or occasional marriage alliances. The Macedonian ruling dynasty apparently became part-Persian after the sister of Alexander I married a Persian noble (their son, Amyntas II, became the next king.[22] On the island of Samos, a Persian military intervention supported the claim of Syloson, the brother of the deceased tyrant, Polycrates, over his appointed deputy.[23] In each case, the assertion of influence or dominance was adapted to local circumstances. Darius' immediate, practical aim was probably to ensure that peoples (especially nomadic populations) at the edges of the empire would not disrupt it. But areas such as Thrace, with its plentiful silver mines, or commercial ports on the Aegean, were also valuable new acquisitions.

Before looking at Persian campaigns against Greek territory, it is worth pausing to contextualize the evidence. The Greek source material, in the shape of Herodotus, gives campaign accounts which highlight and dramatize certain incidents, as did Darius' Bisitun text. The details of intention and strategy that modern readers would like to find in them are not always forthcoming. The stories of conquest on which Herodotus drew in order to write his history may have been influenced by heroic traditions in earlier Near Eastern literature about kings and warfare. For example, in royal annals of the neo-Assyrian empire (934–c.610 BCE), the king's exploratory campaigns to the edges of secure territory were part of his role as a civilizing hero. At that time, one of these shadowy sources of anxiety to the settled plain was the mountainous edge of the Iranian plateau. There are signs that this tradition also developed in the Persian empire.

The wide open plains, bounded by rivers and seas in Central Asia in the east, Thrace in the west and the deserts of North Africa in the south, were a new unknown realm to their Persian rulers. Their potential as sources of chaos and insurrection could be checked with garrisons and military campaigns. The Bisitun inscription and Herodotus both highlight crossings of water into enemy territory, as vivid episodes in the campaigns of Persian kings: 'after that the Scythians who wear the pointed cap, these came against me, when I had come down to the sea. By means of a tree-trunk with the whole army I crossed it. Afterwards I defeated those Scythians' (DB V, lines 22–25).[24] In seal iconography, combatants in Iranian costume are shown matched in deadly combat with Scythians, as if symbolizing a perpetual struggle (fig. 2.10). Herodotus' stories of Cyrus' battles in Central Asia suggest that a significant tradition existed about royal campaigning on the frontier. The historian's later, comic account of Darius' invasion of Scythian Thrace undermines the positive ideology of such campaign stories.[25] In Achaemenid ideology, the incorporation of the edges of the empire was symbolised in the channelling of raw materials and exotic prizes to the central palaces. The movement of material to the centre of the empire could be paralleled in personnel, with skilled advisers from fringe territories enjoying success in the royal court. The reports of Persian clashes with Greek cities mix all these ingredients in a potent tale of royal *hubris* and imperial expansionism.

THE IONIAN REVOLT AND THE FIRST CAMPAIGN IN GREECE

Around 498, over twenty years after Darius' first, insecure years, revolt arose in several cities on the Ionian coast, the furthest western edge of the empire. Herodotus' highly personalized account attributes the entire affair to one Aristagoras, the ruler of Miletus, who persuaded Darius that it would be a good idea to add the Cycladic island of Naxos to his domains.[26] A joint force made up of levies from the Ionian cities on the coast and commanded by the local satrap, Artaphernes, apparently failed to take the island. After their return, reportedly at the urging of a fifth columnist at the Persian court, Aristagoras promptly turned the assembled levies into a force *against* the Persians; he allegedly used his own influence to persuade several cities in Caria and Cyprus, as well as Miletus and Byzantium, to proclaim independence from Persia or from the local rulers who owed their position to Persian patronage.[27] The initial impetus led to a partially successful assault on Sardis, the regional capital defended by the satrap and his Lydian allies (the outskirts were charred, but the citadel was not taken). In the following six years, the rebellious cities were brought back into Persian rule in a number of different ways: early surrender, restored loyalty or military conquest, most severely and famously in the case of Miletus, which was besieged and then sacked.[28] The true complexity of the reasons for such a patchy, but sporadically persistent revolt is difficult to recover from the available sources. Economic competition and internal civic faction fighting have both been suggested as reasons for tension and unrest.[29] The Persian response after reconquest involved a reassessment of tribute; this suggests that there may have been dissatisfaction in certain cities with the spread, among citizens and elite, of both benefits and obligations arising from Persian rule.

The punishments for rebellion did not end at Miletus. According to Herodotus, Athenian envoys visited Artaphernes at Sardis in 507/6, with a view to securing an international alliance. While there, they complied (perhaps without understanding the consequences) with the standard condition for Persian support, an acknowledgement of the king's power by offering 'earth and water'.[30] As a result, Athens was one of those fringe cities seen as nominally friendly to the Persians. So when Athens, along with Eretria on the island of Euboea, sent ships in support of the first phase of the Ionian rebellion, they were held to have also rebelled. To make things worse, Herodotus passes on the tradition that envoys from Darius who

2.10 Two sets of duels are shown on this impression of a fragmentary agate seal of unknown origin. Two soldiers (Persian?) in leather reinforced tunics and robes overcome opponents in peaked caps. Such images are generic rather than representing historical battles. The fragmentary name in the cartouche may be the royal name 'Artaxerxes'. Royal name seals could be owned by officials in imperial administration rather than being wielded by the monarch himself.

2.12 A large mound at Marathon in Attica commemorates Athenians who died fighting a Persian force. Its monumentality illustrates the immense significance that the victory held for Athenian ideas about their historic independence. In contrast, the large numbers of Persians said to have fallen by Herodotus are phantoms, yet to be located in the archaeological record.

2.11 In the sixth and fifth century, Athenian painters of symposium pottery frequently depicted foreigners in distinctive dress. This early red-figure plate by Epictetos shows an Iranian, or generic Oriental, archer in a patterned costume influenced by the embroidered and appliquéd long-sleeved tunics and trousers of the Achaemenid army.

appeared in Greece in 491 asking for earth and water were rudely imprisoned in pits by the Athenians and Spartans.[31] Such uncivilized behaviour could not be tolerated. Besides, the conquest of other islands of the Aegean suggests that the Persian king was seeking a dominant position in the seas fringing Asia. In 490, Darius I sent a seaborne expedition across the Aegean, led by the general Datis, which first laid waste to unfortunate Eretria, then landed on the Attic coast to march towards Athens.[32] Being prewarned, the Athenians, joined by reinforcements from Plataea, met them at Marathon.[33] Herodotus' much later account of the battle is a little difficult to shape into a coherent account – the Persian cavalry that he says was landed from the ships never appears to take part in the fight and his claims of 6,400 Persian dead, as compared to 192 on the Athenian side, are a little hard to corroborate.[34] But the surprisingly strong resistance was apparently enough to prevent the Achaemenid force progressing further.

Compared to other military feats of Darius' reign, the unsuccessful landing of his punitive force at Marathon was a minor event without wider strategic impact. But the encounter's effect on Greek ideas about their own identity, distinct from the peoples of Asia, was enormous; the battle was (and still is) commemorated in the landscape by a huge burial mound built over the cremated remains of the Athenian dead (fig. 2.12). The legend of Marathon was to be further magnified by subsequent events, when Xerxes I led a massive expeditionary army into the Greek mainland in 481. The recurrent signs of resistence and agitation projected mainly from Athens had qualified it for the full remedial treatment of a conquering royal expedition led by Darius' son.

XERXES I, HIS FATHER'S WORK AND THE EMPIRE

King Xerxes proclaims: My father [was] Darius; the father of Darius [was] Hystaspes by name; the father of Hystaspes [was] Arsames by name. Both Hystaspes and Arsames were living; nevertheless, thus was the desire of Ahuramazda – Darius who [was] my father, him he made king on this earth …

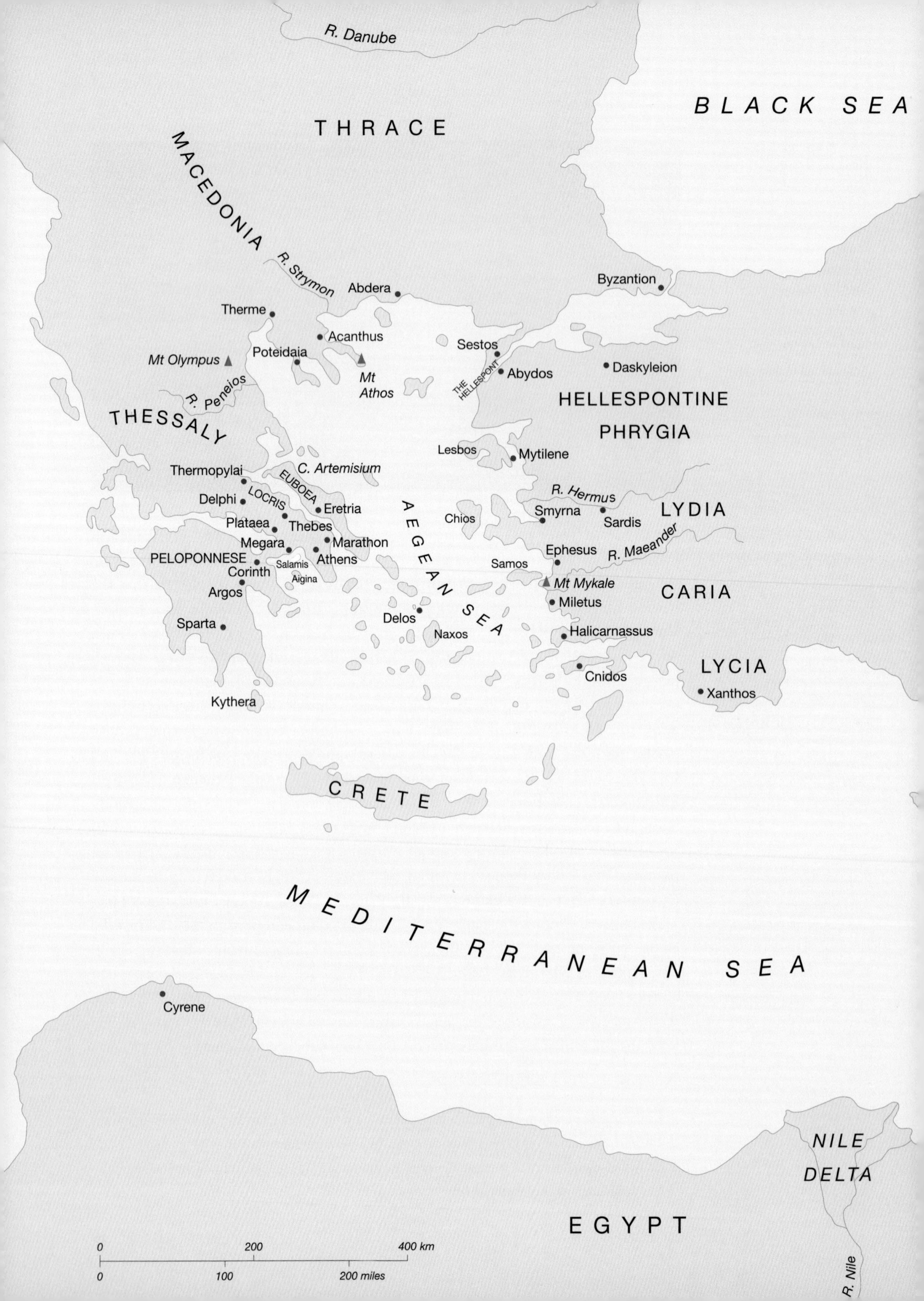

R. Danube

BLACK SEA

THRACE

MACEDONIA

R. Strymon

Abdera

Byzantion

Therme

Acanthus

Sestos

Daskyleion

Mt Olympus

Poteidaia

Mt Athos

Abydos

THE HELLESPONT

HELLESPONTINE

R. Peneios

THESSALY

PHRYGIA

Lesbos

Mytilene

Thermopylai

C. Artemisium

EUBOEA

R. Hermus

Delphi

LOCRIS

Eretria

Chios

Smyrna

Sardis

LYDIA

Plataea

Thebes

Megara

Marathon

Ephesus

R. Maeander

Salamis

Athens

AEGEAN SEA

Samos

Mt Mykale

CARIA

PELOPONNESE

Corinth

Aigina

Miletus

Argos

Delos

Halicarnassus

Sparta

Naxos

LYCIA

Cnidos

Kythera

Xanthos

CRETE

MEDITERRANEAN SEA

Cyrene

NILE DELTA

EGYPT

R. Nile

0   200   400 km

0   100   200 miles

Darius had other sons also; [but] thus was the desire of Ahuramazda: Darius, my father, made me the greatest after himself. When my father Darius went to his [allotted] place, by the favour of Ahuramazda I became king in my father's place.

XPf

Darius died in 486, and Xerxes' accession was incorporated smoothly in the dating of administrative documents in Babylonia by the end of the year.[35] The first royal succession since Darius' wholesale redefinition of the Persian monarchy was not a matter of automatic protocol, since none was established by practice. It was a testing point for the success of his promotion of the Achaemenid ruling family over all other claims. The idea of a princely heir, a king in formation, was displayed visually

2.14 Two large sculpted slabs showing a generalized scene of the enthroned king with his heir and an approaching petitioner took the central places on the two accessible façades of the Persepolis audience hall or *apadana*, surrounded by approaching courtiers, subjects and soldiers. They were moved to a different setting in the Treasury later in the fifth or fourth century. The best preserved was taken to Tehran, the second is still at Persepolis.

towards the end of Darius' reign on the façades of his newly created audience hall at Persepolis. The question of who would fulfil this role may not have been certain for much of Darius' reign and there may have been competition between the king's sons.[36] Xerxes, in his thirties at the time of the accession, argued in his royal inscriptions not just that his accession to the throne was because he was a son of Darius but that his father (and the god Ahuramazda) recognized in him, one of the members of the Achaemenid family, the special qualities of kingship.[37] Xerxes' use of his father's work to legitimize his own rule centred on his filial duty and, in both texts and architecture, developed the idea of a consistent family dynasty.[38]

Xerxes the great king proclaims: By the favour of Ahuramazda, much that is good did Darius the king, my father. And also by the favour of Ahuramazda, I added to that work and built more. Me may Ahuramazda protect, together with the gods, and my kingdom.

XPg

Xerxes finished several major projects at Persepolis, including the audience hall, and building continued there throughout his reign. Glazed bricks on the façade of the audience hall commemorated his completion of his father's work. He planned a new, much larger palace building next to his father's on the edge of the platform, and decisively shaped the approach to and use of the platform with the new 'Gate of all Nations' at the head of the monumental stairway entrance (frontispiece, fig. 7.1).

> Proclaims Xerxes the king: By the favour of Ahuramazda, this Gateway of All Peoples I
> built. Much other good [construction] was built within this *Parsa*, which I built and
> which my father built. Whatever good construction is seen, all that by the favour of
> Ahuramazda we built … Me may Ahuramazda protect, and my kingdom, and what was
> built by me, and what was built by my father, that also may Ahuramazda protect.
>
> XPa, lines 11–20[39]

The inscription shows Xerxes developing Darius' attempt to represent the diversity of the empire's peoples in the structures at Persepolis. His tomb façade reproduced the peacefully co-operative peoples of Darius' iconography. Nevertheless, royal military campaigns formed a significant part of Xerxes' early definition of his kingship. Scattered references suggest that a claimant taking a traditional royal name staged a rebellion in Egypt just before Darius' death.[40] After dealing with the insurrection, Xerxes made his own brother Achaemenes the new satrap. Far more serious than intractability in the west was a revolt in Babylon in the early years of Xerxes' reign. The exact date and duration suggested for this revolt are not easy to establish between scattered Babylonian documents. A hostile tradition about Xerxes' behaviour in Babylon survived in Herodotus' account (where it blended well with his story of the king's invasion of Greece). Herodotus alleged that Xerxes had impiously stolen a golden statue from the temple precinct of the city's patron deity, Bel-Marduk. This tale of plunder has been traditionally interpreted as a punishment of the rebellious Babylon. It is possible that this statue was a symbolic prize taken to a royal palace in order to represent Babylon's part in the empire, but it is unlikely to have been the cult statue itself.[41] Herodotus delighted in passing on stories about the greedy designs on Babylon held by both Xerxes and his father Darius. The emotive tale of statue-theft may in fact have been a small symptom of dissatisfaction over the more impactful transfer of property that occurred after a revolt; tracts of productive land in Babylonia were taken away from disloyal owners, and transferred to Persian nobles and allies.[42]

We know next to nothing about any diplomacy, investment or unrest in the east and north of the empire dated securely to Xerxes' reign. Although annotating specific building projects with his own name, Xerxes did not follow his father in narrating his historical conquests as a new king. One of his major inscriptions found at Persepolis, probably composed later in his reign, restates his and his father's familial and ethnic identity, gives the abstract and canonical list of peoples subject to his power, and adds a new kind of account of his acts as king:

> I ruled them; they bore me tribute … The law that [was] mine, that held them [stable] …
> When I became king, there is among those countries which [are] inscribed above [one,
> which], was in turmoil. Afterwards Ahuramazda brought me aid; by the favour of
> Ahuramazda I defeated that country and put it in its proper place.

2.15 A central virtue of kings was their power to combat destructive chaos, an idea also present among the older Mesopotamian monarchies. Contests with animals symbolized this struggle, although in reality, this ideology also surrounded campaigns against rebels. In this image impressed from a chalcedony cylinder seal from Borsippa, Iraq, a crowned Persian grasps a lion next to a traditional Babylonian-style hero grappling with a bull. Although a synchronized struggle, the Persian was perhaps overpowering the higher-status opponent.

... there were [some] where formerly the *daivas* had been worshipped ... I destroyed that place of the *daivas* and I gave orders: 'The *daivas* shall not be worshipped any longer!' Wherever formerly the *daivas* have been worshipped, there I worshipped Ahuramazda at the proper time and in the proper ceremonial style.

And there was something else, that had been done wrong, that too I put right. That which I have done, all that I have done by the favour of Ahuramazda ...

XPh, paras 3–6

The worship of 'daivas' is used here to describe rebellion, in a way similar to Darius' use of the moral absolute of the 'lie' to explain the actions of those who did not accept his rule; the word comes from eastern Indo-Iranian religious traditions about good and evil, in which *daiva* was a classification of a bad spirit, the flipside to the benevolent protection of the gods. This binary opposition could place peoples in and beyond the empire into two categories: those (positive, peaceful) groups with the Persians and their allies and those (evil, violent) against them.

The symbolic struggle against human evil or natural chaos in the maintenance of civilization was a core ideal of Near Eastern kingship. The real boundary between anti- and pro-Persian, however, could be much more fluid and ambiguous; ideology and reality rarely matched. The Persian invasion of the Greek mainland is one case in point.

Xerxes is best known in the European tradition because of his leadership of this land and sea expedition to Greece in 480 and 479 BCE. Herodotus casts Xerxes in the role of an arrogant and violent despot, but his work, written up to fifty years after the invasion, remains our central source for the order of events.[43] Xerxes mustered his troops in Cappadocia and then at the capital of Lydia, Sardis, in early 480. The army then moved up the coast, crossing the Hellespont near Abydos.

The first two feats of the invasion were performed against natural, not human, enemies. While the army and fleet gathered, work parties composed of local residents and 'men … from all nations in the army' were put to work at the Athos peninsula to cut a canal through the isthmus.[44] The traces of this two-and-a-half-kilometre channel were discovered by archaeological excavation in 2001 (fig. 2.17).[45] Herodotus connects the project with the wreck of the Persian navy around Athos ten years earlier, but canal-building (and path-making) was a traditional feature of the activities of a good king in Near Eastern tradition.[46] More immediately, the working of this canal echoed the Suez canal to the south, another way in which Xerxes followed his father. The second superhuman pathway was formed for the land army. As Darius had apparently built a pontoon bridge over the Bosporus for his land invasion of Thrace, Xerxes went one step further by harnessing the Hellespont near Abydos with two bridges of Phoenician flax and Egyptian papyrus, floating on over three hundred warships each.[47] Both bridge and canal were probably seen as positive kingly deeds, but Herodotus presents them negatively as products of Xerxes' overwheening pride. According to him, the king arrogantly sentenced the waves to a flogging after a storm carried away the first links of the pontoon bridge, and injuries inflicted on the canal-diggers signalled divine displeasure.

The expeditionary force of soldiers, households and provisioners crossed from Asia into Europe in early summer 480; the recorded numbers of over two million were exaggerated, and the entire army would have numbered well under a hundred thousand.[48] Much of the progress into mainland Greece was taken up with diplomatic rather than military activity. The area of Thrace into which Xerxes crossed was a territory containing subjects of the king, some of whom were duly conscripted. The army, in three divisions, followed the coast westwards, crossing the river Strymon with another pontoon bridge and making a rendezvous with the fleet at Acanthus and again at Therma in Macedonia (still in friendly territory). On reaching Pieria, near Mount Olympus, Xerxes received news that several cities and peoples of central Greece, including Thebes, Locris and Thessaly, had submitted to his demand for earth and water. After the war, this co-operation was vilified as 'Medizing' by other Greeks who had resisted or at least remained neutral in the face of the Persian advance. There were many Medizers, not least the Greeks in Xerxes' entourage, including exiled Athenian aristocrats and Demaratus, a former king of Sparta. Both at the outset and in the later stages of the invasion, the cities and peoples of Greece were not united in opposition to Persian rule, but resisted, co-operated or assisted according to their own rivalries, fears or expectations of benefit.

The first military engagements came on land at Thermopylae, where a small Spartan force was quickly overwhelmed, and at sea nearby, off the headland of Artemisium (which the fleet had reached after apparently suffering storm losses).[49] The sea fight was damaging to the Persians, who lost vessels both to the Greeks and to further storms. As the land army advanced, the peoples of the Peloponnese devoted their energy to building a defensive wall across the isthmus. The Athenians took to the drastic strategy of evacuating Attica, retreating to Troezen in the Peloponnese, and the

2.16 A calcite jar is inscribed with the name of Xerxes in four languages: Old Persian, Elamite, Babylonian Akkadian and Egyptian Hieroglyphic. Similarly inscribed stone vessels were found smashed in the Persepolis Treasury, but, like royal name seals, such prestigious objects could circulate widely across the empire. This example was found in Bodrum (Halicarnassus).

2.17 The line of vegetation in the landscape here marks the low land showing the route of Xerxes' canal through the Athos peninsula, discovered in 2001. The excavators suggest that the canal was not long in use. Xerxes' victory over this landscape may have been symbolic rather than practical.

nearby islands of Salamis and Aegina. About four months after crossing the Helle-spont, the Persians occupied Attica and the city of Athens, finally delivering the pun-ishment for their disloyalty by sacking the religious buildings on the Acropolis and carrying off statues from there and the marketplace. Athenian exiles who were travel-ling with the Persians were then invited to make the proper sacrifices on the Acropolis;[50] from the conquerors' perspective, the rebellious stain had been removed from Athens, and those righteous citizens who would uphold the correct order (on behalf of the king) piously reinstated their customary ritual.

But the Greek fleet remained close to the occupied shore, using the island of Salamis as a base, as the sailing and campaigning season drew to a close. The Persian navy met them in the narrow strait between the coast and the island. The action of the sea battle is difficult to reconstruct. Herodotus describes masses of wounded hulls and splintering timbers, suggesting that the larger numbers of Persian ships were ren-dered useless in the cramped coastal waters and suffered a heavy defeat. Nevertheless, the Halicarnassian author takes the time to showcase a local royal heroine, Artemisia, who personally commanded a ship among the Persian forces in the battle (to rather self-destructive but impressive effect).[51] This maritime setback did not immediately affect the situation on land, although the navy was withdrawn to Asia Minor. The Per-sian army was settled in Thessaly for the winter of 480–479, under the command of

Mardonius, kinsman of the king. Xerxes, meanwhile, took the long land route back to Sardis, apparently returning to the business of the empire.

After inconclusive diplomatic discussions throughout the spring, Mardonius led an occupying force back into Attica for part of the following summer, but, on withdrawing, was followed back into central Greece by an allied force led by the Spartan general Pausanias. Uneven skirmishes between different segments of both forces (with successes and setbacks on both sides) led eventually in August to a full-scale battle on the plain of Plataea in which Mardonius was killed.[52] Herodotus envisages him on a white charger fighting in the midst of picked soldiers. The death of the king's nominated leader led to a general Persian retreat, leaving behind his royal tent full of the trappings of the highest status. Stories of the Greeks' response to this and other symbols of Persian wealth show both strong fascination and scorn.[53] This combination of influence and assertive difference was to become characteristic of many Greek responses to their neighbouring power over the following century and a half.

The retreat of the Persian land army and the withdrawal of the fleet around mainland Greece drew aggressive Greek expeditionary forces out into the eastern Mediterranean. Mykale, operational base for the Persian navy across the sea from Samos, was successfully targeted, along with Sestos on the European side of the Hellespont, a particularly strong Persian administrative centre after Xerxes' invasion.[54] These limited but effective raids across the length of Persian territory were part of a new attempt to follow up Greek success on the mainland, fostering insecurity in locations that would otherwise provide bases for a counterattack. Islands such as Samos committed themselves to political alliance with other Ionian islanders and Athens, in order to form an organized front against future Persian encroachment.[55] The assertion of independence from Persia in the Ionian cities and islands did not spread further east; there is little sign that traffic and trade along this western edge of the empire was affected. The allegiance of the Ionians of Asia Minor was to change again within a century; the most lasting impact of their secession was not independence but rather a close acquaintance with Achaemenid diplomacy and a theoretical idea of Persian vulnerability in the face of Greek independence.

Herodotus and two later authors say that, after the defeats at Plataea and Mykale, Xerxes left Sardis to journey back to one of his central capitals: Susa, Ecbatana or Babylon. In the latter city there may have been political unrest to draw his urgent attention.[56] Herodotus obscured the following fifteen years of his reign with stories devoted to dynastic intrigue, while practical changes in the empire are not mentioned at all.[57] In fact, a number of the surviving inscriptions of Xerxes were probably composed during this period; construction at Persepolis continued. The construction and maintenance of a strong Persian fleet in the west was sustained in response to further Athenian campaigning directed at dominating the Aegean and its fringes.[58] Away from the glitter of the battlefield in Greece and the elaborate dynastic soap opera of Herodotus, the long-term trends of archaeo-

2.18 The luxury of the Persian dining experience fascinated the Greeks when they looted court trappings from the battlefield. Movable wealth in the form of silver bowls would have been particularly evident. This example shows the sharply defined shoulder and defined, flared lip that were characteristic of Achaemenid period drinking bowls. Similar vessels have been recovered from tombs and cemeteries in western Asia Minor, Syria and the Levant.

logical and administrative data illustrate a continuing stability and productivity during Xerxes' reign.[59]

The king's life ended violently, within the court in the late summer of 465.[60] Laconic Babylonian notes in the contemporary astrological diaries say that Xerxes was murdered by his son, without naming him (we know of three sons) (fig. 2.20).

Dramatic Greek stories cloak the event in court stories of intrigue among the Persian advisers closest to the king.[61] They suggest that a Persian noble called Artabanus may have laid some claim to the kingship, while blaming Xerxes' murder on his oldest son, Darius.[62] In these tales, the eventual legitimate successor, Artaxerxes, righteously avenges the deaths of his father and brother. As in stories of the death of kings, events are buried away in the palace buildings; the political reality also lies hidden from view.[63] After the deaths within the royal family, there may have been further unrest in Bactria, where another royal son was satrap, but rebellion did not spread in the heart of the empire.[64] The accession of this new king was seen as an opportunity to alter or renegotiate provincial relationships with the central monarchy, as if seeking new benefits through the change in management.[65] In the most extreme instance, a rebel called Inaros in lower Egypt took advantage of the change in rule to seize power in part of lower Egypt, a rebellion that, although it failed to eject Persian forces from the province, continued for approximately eight years. Inaros' son ultimately became a client-king of the Persians.[66]

The events in the reigns of Darius and Xerxes forged a new identity for Persian imperial rule. Events on the western edge of the empire left a legacy of consciousness of the difference between Greek-speaking peoples and those in Persian territory. In the European tradition, this merged with a wholesale distinction between the culture and politics of the East and West; but the Persian empire's relationship with its neighbours and dissident groups was always more complex. In the long reign of Artaxerxes I, Greek conflict and Persian diplomacy would again become intertwined; cultural relationships also became complex. Imaginary Medes, Persian politicians and their fabulous trappings form a glamorous thread, envied and vilified, running through the words and images of classical Greece. Returning to the centre, in Mesopotamia and the Iranian plateau, the vision formed by the Achaemenids of themselves crystallized in the palaces of their capitals.

2.19 A black glazed *phiale* or bowl excavated in the Athenian *agora* shows the influence of contemporary Persian luxury vessels; its defined shoulder is derived from metal originals. The horizontal fluting also imitates a common feature of Achaemenid metalware decoration. This example dates from before the second Persian expedition.

2.20 The date of Xerxes' death, in 465 BCE by modern reckoning, was noted by a Babylonian scholar in his daily observations of planetary and climatic events. This data collection was designed to match signs with the events they predicted in order to build a reference library for predictions.

3 ROYAL CAPITALS

As to the ruins in particular, I have mentioned all that I could give any Idea of: but if the curious think it not enough, or that it is a little confused, I pray them to consider … that it is very hard to observe much order in the relation of things, which the process of many Ages, the weather, and even the malice of Men, have put into extream confusion.

Jean-Baptiste Tavernier[1]

The Achaemenid kings used up to five different royal capitals as residences and places of audience with their court and subjects. These capitals, the cities of Babylon, Susa, Ecbatana, Pasargadae and Persepolis, became near-legendary destinations of unimaginable glamour to those on the edges of Persian territory. It was the progress of Alexander of Macedon through the heart of the empire that brought them to life in Western tradition; with each surrendered city, he accumulated greater riches from each palace treasury. Persepolis, whose rich palaces were looted and burned by Alexander, was the first site whose remains were reconnected with accounts of Achaemenid history, after European merchants and embassies began to travel in greater numbers past its stone ruins in the late sixteenth century. Over the next two centuries, the less obvious remains of the other centres were tallied with ancient geographical descriptions and identified. Each lies in very different terrain, in the low Mesopotamian plain or across the Zagros mountain range on the Iranian plateau, scattered in strategic positions across this spine of the empire. The nature and extent of the remains from which we can reconstruct the physical world of Persian kingship at each capital vary a great deal. Yet it is from the fragments of the palace audience halls and courts that the Achaemenid kings' image of themselves and their subjects has begun to emerge.

According to the ancient sources, Greek and Persian, the Persian kings used all four main cities as royal residences in a seasonal progression between suitable climes.[2] The precise calendar of movements varies from author to author, but they suggest that the migration could often be regulated according to season. The hot summer months were best spent in Ecbatana, high on the Iranian plateau and encircled by mountains, while winter, which could be harsh and snowy over the Zagros mountains, was temperate in Susa, on the edge of the Mesopotamian plain. The schedule of travel and duties at each palace varied over time and included spells outside the regular circle of royal palaces, for example on campaign or in regional capitals. The king's passage between destinations was not merely a travel interlude but an almost ceremonial procession which displayed the full hierarchy of the court on the move.[3] The court probably functioned as fully on the road as within a built-up

59

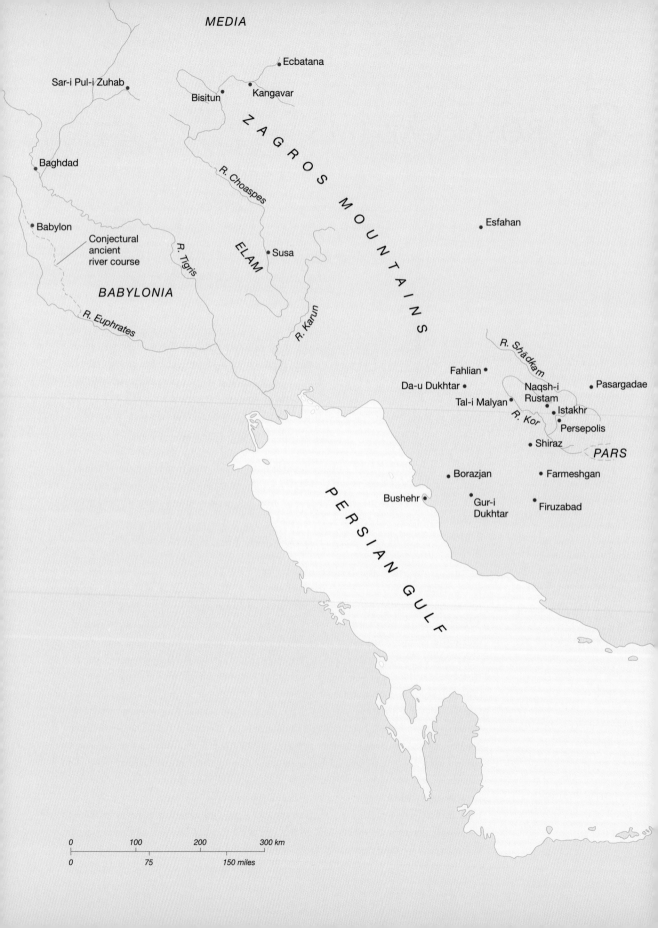

MEDIA

Sar-i Pul-i Zuhab •

• Ecbatana
Bisitun • • Kangavar

Baghdad •

Babylon •

Conjectural
ancient
river course

R. Choaspes

BABYLONIA

R. Tigris

R. Euphrates

ELAM

• Susa

R. Karun

Z A G R O S   M O U N T A I N S

Esfahan •

R. Shādkam

Fahlian •
Da-u Dukhtar •
Tal-i Malyan •

Naqsh-i
Rustam

• Pasargadae

R. Kor

Istakhr •
Persepolis •

Shiraz •

PARS

Borazjan •

• Farmeshgan

Bushehr •
Gur-i
Dukhtar •

• Firuzabad

P E R S I A N   G U L F

0   100   200   300 km

0   75   150 miles

3.2 Southern Mesopotamia and southern Iran. Royal complexes were built at Persepolis, Pasargadae, Ecbatana and Susa, and developed at Babylon; smaller monumentalized sites scattered across southern Iran turned the wider landscape into a setting for the monarchy.

capital. The alternation of architectural and nomadic settings for the king and his court was partly a result of the unique territorial and cultural make-up of the Persian empire. It is likely that the built-up centres that were developed during the reigns of Cyrus, Cambyses and Darius I were not conceived of as urban islands in which the king's power was concentrated. In Fars, for example, monumental masonry remains, including foundations, stone column elements and small sculptures, have survived at several small but prominent sites scattered across the landscape.[4] These small patches of palace architecture dotting the landscape may have been the stone-built section of travel way stations, used by officials and the court, spanning the province. But their special architectural development is best seen as an extension of the kind of widely spaced planning undertaken at Pasargadae and the Achaemenid tendency to see power and kingship as invested in the setting of the formal garden or the semi-controlled hunting ground. These occasional pavilions perhaps served as architectural beacons designed to express how the entire landscape of the home province of the Persians lay at the heart of Achaemenid power.

Of the four capitals with royal residences (dating from Darius I onwards), three carried associations with earlier monarchies – Susa, Babylon and Ecbatana. The Mesopotamian basis of the older Assyrian and Babylonian empires was now counterbalanced with the homelands of Iranian power in Media and Parsa. Each capital represented a different facet of Persian territorial power. The cities and palaces may have had roles that differed from each other. The nomadic (if highly elaborate and sophisticated) lifestyle of the king and his court for part of the year may have affected the way permanent buildings were used. Even the extent to which each palace complex might have been inhabited and developed as a populated centre, in the sense that we understand permanent cities, is still a matter for debate.[5] The functions

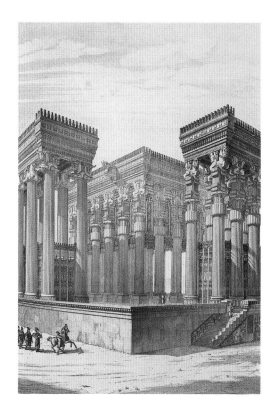

3.3 The architecture of the Achaemenid palaces combined sculpted stonework with massive mud-brick walls. This nineteenth-century reconstruction of Persepolis (by Flandin and Coste) imagines open porticoes, illustrating early debate about architectural form.

of palace complexes, individual buildings or rooms are still open to speculation.

For example, what were specific buildings in the complexes called? We know them now by names produced by a mixture of archaeologists' assumptions about use and from unevenly applied ancient words. There are three words used by the Persian kings in their inscriptions to name their buildings: *hadesh*, *tachara* and *apadana*. The exact architectural meaning of *apadana* is not clear in the few inscriptions in which it appears.[6] It was used first by excavators for the large, columned audience hall at Susa because it was inscribed on column bases there by Artaxerxes II in commemoration of his restorations. Archaeologists have come to apply the word more widely to the largest Achaemenid columned halls as a building type.[7] *Apadana* is found elsewhere only on an isolated column base of Artaxerxes II, from

Hamadan. *Hadesh* and *tachara* are equally opaque, since they are not systematically used for one distinct type of palace building.

Apart from the royal inscriptions on the buildings themselves, most detailed literary descriptions of the topography and palaces of these capital cities were quoted or created by authors writing long after the disappearance of the monarchy that constructed them. Visions of these lost worlds appeared in the Biblical book of Esther (set at Susa), a compendium on luxurious dining (the 'Deipnosophistai') assembled by Athenaeus, and the universal histories and geographies of Diodorus of Sicily and Strabo; the last three texts all date to the Roman period. All of these descriptions focus on the unparalleled luxury of the king's environment – the golden canopy over his bed, his rich hangings and precious metal dinner service. While the king's possessions and palace fittings were undoubtedly key elements in making him distinctive and powerful, these second-hand descriptions do not give us the full picture of the Achaemenid royal palaces. Another part of palace life has been recovered in writing from Persepolis, where thousands of clay tablets have been discovered, inscribed in cuneiform writing in the Elamite language. These administrative documents detail the bare bones of the processes of building, travel, business and religious ritual taking place within the palace and city. For the flesh on these bones, we must look at the whole picture made up of many different sorts of evidence.

ECBATANA

Ecbatana, or in Persian Hegmataneh, was the royal capital on the site of the modern city of Hamadan in north-west Iran. Xenophon and several other authors call it the summer residence of the Achaemenid court.[8] At an altitude of over 1,800 m, the city is overlooked by a mountain range, of which the greatest peak at 3,600 m is Mount Alvand (in Greek sources, Mount Orontes). Ecbatana is surrounded by paradoxes. Coherent, clearly Achaemenid ruins have never been excavated there, yet 'Hamadan' is one of the most frequent names to appear on the museum labels of Achaemenid objects scattered in collections across the world. Numerous Achaemenid architectural fragments have come to light in the vicinity of the town, yet none can be placed in any reconstructed ground plan.

In an attempt to fathom the layout of ancient Ecbatana, historians and archaeologists examine the descriptions of a Greek author, who never visited it, Herodotus. Though writing at the height of Persian power, he may not have given an accurate report of the city topography. His description of the seven concentric city walls of 'Agbatana', with variegated battlements and silver and gold plating, is part of his tale of the origins of a monarchy in Media.[9] The encircling walls symmetrically progress to an inner circle containing the palace and treasury. He attributes these fantastical fortifications to the Median founder-king, Deiokes, who, he says, also created court formalities to protect the throne. In his later references to the city in the Persian period, Herodotus gives no further details of its palaces or setting. Ctesias, writing a few decades later, also placed the building of Ecbatana in a

3.4 An aerial view of
Hamadan taken by the
Chicago expedition in 1935
shows the high Mosalla hill
at the upper edge of the
picture. The area of the
Hegmataneh hills, now
partly excavated, lies below
the main road arteries at the
bottom edge of the
photograph.

3.5 'By the favour of
Ahuramazda, Anahita and
Mithras, this palace I built.'
Fragments of two column
bases preserve building
inscriptions of Artaxerxes II
in Old Persian and
Babylonian (top, centre and
left) and Elamite and
Babylonian (bottom, centre
and left). Emerging from
Iran in the late nineteenth
century, they were said to
come from Hamadan;
similar fragments have been
found there.

period before Achaemenid rule.[10] In his account, the semi-mythical figure of
Queen Semiramis was said to have constructed the palace there, one in a series of
immense transformations of the Median landscape.

In fact, a number of inscriptions about royal building projects dated to the
Achaemenid period have been thought to come from Hamadan. Most of them are
inscriptions of Artaxerxes II, inscribed on fragments of stone column bases found
scattered around the town. Travellers began noting
column bases in the vicinity of Hamadan in the
early nineteenth century. One which resembled
those at Persepolis was seen by the side of
Tappeh-ye Hekmataneh, a long, uneven mound
to the north of the centre of town. More recently,
archaeological exploration in the same area has
brought to light a new inscribed column base.
Although excavations on top of this mound have
revealed a mud-brick wall and a complex of rooms,
the style of the buildings is not Achaemenid and
may be much later.[11] Tappeh-ye Hekmataneh is
not the only candidate for the site of an ancient
building in town. The higher, more striking
Mosalla hill to the south-east of Tappeh-ye Hekmataneh has also often been considered as the site
of the ancient palace. But although it was the site

of later fortresses, the Mosalla hill has not produced a large number of remains, beyond scattered architectural fragments similar to those found all over the town.

The incoherent evidence makes it difficult to imagine the ancient city, but comparative evidence can help us begin to map it out. The plans of other Achaemenid centres and Median remains suggest that the fortress and palace may have occupied separate locations. Perhaps both the Mosalla and Hegmataneh hills originally defined the ancient city's shape. The river may have also been a focus for both constructions; Artaxerxes II's palace may have been situated by the river like its counterpart in Susa.

The near-mythological, early Persian history woven around the site in Greek literature reappears in other, rather more mysterious inscriptions said to come from

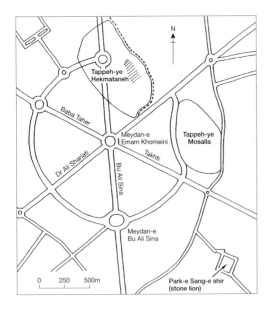

3.6 This sketch map of the modern Hamadan town centre shows the location of current excavations and finds. The point of view of the aerial photograph looks southward from the northern edge of this map. After Knapton, Sarraf and Curtis 2001.

Hamadan. Two gold tablets inscribed in Old Persian cuneiform record the names and lineages of Ariaramnes and Arsames, two of the early kings who appear first in Darius I's Bisitun genealogy, connecting his ancestors with those of Cyrus II.[12] One was first published by the archaeologist Ernst Herzfeld in 1931, before he began his excavations at Persepolis, and the tablet found its way to Berlin. The second surfaced publicly in the 1940s and was described for a general audience by Arthur Upham Pope in the *Illustrated London News*. As with many objects that became known in similar ways, there is no guarantee that the objects are ancient, and the tablets are certainly incongruous. Why should these ancient kings be writing in Old Persian that *should* be dated after Darius I? Why should inscriptions of archaic Persian kings come from a city that would have been ruled by Median kings? Yet another possibility is that the inscriptions could in fact be ancient forgeries. The clue lies in later inscriptions of kings in the fourth century.

Rulers such as Artaxerxes II and III recited their whole lineage in their building inscriptions, showing the long inheritance they felt they were upholding. Like the Greek tales of Ecbatana's origins, these kings wanted to portray a rich past for their capitals.

The history of these inscriptions is an example of the omnipresent murk surrounding the precise origin and nature of many objects said to have come from Hamadan. After the increased exploration, excavation and blatant plundering of ancient sites in the nineteenth century, some entrepreneurs woke up to the benefits of selling ancient objects of all periods taken from the ground across the country. Hamadan became a major centre where antiquities, and some modern forgeries, surfaced for sale on the local or international market.[13] Many may be authentic, but their potential contribution to our knowledge about ancient Iran is greatly diluted by the uncertainty surrounding the city.

However elusive, the palaces of Ecbatana were a crucial hinge in Achaemenid geopolitics. The city's name was well enough known as a centre of Persian concerns for a late fifth-century Athenian comic to proclaim that a luxury jacket came 'straight from Ecbatana'.[14] When the monarchy of Persia came under threat, Ecbatana seems to have been a pillar of the regime. When Artaxerxes II had to fight his brother Cyrus for the throne, he marshalled his loyal troops there. Ecbatana was supposed to be a rallying point for Darius III after the loss of Mesopotamia and the western half of his empire to Alexander. His hoped-for reinforcements from the Caucasus and the Caspian failed to arrive, and he abandoned his last capital to flee eastwards to his death. In 521–520, Darius I's army had overcome and executed his rival, the pretender Phraortes, in public on the walls. In a turn of historical symmetry, two hundred years later, Ecbatana was again the site of the final symbolic obliteration of rebellion. The last aristocratic Persians to attempt to preserve an Achaemenid monarchy in the furthest east of the empire, Bessus and his accomplices, were sent to Ecbatana by Alexander, and executed there in the palace that had housed their king.

Ecbatana's significance did not end with the Achaemenid dynasty. Nineteenth-century travellers' reports of large limestone and marble columns on the fringes of Hamadan suggest that monumental stone buildings were constructed there in the following Hellenistic and Parthian periods.[15] It is the more or less continuous occupation of the same site that has proved such a problem in reconstructing the city's Achaemenid form. The continuity occasionally surfaces strikingly. At the Park-e Sang-e Shir, in the south-west of the town centre, a stone statue of a lion is displayed. Its mouth is worn smooth by the touch of many hands – the lion has long been locally regarded as a talisman of marriage and childbirth. A closer look reveals a style of carving similar to Greek funeral monuments of the fourth to third century BCE. Historians have traditionally connected the lonely beast with the burial of Alexander's friend or lover, Hephaestion.

Susa

> This palace which I built at Susa, from afar its ornamentation was brought. Downward the earth was dug, until I reached rock in the earth … At Susa a very excellent work was ordered, a very excellent work was accomplished.
>
> DSf, lines 22f, 55f[16]

Like Ecbatana, the Achaemenid centre of Susa was grafted on to a city with a longer history as a local capital. By the time of the Achaemenid remodelling of the site, there had been an urban settlement at Susa for three and a half millennia. Situated on the border between the Mesopotamian plain and the Zagros mountains, Susa today is on the north-eastern edge of the modern province of Khuzistan. Historically, this region was known as Elam, after the language and culture of successive states that straddled the marginal territory reaching between southern Mesopotamia and the western edges of the Iranian plateau.

In keeping with its location, Susa was linked with political authorities and cultural influences from both of its regional contexts. As part of the Elamite world in the second millennium, Susa's connections included religious and urban sites in Fars, such as Naqsh-i Rustam, Kurungan and Anshan (Tal-i Malyan), near Persepolis. Despite its long history of settlement, Greek authors do not show much consciousness of Susa's antiquity, in contrast to their visions of an archaic Ecbatana. Nevertheless, Susa was relatively well known as the central Persian capital and was seen as the ultimate eastward destination for embassies on the Royal Road from Sardis.[17] Susa was the glamorous setting for the tale of Esther in the Persian court. It was this Biblical association that led British and French excavators to the site (in 1852–54 and the 1870s) in search of the royal palace.

The two mounds on which there are remains of the Achaemenid royal buildings are only part of the vast *tell* (hill). The brick citadel on the Acropole, the highest part of the site, was built by the French archaeological mission in 1898 in order to provide protection against tribal raids. At that time, Susa lay close to the permeable border with Ottoman territory. French excavators, first the pioneering Marcel and Jane Dieulafoy, followed by the Délégation Archéologique en Iran, worked in Susa and surrounding areas from the 1890s until 1979 and bequeathed the names by which the main features are known.[18] On the Acropole are piled successive brick temple foundations, but for the Achaemenid period only burials have been found there.

3.7 Susa from an altitude of 534 m, autumn 1935, from the south (Oriental Institute, Chicago). The remains of the Achaemenid palaces stand on the mound furthest from the camera. In the foreground is the French mission's château and the heavily excavated Acropole mound. The Ville Royale area extends towards the east. The then unexcavated site of Artaxerxes II's palace lies opposite the *apadana* mound across the Shaur river.

To the north of the château and Acropole lies the gravel, rubble and mud-brick platform which supported the Achaemenid audience hall, or the *apadana*, and royal palace complex. East of these is the expanse of mud-brick remains of many periods, called the Ville Royale; at its southernmost tip stood a late (Hellenistic, Parthian or Sasanian) building known as the Donjon. Further east of the Ville Royale, beyond an intervening channel, lie further partially excavated buildings called the Ville des Artisans.[19] The site today is approached from the west, where the modern city has grown, centred on the Shaur river.

> Darius the king says: By the favour of Ahuramazda, much handiwork which previously had been put out of its place, that I put in its place. A town by name … [its] wall fallen from age, before this unrepaired – I built another wall [to serve] from that time into the future.
>
> DSe, lines 41–49[20]

Many tablet fragments found at Susa, in three different languages, combine to form translations of the same words of the king. A great variety of inscriptions of Darius I are attested here, at his earliest building project. The last few lines of this inscription (above), describing the extent of Darius' rule and his restoration of order after the rebellions against him, reflect his desire to be seen as the restorer of ancient Mesopotamian cities. This traditional kingly quality was joined with Darius' desire to forge a new-look monarchy at Susa.

The extensive remodelling of the Achaemenid period is still visible in the steep, reinforced faces of the *apadana* mound, which set it apart from the surrounding landscape. The elevation of over 15 m above the river plain would have accentu-

3.8 This map of the central archaeological area of Susa shows the three principal mounds separated from the fourth-century Achaemenid palace of Artaxerxes II by the Shaur (or Chaour) river. The prominence of the columned *apadana* or audience hall is illustrated by its position on the northern edge of the main palace complex. After Boucharlat 1997.

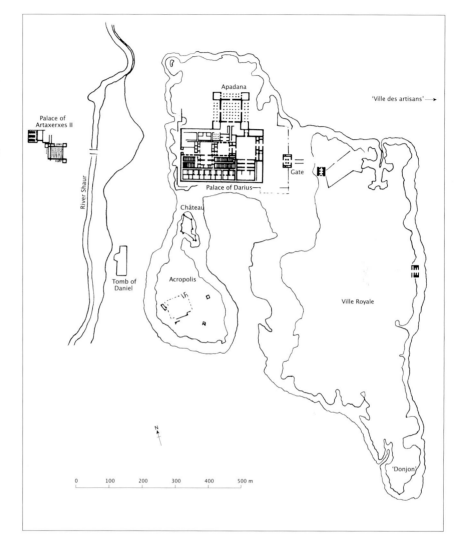

ated the columns, 20 m high, of the prominent audience hall, visible from three sides of the approach to the terrace. A bridge, 30 m long, led from the Ville Royale towards the royal palaces. Four gateways or entrances have been uncovered. Three tall structures, which are known mainly from their huge foundations, trace a route into the Ville Royale, then from it on to the *apadana* mound, flanking the bridge. Remains of a fourth monumental, decorated stairway have been discovered in recent Iranian excavations; this seems to have formed a splendid entrance on the north-western side of the *apadana* mound. People climbing up to the terrace on the decorated stairway could have moved around or through the audience hall, to exit at the tall gate on to the Ville Royale. At least one larger-than-life statue of Darius beside the inner gate here gave those passing through it a last brush with royalty. The entire area around the palace was transformed into an experience of royal power.

A second, longer inscription recovered in many forms (DSf) celebrates the massive earth-moving and manifold skills required to create the new environment:

> When the excavation had been made, then rubble was packed down, some 40 cubits in depth, another [part] 20 cubits in depth. On that rubble the palace was constructed. And that the earth was dug downward, and that the rubble was packed down, and that the sun-dried brick was moulded, the Babylonian people – it did [these tasks].

DSf, lines 24–30[21]

3.9 The nearly 1.5m-high spearbearers found pacing the palace walls at Susa are often interpreted as the king's guard. A high status is indicated by their gold bracelets and ornamented gowns. The decorative motifs of the guards' clothing echo the larger borders, which frame them in this reconstruction. Their original location may have been around the western entrance to the palace, where they were found.

This famous building inscription was present all over the mound, visible on glazed bricks on the palace façade, on marble tablets designed to be turned and read on rods. The text permeated the structure, on clay tablets and cylinders deposited in the foundations, as a new, multimedia, international version of the royal foundation documents traditional in Mesopotamian cities. In it, Darius detailed the contributions of peoples and countries across the empire to the construction of the palace: 'The cedar timber, this – a mountain by name Lebanon – from there was brought. The Assyrian people, it brought it to Babylon; from Babylon the Carians and the Ionians brought it to Susa' (DSf, lines 30–4). The highlighted sources of building and decorative materials are at the geographical extremes of the empire – the far west, east and furthest south. Ivory came from Ethiopia, India and Arachosia. The distant edges were combined in a physical demonstration of the king's power in the very centre. Assyrian kings had celebrated similar harmonious palace creation using material from the regions they had conquered, but the Persian buildings at Susa encompassed vast new territories and peoples.

> The stone-cutters who wrought the stone, those were Ionians and Sardians. The goldsmiths who wrought the gold, those were Medes and Egyptians. The men who wrought the wood, those were Sardians and Egyptians. The men who wrought the baked brick, those were Babylonians. The men who adorned the wall, those were Medes and Egyptians.

DSf, lines 49–55

This emphasis on the skills of individual peoples is also a new feature compared to older building inscriptions. It was designed not just to demonstrate the King's power but perhaps also to ignite the pride of different ethnic groups in their participation. The inscription may give some clues to what work was performed by which people but it may also be an artificial simplification. Like other Achaemenid inscriptions, the text is highly tuned to express an ideal image of the monarchy over a long period of time.

Some of the ornamentation of the palace referred to in Darius' inscription was recovered during the excavations, scattered in fragments through layers of reused material. Interior and exterior walls carried an eye-catching mixture of colour and texture, produced using a variety of moulded and fired brick. Brick wall-facing in relief was both left unglazed, perhaps inside, and tinted with vivid colours under glaze. Still ranks of robed archers covered a recessed façade, possibly the outer palace wall (fig. 3.9). The interior courts of the palace were lined with seated sphinxes and pacing lions (fig. 3.10). Fragmentary bricks showing servants or peoples of the empire mounting a staircase seem to have come from the destroyed monumental entrance at the north-west of the site.[22] Features and details of clothing were both

3.10 These glazed-brick pacing lions, which possibly lined an inner court at Susa, owe a clear debt to the sixth-century brick ornamentation of Babylon. But they differ in colour scheme and manufacturing technique – these bricks were created in three firings, with the relief decoration and glaze being applied in separate stages.

depicted in shallow relief and picked out by black borders lining each segment of colour. Numerous fragments of glazed colour tiles and decorative borders show that the framed decoration extended perhaps over entire walls and interior details; some interior walls may have been lined with tiles imitating veined stone.

The striking brick glazing technique, an adaptation of Elamite decoration, is now often referred to as 'cloisonné' after the technique of inlaying jewellery with coloured stone.[23] In fact, roughly contemporary inlaid jewellery has some parallels with the relief-glazed cloisonné brick at Susa. The matching colours and motifs of jewellery from a grave on the Susa Acropole show a desire to make visual displays on the large and small scale mirror each other.[24] Flat glazed tiles in colour recovered from the mound also show vivid patterns and images, such as lion-heads and rosettes, that can be found elsewhere in stone, gold and inlay.[25]

The plan of the royal complex shows the same combination of the needs of the Achaemenid monarchy with Mesopotamian tradition as in the associated texts and ornamentation. The columned audience hall, 109 m square (the *apadana*, in Artaxerxes II's words), is an enlarged, adaptation of the pavilions of Pasargadae. The interior was filled with thirty-six columns on square bases; the three exterior porticoes contained twelve columns on distinctive bell-shaped bases. A few of the massive bull-headed column capitals, which supported the cedar-beam roof-structure, were recovered in pieces from the vicinity of the hall. The remains of a base to the south of the hall probably indicate where a raised throne stood. Behind the throne, a door leads into a very different structure. In contrast to the open porticoes and aisles of the audience hall, the palace behind grows in small units around one large and two smaller courtyards. This kind of plan is Mesopotamian in origin; a similar series of courtyards and compartments can be seen in the earlier neo-Babylonian complex at Babylon. The storage complexes visible here, and the likely upper storeys, could have been the residential palace for the king and his court. The vivid decoration that turned the internal courtyards into wells of imagery and colour indicates they were probably intended to be partially public, perhaps to privileged visitors who could progress further than the audience hall. Unfortunately, very little material was found here that illuminates life in the palace. Only a solitary administrative clay tablet written in Elamite has surfaced in Susa.

Additional inscriptions of Xerxes indicate the continuing use and development of the capital after Darius' initial transformation. A major addition to the landscape was the small riverside palace of Artaxerxes II, probably begun early in the fourth century.[26] About a third to a half of the plan of this palace has been excavated. This new construction faced the main palace platform from across the Shaur river, and its small columned hall was open to approach on three sides. The fourth side offered a more restricted route to a small residential or ritual complex and an area

3.11 One of the more complete bull's head *protome* capitals from Susa. The massive cedar roof beams rested on the bull's 'back'. Looking down from some 20 m, the apotropaic figures guarded dark corners of the palace space. Although the style of the figures recalls Babylonian and Assyrian examples, their presence on the columns parallels the much wider use of animal *protome* decoration in Achaemenid architecture and adornment.

71

that was possibly a garden. The palace was decorated with carved stone reliefs (on the stairways of the complex), glazed brick and wall paintings. The small fragments of surviving painted plaster suggest that the design reproduced figures representing the king's subjects, comparable to examples in stone at Persepolis (fig. 3.12). Artaxerxes II had the stone column bases of the hall porticoes inscribed with a text describing his creation: 'By the favour of Ahuramazda this is the palace which I built in my lifetime as a pleasant retreat. May Ahuramazda, Anahita and Mithras protect me from all evil, and my building' (A2Sd, lines 2–4). The phrase 'pleasant retreat' is a translation of the word *paradayadam*, known in slightly later Avestan Persian as *pairidaeza* and borrowed by Greeks describing Persian gardens and game parks, as *paradeisos*, or paradise. Here, the word probably referred to well watered grounds near the river, within the bounds of the palace, whose greenery acted, like the garden at Pasargadae, as an extension of the setting for the king. The plan of this late palace combines different features of earlier palaces in Susa, Persepolis and Pasargadae.[27]

The relationship of the palace area to the surrounding town and country is mysterious. The early excavation of the site was done with little recording of mud brick, the key construction material of ordinary and royal buildings alike. The continued reuse of the area also probably destroyed the remains of buildings without durable foundations and decoration like those of the palaces. Recent finds of the shattered monumental staircase and sling-shots made from broken columns suggest that the central city may have been more fundamentally damaged by wars in the wake of Alexander's conquest than was previously thought. Yet material remains of the service sector supporting the palace are so scarce that one suggestion holds that there may have been no concentrated settlement in the centre of Susa at that time. The small 'village' situated beyond the Ville Royale shows that some living and working quarters were used from the late Elamite to the Achaemenid periods. Further excavation may reveal more about settlement patterns in and around the city – it is possible that the population here may have been more rural or transient than at other capitals. As at Ecbatana, the wider urban context for the royal palaces has yet to appear and our verdict must remain open.

3.12 One of several fragments of wall painting from the fourth-century Shaur palace shows a figure, perhaps a subject, servant or official, wearing a cylindrical headdress covered with fabric reaching around his chin.

PERSEPOLIS (PARSA)

The Sultan ... the Light of the Garden of the Sultanate ... Abu Abdullah ... visited this strange place and astonishing edifice at the beginning of Moharram in the year 773 [1371 CE].

Graffito in the Palace of Darius, Persepolis[28]

Persepolis is the best preserved of the Achaemenid palace complexes; the ruins were not built over after their destruction and, of all the palaces, it incorporates the most stone in its structures. The skeletal doorways and columns mounted on their rock platform below the Mountain of Mercy, visible from across the vast Marv Dasht plain, have been a magnet to Iranian and foreign travellers alike across the centuries. The Palace of Darius alone is covered with Persian and Arabic inscriptions documenting over fifteen hundred years of visitors. The city was known as

3.13 The raised terrace on which stand the surviving royal structures of Persepolis, viewed from its north-west corner. Irregular rock outcrops were built up and levelled using stone and rubble excavated from around the site. The palaces of Xerxes and Darius (in the background) stand on naturally higher ground. Two royal tombs of the fourth century are carved into the hillside (the Shah-e Kuh).

Persepolis in Greek sources after its destruction in 331 BCE by Alexander; its reputation in these sources as a doomed, decadent city has dominated descriptions of it until recently. Before the Macedonian invasion, it was known in Persian by the name of Parsa, like the whole region (this was adapted into Greek in the fourth century as Persai).[29] To those at the edge of the empire, it was less well known than Susa and Ecbatana, but, of all the capitals, it was closest to the identity of the dynasty. It was built in the province of Parsa, the Persian homeland where Cyrus the Great's capitals of Pasargadae and Anshan were situated. The kings and members of the immediate royal family were returned to be buried there in the family tombs at Naqsh-i Rustam and the hill overlooking the city.

The ruins became known in the modern world as Persepolis at the very beginning of the seventeenth century. Despite intensive interest, exploratory digging to reveal more about the buildings there did not take place until the nineteenth century. Full-scale excavation of the terrace, uncovering the major buildings and a large number of finds, was undertaken by the Oriental Institute of Chicago from 1931 to 1939, after which supervision of the site passed to the Iranian Archaeological Institute established there. Iranian excavations brought to light more structures

and finds on the terrace and in the plain below. In the course of the 1960s and 1970s, an Italian-led restoration team (IsMEO) conserved, rebuilt and investigated several structures. Some of the conservators who now care for the site first worked in this team.[30]

> Darius the king says: On this terrace, where this palace was constructed, here no palace had been constructed before; by the grace of Ahuramazda, I built this palace … It was built well and soundly and exactly as I decreed.
>
> DPf, lines 1–3, 6–7[31]

This Elamite inscription of Darius I on the south wall of Persepolis celebrates his construction of a small palace and *apadana* at the heart of a complex that was to grow into a panorama of halls and courtyards. The text contrasts with those from Susa; here Darius emphasizes that no king has built here before. His claim to have

3.14 Bas-reliefs cover the external faces of the *apadana* or audience hall platform on the north and east. They were carved by teams of sculptors working in sequence on a predetermined design. Groups of subject peoples distinguished by dress (here, probably Scythians and Babylonians) carry local goods, animals, Achaemenid vessels and jewellery towards a central staircase, led by figures in standard court or riding costume. Facing reliefs feature courtiers, servants, chariots and troops of the king.

begun afresh conceals a link with Cambyses. In the plain, 4 km from the terrace, lie the low foundations of a columned palace and a platform, the Takht-i Rustam, similar to the base of the tomb of Cyrus (fig. 1.19). Their style of construction mirrors that at Pasargadae, and their unfinished state suggests that they were begun by a king whose reign was unexpectedly short – Cambyses. While the development of Marv Dasht may have begun in this area, Darius ultimately chose the more physically imposing terrace as the site of his construction.

One of the original entrances to the terrace was situated at the south, near this building inscription. But with the completion of the massive terrace walls, a new, grander entrance was built at the north-western corner. This shallow-rising, double staircase was topped by an isolated gateway building inscribed by Xerxes (fig. 7.1). His 'Gate of all Nations' incorporated giant guardian bulls and bull men; like a similar gateway that may have existed at Pasargadae it was inspired by the massive and decaying ruins of the Assyrian palaces destroyed a hundred and fifty years before (fig. 1.1). They probably fulfilled the same role to ward off evil, although, rather than leading into a restricted palace interior, this detached gate gave on to an open area, the northernmost third of the terrace. Turning right from the gate, a visitor would be faced with the columned north portico of the audience hall, its stone base carved with a frieze of processing figures, soldiers and subjects of the king.[32] The other exit gave access to administrative offices in mud-brick buildings behind the fortifications to the left. Thousands of tablets were found here recording transactions of goods and food, and official travellers passing through Persepolis in its early years; the excavation of this area was never completely documented and the decaying walls now give little idea of the context of the finds. By the fourth century, the adjoining open area was fringed with smaller shady columned porticoes at the foot of the mountain. A formal route through this open space was defined in the late fifth century with the addition of a second gate guarded by bull guardians (the carving remained unfinished). This approach directed people first at the portico of the Hundred-Columned Hall, also known as the Throne Hall (fig. 3.1).

Bull guardians also flanked the wide, double doors leading to this hall, built mostly during the reign of Artaxerxes I. Unlike the *apadana*, it was not raised above the terrace ground level and had only one portico; its other three sides are punctuated with square niches and monumental doorways with carved jambs. Reliefs showing ranks of soldiers, topped by a scene of a petitioner approaching the enthroned king, towered over visitors entering from the terrace. The side doors leading into concealed corridors were guarded by massive combat scenes: the king pictured as an uncrowned hero plunges his dagger into four different threatening fabulous creatures (fig. 3.17).

3.15 The northern part of the Persepolis terrace, seen from the hillside, above, showing the Thirty-Columned Hall in the foreground, and the monumental way on to the terrace, from the Gate of All Nations (top left). Small administrative buildings were situated behind the modern *son et lumière* seating (top right).

The back doors (at the south) mirror the front in size and subject, showing the enthroned king supported by ranks of figures representing the peoples of the empire. But these doors led only to a narrow corridor, and restricted access to the buildings at the south of the terrace – the hall faced its mass audience like a stage set.

A third building, begun by Xerxes and finished under Artaxerxes I, fills the space between the open north and the palaces of the southern terrace (fig. 3.18). The Central Building is also known as the Tripylon (after its three doorways) and the Council Hall, because of the stone benches which lined its north and south porches. It is on a level with the *apadana* and its double stairway and recessed façade give on to a small courtyard formed by the walls of its larger neighbours. The façade designs combine lion–bull combats with lines of guards, who converge on a central panel. Here the visitor encountered an over-life-size bas-relief king walking beside him through doorways. The stone king was ornamented with the gold torque and bracelets that distinguished his status in person.

3.16 The buildings on the Persepolis terrace (after Roaf 2004). Additional structures spread across the Shah-e Kuh to the east (fortifications, water channels and cistern) and below on the plain, to the north and south (including monumental structures). Additional settlement traces have been found a few kilometres west, in the plain.

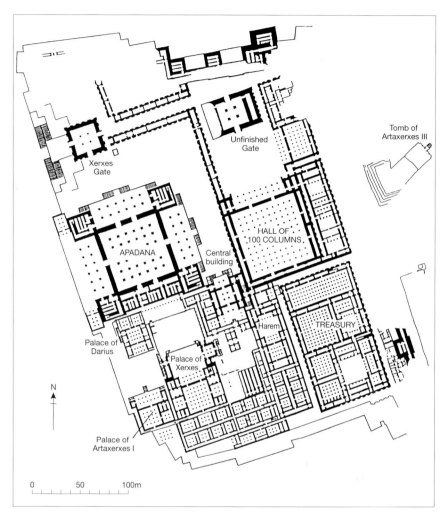

3.17 In four doorways of the Hundred-Columned Hall, a hero grapples with four different fearsome creatures, here a lion. Although the hero is not dressed as the king, he seems to represent an aspect of royal power. The image was substantially adapted from a neo-Assyrian motif, once used on royal seals and palace walls.

Behind these three buildings were two important sectors of the complex. To the left (the east), securely stationed under the fortifications of the Mountain of Mercy, the halls and corridors of the Treasury concealed the distribution of silver and other goods, and the careful hoarding of gifts and relics associated with past kings.[33] This low mud-brick building changed shape several times over its lifespan, its walls kept unusually isolated from other construction on the terrace (fig. 5.3).[34] It eventually possessed an ornamented entrance hall complete with painted walls, hard, glossy red floor and free-standing and relief sculpture. Apart from its administrative function, the building had a prestige of its own within the royal system.

The south-west corner of the platform, behind the *apadana*, was the site of successive palace building right through the history of Persepolis. It began with the palace of Darius I, a small compact construction raised to be visible from the plain on both the west and south. Its sculpted, polished walls have always been visible to visitors and in Persian it was known as the House of Dārā or the Hall of Mirrors (in Old Persian, Darius called it a *tachara* and Xerxes a *hadesh*). Its doorways show a clear adaptation of Egyptian architecture and its small niches were perhaps models for those in the Hundred-Columned Hall (fig. 3.19). Here, the king is closer than ever, walking with servants through the doors, the patterns on his clothes picked out by engraving and paint.

Xerxes continued to develop this area with two palaces. One was an expansion of the private palace model of Darius' structure, with a grander central columned

3.18 A reconstructed view, by Friedrich Krefter, from the Central Building stairway of the space between the *apadana* or audience hall (left) and the Hundred-Columned Hall (right). In the background (centre) stand walls built later in the fifth and fourth centuries to define the approach to these large halls. The *apadana* corner towers were at least partly decorated with glazed tiles. Sociable courtiers populated the inner parapet, while soldiers and animal combats guarded the outer face.

hall. It is positioned on the highest point of the terrace, and far less of the sculptured decoration of this palace survives. Xerxes was also responsible for an extensive series of blocks known in some modern accounts as the harem.[35] There is no particular evidence for the use of these rooms as a separate residence for court women; the series of small rooms and corridors of the extensive west wing suggest that it may have been a residential building. The main body of the complex was restored, first as the Chicago dig house and then as a museum and research centre. The low entrance and colonnaded enclosed courtyard produce a pleasantly cool space. Carved door jambs of servants and the king-as-hero in combat with beasts show that the hall was another adaptation of Darius' original model.

At least two further palaces along these lines were built in three areas now characterized by scanty remains and open space. The recovery of their layout was confused by extensive remodelling in the fourth century, both before and after the conquest of Alexander. The complicated building history of many of the structures, with sections added and completed by different kings, means that surviving royal building inscriptions cannot always be relied upon to present a clear sequence of construction. The Chicago and IsMEO investigations tried to unravel part of the story. Inscriptions and foundation lines indicate that a palace of Artaxerxes III first stood on the site now labelled Palace G between Darius' *tachara* and the Central

3.19 Evening sun illuminates the doorways of the palace of Darius I, viewed from the western side of the building, adjacent to the terrace edge. Their cornices clearly show Egyptian influence, while the door jambs carry bas-reliefs of the king, his attendants and heroic combats. At the palace's southern side, soldiers and servants or officials were carved into the façade and stairway.

Building. The façade of this building, together with parts of the other palaces, was rearranged in a new pavilion perched on a rubble base in the south-west corner of the terrace, a site known as Palace H, some time after the end of the Achaemenid period. Numerous fragments of an earlier buiding indicate that Palace H was originally the site of a palace of Artaxerxes I.[36] Despite the apparently independent planning and revision of blocks of building on the terrace, the palaces and rooms of this area became more interconnected through stairways and corridors as they were adjusted to fulfil their functions.

The way in which these royal buildings were actually used remains a lively debate. Evidence for the practice of religious ritual survives in the Persepolis Fortification Tablets, but their location cannot be narrowed to a particular building on the terrace, rather than elsewhere in the area. Doubts about the suitability of even the so-called 'private' palaces as everyday residences have led to a number of uses being proposed for them: meeting rooms, banquet halls or ritual places. Seas of tents and temporary structures have been imagined on and below the terrace, to accommodate the entourage of a nomadic court. Nevertheless, other parts of the terrace seem to have been designed very practically, such as the storage and guard-space in the *apadana* towers, side access corridors and halls by the Hundred-Columned Hall, garrison quarters and administrative rooms in the shadow of the hill and fortifications.

The absence of obviously specialized room use may mean only that the mobile court was well adjusted to using space flexibly. The building plans in general show a desire to accommodate a large audience and to exert control over access to and the visibility of the king and his inner court. Specific answers about usage have often been sought in the elaborate carving of a great population of peoples, servants, and the king in various guises, along the walls and door jambs of many of the palaces.

The best-known idea is that Persepolis was the site of a No-Ruz gift-giving ceremony. No-Ruz is the festival celebrating the Persian new year on the spring equinox, usually on 21 March in the Western calendar. The interpretation of Persepolis as a No-Ruz location originates in the Iranian tradition that the legendary King Jamshid instituted the first of such processions there. The idea is in itself is an interpretation of the ranks of processing peoples visible to all visitors on the north façade of the *apadana*. The notion was repeated by European travellers to the site from the eighteenth to the early twentieth century, often with references to contemporary gift-giving practices that they themselves witnessed.[37] Persepolis might well have been the site of royal ceremonies, but date and participants are debatable. Religious and royal rituals that claim age-old stability can in fact change surprisingly fast, and the use of Persepolis probably evolved over its lifetime. The best-attested new year festival of the Achaemenid period, the *akitu* festival, actually took place in Babylon.[38] Several Classical authors describe formalized processions involving the Persian king, but these occur in a variety of locations and circumstances.[39] Instead of directly representing a real event, the Persepolis reliefs might have more of a symbolic value.

3.20 A photograph from the Oriental Institute of Chicago's excavation archive apparently shows gold and silver foundation tablets inscribed in the name of Darius I at the moment of their discovery buried at the corner of the *apadana*; to the left crouches Friedrich Krefter. The trilingual tablets were enclosed with late sixth-century coins in stone boxes.

The representation of ethnic groups on the *apadana* is, like the building inscription at Susa, a way of incorporating the entire empire into the fabric of the palace. They are part of the frozen world that the planners of the sculpture ensured would permanently surround the king: courtiers, soldiers and subjects. The objects and livestock in their care could be symbols of their gifts, or possibly they were already thought of as within the king's care. The vessels, furnishings, even exotic livestock, are all examples of what the king aspired to collect in his palace after its foundation. Darius' work on the platform was begun with an desire to demonstrate the empire's span. Underneath the foundations of the audience hall, gold tablets in stone boxes sealed his power in the roots of the palace:

> Darius the king says: This is the kingdom which I hold, from the Scythians who are
> beyond Sogdiana, to Ethiopia, from Sind to Sardis, which Ahuramazda, the greatest of
> the gods bestowed upon me.
>
> DPh, lines 3–9[40]

Scattered evidence across the plain of Persepolis testifies to some settlement around the palace platform. Large halls with stone architectural elements that may have been elite residences have been excavated to the north-west and south of the platform, although a pine forest planted by the last Shah now obscures much of the adjoining plain.[41] Artisans and administrators of all nationalities were certainly resident at the site for the intensive building and development of its first thirty to forty years. Test trenches at the nearby remains of the medieval city of Istakhr, a mass of layered mounds marked with an old caravanserai's dissolving mud-brick walls, have revealed Sasanian levels. An Achaemenid settlement may lie underneath, or nearby at Firuzi; references to nearby centres in the Persepolis Fortification Tablets provide an important reminder of the continuity of settlement in the area, which is unlikely to have been emptied by the end of the empire. When Alexander fell on Persepolis after a difficult passage through the mountains, Diodorus Siculus implies, it offered a comfortable and undefended prize for an army ravenous for plunder:

> It was the richest city under the sun and the private houses had been furnished with every sort of wealth over the years … many of the houses belonged to the common people and were abundantly supplied with furniture and wearing apparel of every kind … The citadel is a noteworthy one and is surrounded by a triple wall … At the eastern side of the terrace at a distance of 4 plethra is the so-called royal hill, in which were the graves of the kings … Scattered about the royal terrace were residences of the kings and quarters for the great generals, all luxuriously furnished, and buildings suitably made for guarding the royal treasure.[42]

Diodorus' late description does seem to tally at certain points with the general topography of Persepolis and Naqsh-i Rustam, but with a few troubling inconsistencies. He has perhaps confused the cliff of Naqsh-i Rustam, 6 km from the terrace, with the mountain behind the terrace on its eastern side, because both were mentioned in his sources as containing royal tombs. Generations of visitors have striven (some with great imagination) to see the triple wall he describes surrounding the 'citadel' (a correct term, since in Elamite tablets the palace terrace could be referred to as a 'fortress'), the most plausible rationalizations suggesting he has misrepresented the three main faces of the platform wall, or the successive, stepped battlements on the platform, *apadana* and mountain ridge. Diodorus provides us with a fleeting mirage blurred by time and distance.

BABYLON

> There are many ways by which I can show the power of Babylon, how great it is … Rule over this country … is of all the satrapies far the greatest.
>
> Herodotus, 1.192

The rich and flourishing city of Babylon and its hinterland was a prize conquest of Cyrus and Darius; Herodotus devotes much space to their assaults on the city.[43] Its fortunes under the Achaemenid dynasty ranged from rebellion to privileged loyalty. The city first became pre-eminent in southern Mesopotamia in the eighteenth century BCE, but by the early first millennium it was dominated by the Assyrian monarchy to the north. In the late seventh century Babylon became independent and inherited the territories previously subject to Assyria. Babylon's status as an imperial city immediately before its incorporation made it a prestigious but problematic possession of the Achaemenid kings.

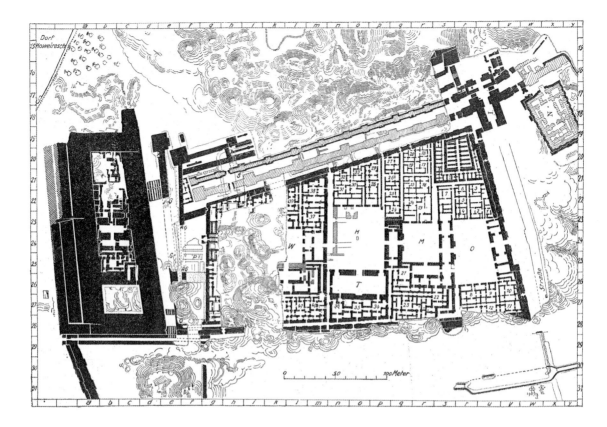

3.21 Part of the neo-Babylonian royal palace complex was situated in the 'Südberg' of the palace of Babylon, abutting on the Euphrates to the west and the Ishtar gate (top right). The enclosed courtyards show the type of plan that influenced the Achaemenid palace at Susa. A fourth-century Achaemenid extension was added to an entrance to the palace (in the area marked 'P' on this early twentieth-century plan, after Koldewey).

During the revolts against Darius I, the city produced a new claimant to the Babylonian throne, allegedly descended from its own older and legitimate royal line. Perhaps in response to this, a copy of the Bisitun relief and inscription proclaiming Darius' legitimacy were placed in glazed brick along the main processional way proceeding from the Ishtar gate. The city rebelled again at least once under Xerxes, after which Babylonia was made a separate satrapy. The ambivalence of the early Persian kings' relationship with Babylon may be illustrated by an anecdote included by Herodotus in his negative account of the city's treatment by Darius and Xerxes:

> [Nitocris, a legendary founder queen of Babylon] contrived this trick: she had her own tomb built suspended above the busiest gate of the city. She had the following inscription engraved on the tomb: 'If any of the future kings of Babylon should be short of money, let him open this tomb and take as much as he wants. But if he is not really short of money, in that case let him not open it; it would be worse for him.' This tomb was undisturbed until royal power passed to Darius. Darius found it strange that he never used this gate and that – with the money lying there and this inscription inviting him – he should not take it. He never used this gate because the corpse would be above his head as he passed through. So he opened the tomb but found no money; instead there was a dead body and the following inscription: 'If you were not so shamefully grasping and greedy for money, you would not have breached the resting place of the dead.' This is the kind of person they say queen was.
> 1.187

It is typical of Herodotus to turn a story or fable into a joke at Darius' expense. The historian was adept at parodying themes of Eastern kingship and this story uses several centred on the kingship tradition of Babylon; Nitocris' trick is played through the medium of the eternal, inscribed conversations of past kings with the present. The taboo about Darius passing under a corpse plays on the potential restrictions on the king's movements placed by the long-lived practice of scholarly interpretation of omens.[44]

Babylon was steeped in a number of age-old kingship roles which the Achaemenid dynasty partially adopted, but we cannot be sure that Babylon was used as a full royal capital in the first century of Persian rule. By the end of the fifth century, however, the city seems to have become a central resource of loyal support for at least part of the Achaemenid family. When in 401 BCE the younger Cyrus marched against his brother Artaxerxes II, in a challenge to his accession, the rebel army burned the residence and 'paradise' grounds of the loyal Babylonian satrap, Belshunu.[45] It was unusual for such an important satrapy to be under the care of a non-Persian, but some of Babylon's eventual success as a royal centre seems to have resulted from a conscious blending of Achaemenid politics with strong local traditions.

3.22 A reconstructed elevation of the Achaemenid columned hall added to the edge of the royal palace in the reign of Artaxerxes II, based on the foundation ground plan and fragmentary surviving decoration (after Koldewey). Pieces of glazed-brick figures and motifs have survived, but the overall decorative scheme is conjectural.

By the end of the fifth century, authors such as Ctesias and Xenophon relayed stories which linked the rise of Median and then Persian power to Babylonian support rather than opposition.[46] The Cyrus Cylinder had included an official attempt to connect a Persian ruler with an archaic king, exploiting a convergence of Assyrian monarch and the city of Babylon.[47] But the Greek stories, partly sourced perhaps both in the Persian court and in the highways and byways of the empire, suggest that a popular history grew up which fully blended Babylon with traditions about the end of Assyria.[48] One of the best-known examples of this is the legend of the Hanging Gardens of Babylon, which were said to have been constructed by an *Assyrian* king, for his *Median* bride, in *Babylon*.[49] Whatever the kernel of truth behind the story, it resembles many of the new, blended histories of the succession of empires leading to Persian rule.

These popular histories show how the great antiquity of Babylon and the cities of Mesopotamia, so immediately apparent in their urban landscapes, were linked with the Achaemenid world. The great neo-Babylonian palace complex, built for Nebuchadnezzar II at the northern edge of the 'Südberg' or Southern Citadel, and the surrounding monumental gates and processional ways continued in use throughout the Persian and into the Hellenistic period. Darius II may have begun to build an addition to the existing palace, but a Persian-style columned portico was added by Artaxerxes II. Fragments of foundations, column bases and fragments of glazed brick decoration of this building survive.[50]

PASARGADAE

Pasargadae, as described in Chapter 1, was in fact not one of the canonical list of three or four capitals usually mentioned in Greek authors as the king's residences. It was sometimes confused with the slightly later complex at Persepolis, and it is possible that their geographical proximity meant that spells of residence there were not distinguished as separate excursions in the sources known to the Greeks;[51] tablets at Persepolis show that it was part of the same administrative region.[52] But the dominance of Persepolis does not mean that the earlier palace became a forgotten backwater. Both historical and archaeological evidence demonstrates its active use up to Alexander's conquest.

The addition of cuneiform inscriptions to the pavilions of Pasargadae proclaiming 'I am Cyrus the king, the Achaemenid', probably in the reign of Darius, strengthened his claim to the kingship in the immediate political circumstances of his turbulent accession. By these inscriptions or through ritual and oral tradition, the memory of the empire's founder was shackled to the site for at least the following two centuries. Pasargadae reappears in Greek narratives twice in later Persian history. In both stories, surrounding the accession of Artaxerxes II in 404 BCE, and a late stage of Alexander's invasion in 324 BCE, the site's associations with the origins of the monarchy become mixed up with contemporary turmoil over the throne.

The first tale is a brief reference by Plutarch to a trip to Pasargadae made by Artaxerxes II very early in his reign (it is associated in his story with the first plot that Cyrus the younger made against his brother). Artaxerxes' activities at the palace are intriguing. Plutarch says that the king, whose accession had already been recognized, and who had already assumed a throne name, went to Pasargadae to complete 'royal ceremonies' in a religious sanctuary there.[53] This was apparently dedicated to a 'warlike goddess', who may have been Anahita. The elements which Plutarch passes on are intriguing:

> [the new King] must pass into this sanctuary, lay aside his own cloak and take up the one which Cyrus the Great wore before he became king; he must also eat of a fig-cake, chew on turpentine-wood, and drink down a cup of sour milk. Whatever else they do, apart from this, is not known to others.

We cannot be sure of the accuracy of this passage, like that of many cryptic Greek reports of Persian religious practices. Since the account does not mention that Artaxerxes then reassumed his royal regalia, this appears more like a royal initiation ritual than a full-blown public coronation. We have evidence only for Artaxerxes II undergoing this initiation, although we may assume that it became traditional at some point in the dynasty's history. The harsh and simple foodstuffs symbolized poverty, the subsistence food of the tough mountain lifestyle of his ancestors. Their consumption, and the wearing of the (allegedly) authentic robe of Cyrus from before he was king, suggests that the present king was symbolically echoing the rise to power of the empire's founder. In the palace of the founder, the legendary origins of the dynasty may have been associated with each new king's possession of the throne. The report of the initiation of Artaxerxes probably became most important after his brother challenged him to the kingship.

The second time Pasargadae emerges as the setting for royal drama is in the aftermath of Alexander's invasion of the empire. On his first visit to the city in 429, Pasargadae was spared the violent destruction inflicted on neighbouring Persepolis. When Alexander returned from the eastern satrapies six years later, he consolidated his rule at Pasargadae with the execution of rebels. While describing these events at Pasargadae, Arrian gives the fullest ancient description of the royal grounds surrounding the tomb of Cyrus, apparently taken from the eye-witness Aristoboulus. The detail devoted to the description of the tomb and its surroundings contrasts with the complete absence of the palaces from the picture:

> In the royal paradise in Pasargadae was the tomb of this Cyrus; around it was planted a grove of all species of trees, which was irrigated with running water and a meadow sprouted thick grass. The base of the tomb was rectangular, built of stone slabs cut square; on top was a roofed chamber, also built of stone, with an extremely narrow doorway so narrow that only one man at a time – and a little one at that – could manage, with great difficulty, painfully to squeeze himself through. Inside the chamber there was a golden trough in which Cyrus' body had been interred, and by this was a divan with feet of worked gold, spread with Babylonian carpets, and underneath it were strewn purple robes. On top were laid luxury coats and Babylonian-made shirts. And [Aristoboulus] says there were also Median trousers, robes dyed in amethyst, purple and all sorts of colours, torques, short swords, and golden earrings inlaid with stones. A table stood by it, and the trough holding Cyrus' body was placed in the middle of a platform. Within the precinct, by the approach to the tomb, a small house had been built for the Magi who guarded the tomb of Cyrus; ever since the time of Cambyses son of Cyrus, this guardianship has been handed down from father to son. They received a sheep every day from the King, along with measures of wheatmeal and wine, and one horse a month to sacrifice to Cyrus. Written on the tomb in Persian letters ran the following, in Persian: 'O man, I am Cyrus son of Cambyses, who founded the empire of Persia and ruled as king over Asia. Do not grudge me my monument.'[54]

No ancient inscription has ever been discernable on the tomb building; Aristoboulus' 'translation' is probably an interpretation of the cuneiform inscriptions on the palaces of Pasargadae. The inscription's theme is common to other imaginative readings of inscribed Near Eastern monuments in Greek authors. As for the luxury appointments of the tomb, they are consistent with the status trappings of the royal court. If their quantity was not completely exaggerated, they may have been deposited at the time of Cyrus' burial, or during ritual openings of the tomb since then. Their alleged theft was a serious business, since such artefacts were uniquely imbued with royal charisma. The accusation and execution for tomb robbery of a Persian noble of royal descent, named Orxines, coincided with Alexander's restoration and sealing of Cyrus' monument (fig. 6.13).[55] The new ruler was both cutting off potential challengers to his position and taking over the supervision of a powerful ideological site. At Pasargadae, the memory of the beginning of Persian imperial power converged with the final moments of its end.

4 THE RIVALS: REGIONAL RULERS AND REFLECTIONS OF POWER

These are Medes and the centre of Babylon and the royal standard of the gold eagle on a shield, and the king on a golden throne embossed with ornamentation like a peacock … The court is also gold, for it seems like it is not painted, but it is so painted to look like a real structure – we breathe in incense and myrrh.

Philostratus, *Imagines* 2.31

4.1 The warm tones of a surviving pile carpet illustrate the richness of the textiles furnishing the tents and palaces of the Persian court. The colour scheme, animal and abstract motifs all closely echo Achaemenid imagery. The procession of horses in the border has parallels at Persepolis and on seals and other miniature objects from across the empire. This sheared wool carpet was found preserved in one of a series of rich tumuli burials in the Pazyryk valley in the Altai mountains, on the fringe of Outer Mongolia. An origin for this exotic import in Iran, Mesopotamia or Bactria has been suggested.

Long after the fall of the Persian empire, a dilettante writer of the second century CE imagined a glittering mirage of the Achaemenid court as the subject of a historical wall painting. The occasion for his rich description was the Persian king's audience with the general Themistocles; once an enemy, now an exile from his city, the Athenian was to have a successful later career within the Achaemenid ruling class, settling in the city of Magnesia on the Maeander.[1] The architecture of the capital around him is evoked with broad descriptive strokes, but small details of trappings and clothing attract the writer's inner magpie-eye. The same palace walls may still be just about discernible to us, but the trappings that gave them and the mobile court a distinctive atmosphere of wealth and power are mostly vanished. The huge reservoirs of worked bullion and cloth that filled palace treasuries at the end of Achaemenid rule were liquidated in the course of the invasion of Alexander of Macedon. Only scattered or fragmentary finds from Iran hint at the luxury objects commissioned or manufactured by the personnel of the court. Instead, finds from across the king's territory, and far beyond, mirror or recall the styles of the court. They illustrate a widespread appetite among local elites for prestige possessions that identified them as belonging to the highest society.

The designers of the reliefs from the *apadana* platform at Persepolis showed the king's wealth through subjects displaying distinctive metal vessels and jewellery alongside regional products. The shapes of the vessels derive from some styles both in use in the Assyrian empire and in earlier ceramic and metal-working cultures of Iran. The carinated bowl is one of the most distinctive forms; developed from styles used earlier in the neo-Assyrian court, it was made in metal, glass and ceramic during the Achaemenid period. Fluted bowls, beakers and elaborate vases or *amphorae* are exhibited at arm's length by several different subject groups. The reliefs, along with excavations of the shattered remains of the Persepolis treasury, show that metal artefacts were part of a wider selection of valued items stored up in the royal palaces, including polished stone vessels, cloth and other objects sourced from different conquered territories. The associations of such treasure, as the king's possessions, or royal booty from specific and distant locales, may have added to its significance. A few items from Persepolis are identified by their style or inscriptions as coming from neo-Assyrian, Babylonian, Greek or Egyptian centres, as if they served as material symbols of the transfer of power. Some surviving Achaemenid vessels carry royal inscriptions of Xerxes I or Artaxerxes II (and, possibly, Darius I); they were perhaps intended as contributions to an archive of royal wealth, in which age as well as material or manufacture added to their value.

Such material culture, although accumulated in unique wealth and elaboration in the palaces, was far from being exclusive to the immediate circles of the king's court. Drinking from precious metal and glass vessels during official entertainments was part of the diplomatic experience for foreigners travelling within the empire.[2] A high-class dinner service was part of the basic equipment for important social and political occasions, when the rulers' status was demonstrated by their superior wealth and hospitality. At royal banquets, even the king's wine bowls or platters, as well as the fine beverages and food they carried, were apparently distributed to honoured guests.[3] This luxury dining culture influenced the aspirations of the ambitious rich both within and beyond the empire. Precious metal vessels echoing Achaemenid styles became desirable collector's items, used for the exhibition of high social status both in life and (the display most often visible to us) in death.[4]

In Athens, a comic poet could poke fun at a member of the *nouveaux riches*, for boasting of the number of Persian bowls he had collected.[5] A letter attributed to Themistocles enquires after precious bowls inscribed in Aramaic, as if the addition of an authentic eastern inscription made for an even more sought-after specimen.[6] Excavated tombs of the fifth to third centuries in the territory of ancient Colchis (Georgia) and Scythia (both in Thrace and north of the Black Sea) have produced bowls and vases strikingly like those depicted on the Persepolis reliefs, or found in the empire's heartlands. For example, another vessel inscribed with the name of

4.2 One of four nearly identical shallow repoussé silver bowls or *phialai*, called a *batugara*, or wine-drinking vessel, in its Old Persian inscription in the name of Artaxerxes (diam. *c.*21 cm). A suggested origin in one of the royal capitals, Hamadan, cannot be verified as the dishes were sold privately in Iran in the 1930s.

4.3 A beautiful glass rhyton-shaped cup, excavated near the Persepolis platform, terminates in a lion sinuously wrapped around a bull (shown here with a partially restored cup section). Vessel shapes well-known in metal are occasionally found finely worked in polished translucent glass.

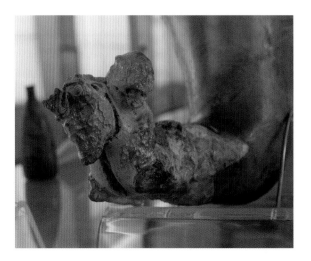

4.4 'Goat-stags', 'horse-birds' – the Greek terms for these Achaemenid vessels, derived from shapes found in western Iran, were confused. Their generic name is *rhyton* after the Greek word 'to pour', while the Old Persian term does not survive. This gilt silver example has horizontal fluting and a fantastic horned griffin characteristic of Achaemenid ornamentation. Said to be from Erzincan.

4.5 (left) & 4.6 (right) Small translucent glass bowls with engraved lobe or petal decoration, echoing Achaemenid metalware shapes, have come to light in tomb goods from Turkey, Libya, Georgia and Iraq. Their place of manufacture is unclear, but there were long-standing traditions of glass-working in Mesopotamia, Egypt and the Levant. The fragments here were found in the fill of the rebuilt Artemision at Ephesus (fourth century BCE) and the shallower complete example came from Cumae, Italy.

Artaxerxes I, this time written in Egyptian hieroglyphs on a large flask or *alabastron*, was found in Orsk, Kazakhstan. The high mobility and long-distance desirability of these vessels means that it is extremely difficult to discover where they were originally made. Collections deposited in different corners of the empire, such as in tombs along the Hermus valley near Sardis, Tell el-Farah (near Gaza), sites in eastern Georgia or the Oxus region, all contain vessels strongly echoing the styles or iconography of the palace centres.[7] In most cases, these desirable prizes were found alongside objects more obviously of regional use or manufacture.

The culture of the Achaemenid rulers, in most cases, did not consist of a comprehensive set of habits and styles adopted by all their subjects at all levels of society. Nevertheless, it was a highly desirable form of display used by regional elites to advertise their social status. These elites could be local groups who had gained an upper hand in dealings with the Persians, or Persians themselves, settling in the cities and on redistributed land. As time went on, family networks with some investment in Achaemenid rule are more and more likely to have been linked in some way with a Persian diaspora across the empire. Any kind of demographic survey of the ethnic mix in different parts of the empire is difficult and subject to assumptions about the equivalence of names with identity.[8] Our historical evidence shows that, by the fourth century, some prominent commanders in the Achaemenid army were the product of marriages between Persians and regional families, from Scythia to Rhodes. For example, Memnon, the general who was to defend Asia Minor against Alexander, was from a Rhodian family linked by marriage to the Achaemenid royal family; he owned estates in the Troad. Datames, the subject of a fascinating late biography in Latin by Cornelius Nepos, was reportedly the product of a mixed Perso-Scythian marriage.[9]

Although these threads of Iranian settlement were probably taking root all over the empire, we cannot assume that objects that appear to us very close to Achaemenid court culture were owned only by Persians, or that Persians themselves used exclusively Achaemenid-style objects wherever they settled. The diversity of cultural traditions in the empire was such that a Babylonian could use a seal with an apparently Greek-style image on it, a Libyan could sip from an Achaemenid-style glass bowl or a Persian could pocket a traditionally Egyptian talisman. Even more confusingly, they could potentially have manufactured them too. Nevertheless, court style may have been the source of regional fashion trends. Signs of far-flung aspirations to the styles of high society can be seen reflected in some styles of ceramic, for example. In Sardis, fine, deep carinated bowls became more popular than traditional plates, indicating a change not just in dining styles but in the food consumed.[10] Athenian potters, in contrast, adapted Achaemenid grooved and carinated bowls to their own formal dining experience, the symposium (fig. 2.19).[11] The decoration of examples found in Georgia and Iran also recalls the shapes of Achaemenid metallic models.

The quality and amount of decorative metal and cloth adornments worn by the king, his courtiers and members of regional ruling society were also fundamental signs of status. At Persepolis, the king stood out from the crowd in a court robe adorned

4.7 A deep variation (17.4 cm) of the profile that influenced vessel forms in ceramic across the empire from Georgia to the Mediterranean, said to be from Erzincan. The carinated shape is ultimately derived from types in use in the late neo-Assyrian and Babylonian periods, but became a distinctive part of court and elite culture from the sixth century BCE.

4.8 A hemispherical bowl with gold sheet appliqués of crowned archers carrying a blossom and a ring or disk (diam. 10.3 cm). The crowns and rings may indicate an implied royal status. The image of the king was quite often used in a generalized and iconic way in imagery of the Achaemenid period.

with pacing lions, gold bracelets and torque. His courtiers wore simpler torques and bracelets on the *apadana* façades, while subject delegations clasped elaborate examples in their fists. By reproducing figures on the *apadana* platform, or in colour along the outer walls at Susa, the palace designers clothed royal buildings with the ruling group's costume. Small decorative, portable pieces of clothing or jewellery could carry the same motifs as monumental glazed walls and massive pieces of architecture. Compare the griffin bracelets held by a group of subjects at Persepolis (fig. 3.14) with a pair of surviving gold examples from the Oxus Treasure (fig. 4.9);[12] both are magnified to the medium scale in the *rhyton* from Erzincan, while bearing a striking similarity to a monumental hawk-headed column capital at Persepolis.[13] The mobility of the court meant that its visual grandeur had to move with it, beyond the immovable stone halls.

At first glance, such elaborate adornments look like formal court attire that allowed only for limited practical wear. But Xenophon, on campaign with a Persian

4.9 Courtiers and guards on the walls of Persepolis and Susa wear or carry gold bracelets and sometimes necklaces as signs of status (fig. 3.14), as do the king and his companions in the Alexander mosaic (fig. 6.4). This elaborate example, one of a pair, was originally inlaid with gemstones and glass (width 11.5 cm). Part of the Oxus Treasure, from the region of Takht-i Kuwad, Tajikistan.

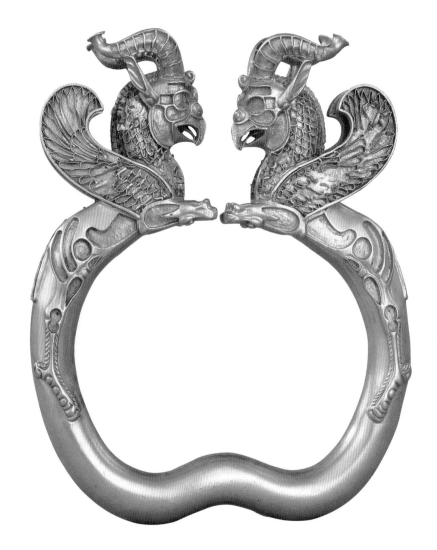

4.10 A gold chariot set from the Oxus Treasure shows a charioteer with a seated figure wearing a soft headdress and golden torque. The 'Oxus Treasure' is a disparate group of objects and the original purpose of this Achaemenid artefact is mysterious; it may have been a religious dedication.

army commanded by the king's brother in 401 BCE, reported that the most favoured nobles wore their splendid garments throughout the most taxing marches and pitched battles. When the royal prince fell in battle, a loyal lieutenant

> leapt down from his horse and flung his arms around him … others say that drawing his dagger he slew himself; he had a gold one, and wore a necklace and bracelets and other things which the noblest of the Persians have … he was honoured … because of his good nature and loyal behaviour.
>
> Xenophon, *Anabasis* 1.8.29

A similarly close focus on a richly attired Persian noble dying for his patron appears in the 'Alexander mosaic' (fig. 6.4), modelled on a painting from the fourth century.[14] There, the king and the closest bodyguards surrounding his chariot wear gold torques and bracelets in the turmoil. After their defeat, these status symbols offered rich pickings to the victors who scavenged dead bodies, or took noble captives alive for ransom.

These adornments were highly visual and portable ways of indicating personal status. They must have been particularly effective in the mobile world of the royal and satrapal courts, whether on campaign or at banquet. That the entire royal decor was encapsulated in a nomadic array is suggested by Greek and Macedonian awe at the kings' tents (that is, those belonging to both Xerxes I and Darius III). Again, the

4.11 Cultures across Persian territory could blend a variety of Achaemenid and outside influences in their self-representation. Here, a fragment from a sixth- or fifth-century building on the Xanthos acropolis shows an Achaemenid-influenced procession sculpted in a Greek style.

high mobility of both artefacts and the designs attached to them obscures our view of patterns of production and use. A pile carpet preserved in the permafrost of the Altai mountains in Siberia may have been made in Bactria or another of the eastern satrapies (fig. 4.1). One of its designs, of pacing horses, parallels not only monumental sculpture at Persepolis but also miniature work in jewellery and inlay.[15] Motifs such as this could travel right from the royal palaces to the furthest corners of the known earth, incorporated freely within home-grown and familiar patterns and possessions.

The transmission of luxury images, textures and forms across Asia was flexible and varied. There are also signs that some elements of the architectural decoration and form of the royal palaces were used elsewhere in the empire. In Sidon, a bull's head capital and a column base were found, neither associated with a recognizable building plan.[16] Some fragmentary reliefs from the satrapal capital of Daskyleion seem to

imitate Persepolitan *apadana* iconography, as do fragments from a building of unknown function on the acropolis of Xanthos (fig. 4.11).[17] Substantial columned halls coinciding with the Achaemenid period at Altintepe, a former Urartian centre in eastern Anatolia, Drashkanakert and Erebuni, the old Urartian capital at Yerevan, are commonly called *apadanas* in archaeological literature.[18] The tentative assumption is that they were used in a similar way to the columned halls at Persepolis and Susa and may have been intended to mirror Persian palace architecture. A clearer example of a deliberate parallel was excavated recently at Gumbati in Georgia, part of a large columned hall that strikingly recalled an Achaemenid *apadana*, even including sculpted column bases imitating those found at the Iranian palace centres.

4.13 Excavations at a number of sites across the Caucasus and beyond have produced grave goods or buildings emulating Achaemenid styles. The plan and part stone construction of this building at Gumbati was influenced by Achaemenid palace architecture (after Knauss).

The halls at some of the sites in Turkey and Armenia can be seen as developments of existing complexes, whereas the Gumbati building, constructed in the late fifth century BCE, was a stone-built architectural form new to the building traditions of the area. Although not seen as officially a satrapy administered by Persian governors in Greek sources, the kingdom of Colchis acknowledged the Great King's authority and supplied contingents for his army. The southern Transcaucasus was well placed to exploit routes and trade between the Black Sea coast, Anatolia and the Caspian provinces which were fostered by the stability of Achaemenid rule. Rich tomb finds from across the area suggest that certain groups benefited from their investment in the empire. The building at Gumbati may indicate that local elites created material echoes of the Achaemenid court setting in order to express their own high status.[19]

Central Achaemenid planning may have initiated or built on organized fortified garrisons, but the evidence suggests that these *apadana* building projects varied, even if they all recalled the same models. Different features may have been chosen by regional planners according to their requirements. They may have considered what would make an impact on a local audience, and what suited their own use of their space. This could be a mixture of what was novel and what was in some ways familiar. The same kind of considerations may have informed tomb design. The tomb of Payava from Xanthos in Asia Minor makes a link in its inscription between the occupant and the local satrap, Autophradates. The monument, a traditional Lycian barrel-vaulted tomb with four reliefs carved in Greek style, includes a battle scene on one face, with an audience scene on the other (fig. 4.14). A scene of audience with a god or king is an old theme in Near Eastern iconography.[20] In Persepolis, a new version was used very prominently on the *apadana* and the Hundred-Columned Hall as the centrepiece of the assembled, stone-carved court and empire. Similar scenes are occasionally found carved, stamped or painted on different objects across the empire, and this was perhaps the kind of view our art critic cited at the beginning of the chapter had in mind. Payava used this way of representing a

4.12 The city of Xanthos in Lycia, the base of a client dynasty with the Achaemenid hierarchy until the 360s BCE, was the site of a number of massive funerary monuments for its elite.

4.14 A Xanthian tomb apparently displays its occupant, Payava, a Lycian notable, in audience with the local satrap Autophradates (left). The format and the satrap's throne, are adapted from Achaemenid audience scenes.

4.15 Another audience scene was set in extensive reliefs depicting a battle covering the funerary Nereid monument for a Lycian occupant. The high status of the leader here, perhaps a Persian included as a nod towards the deceased's international relations career, is distinguished by his throne, footstool, shade and guard; he is greeted from the right by petitioners or advisers.

royal audience to show his engagement with Persian power, underlining the advantage he had gained from his achievements on behalf of the empire. Among the layered battle scenes of the much larger Nereid monument, also from Xanthos, an unidentified Persian commander also sits in audience, closely surrounded by attendants and petitioners, just as the king at Persepolis was flanked by courtiers and subjects.[21]

COURT TALES

The variegated archaeological picture may seem a world away from the overwhelming royal authority highlighted in the royal inscriptions and Herodotus' histories. But the spread of stories about the court in surviving sources is in some way similar. Like material objects, visions of the Persian court were selected and skewed

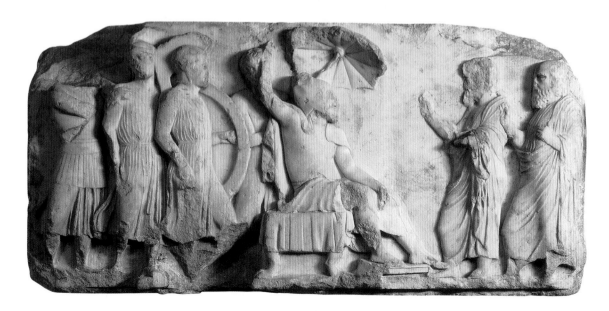

by regional preferences and prejudices. While concentrating on the scandals of the royal family, they were also often designed to boost the reputation of local contacts with the king. The images of the court supplied by Greek accounts from the late fifth and fourth centuries are often simplified and glamorous morality tales of virtue and disloyalty, rather than factual accounts of the centre of government. Several narratives, sourced by Plutarch in the Roman period from the fourth-century writers Ctesias and Dinon, transform court politics into something resembling a gruesome soap opera. For example, the talented and courageous courtier Mithridates committed the fatal *faux pas* of claiming that his king, Artaxerxes II, had not adequately rewarded him for a service performed. Since the service in question was his help in killing the king's rebellious brother, the accusation, which Plutarch relays, he made at a banquet, was extremely subversive, even rebellious. A banquet was an ideological occasion on, in palace or paradise, which the King demonstrated his generosity to his courtiers and subjects, not the other way around.[22] He met a grisly end in the 'torture of the boats', in which, our informant recounts with macabre delight, the victim was kept alive between two hulls until he went rotten in the sun.[23]

The person who reported Mithridates' disloyalty to the king was the queen mother Parysatis. The stories of relentless retribution enacted as the result of the interference of the Persian royal women were popular with Greek authors, who saw them as evidence of the decadence of the Achaemenid power structure.[24] In foreigners' eyes, the profusion of women around the king was evidence of his decadence and devotion to carnal pleasures. Greek reports of cohorts of concubines may conflate those who in fact shared the king's bed with a wider class of female court personnel, who could have worked as courtiers in their own right, for example as singers and entertainers. While the royal women appear to have had their own private apartments, we have no evidence that they were confined to them. On the contrary, some references suggest that royal and noble women could pursue an education, even in physical skills such as riding and archery. They owned property, travelled with entourages across the empire, and wielded seals in order to conduct business. Nevertheless, the behaviour of royal women may have been as closely watched as that of the male nobles around the king, since their role in the legitimacy of the royal household was key. After the reign of Darius I, the Achaemenid kings aimed to create a consistent network of blood kinship around them by marrying within a close circle of nobles and relatives.[25] Royal or very high-status women are depicted on some seals and textiles. Their long, gathered gowns are ostensibly similar to the male court robe, perhaps providing Greeks with further reason to see Persian men as effeminate.[26]

Similarly confusing are tales of courtiers called eunuchs, who frequently appear in Greek texts as founts of devious intrigue. There had been a tradition of employing some castrated men in earlier Near Eastern courts. Since the Achaemenid court inherited many of the interrelated administrative and social networks of their predecessors, it is entirely likely that these specialized roles continued. However, the evidence is ambiguous. The term used for 'eunuch' in Akkadian could have

4.16 Persian women are to be found represented on seals, textiles and small-scale sculpture. Sometimes wearing crowns or long trains hanging from their head (with faces uncovered), they wear their hair in bobbed or plaited hairstyles. These impressions from a chalcedony pendant show how women's gathered robes had some parallels with male court dress.

become a standard court title, leaving us no indication whether the (to us) crucial physical definition still applied.[27] Moreover, the term 'eunuch' in Greece can frequently be mistranscribed for the word meaning 'wine-pourer' or 'wine-bearer' another formal position of the inner court, leaving significant scope for later misunderstanding.[28] In tales set in the courts of Artaxerxes II and even Alexander, the eunuch courtier character is seen as shrewdly watching those who threaten to overreach their status. The amount of malice, injustice or righteous suspicion attributed to the eunuch's involvement in courtly proceedings varies. On other occasions the eunuch is the disposable accessory to a change of kings and the enabler of the next king's success. In the sources, such stereotypical roles stretch between reigns and elide individual personalities.[29] Two trends may have contributed to the pervasive influence of the cunning eunuch in the majority of court stories. The strong tendency in Greek literature to stereotype all Persian court personnel as effeminate and unmanly is one. But another possibility is that the stories

4.17 Decorated scabbards for the *akinakes* or Persian dagger are depicted in great detail on the Persepolis reliefs. This surviving gold scabbard overlay, from the Oxus Treasure, shows finely detailed scenes of a lion hunt with horsemen in Assyrian-style garb. The composition and its style have been used to argue for a date of manufacture in both the seventh and the late fourth century BCE.

were all gradually reshaped in order to fit a popularly understood model of court society.

These colourful court tales contributed to an overwhelming Orientalist tradition about the Persian monarchy. But they may also give us an idea of the social ideals governing the lives of those around the king. The king's female relations and companions, and his close male advisers (whether eunuchs or deposed kings) were two groups who interfered in affairs of betrayal and individual rebellion within the ruling class. What the stories emphasize is the presence of a circle of protecting figures around the king. The stories also place the highest value on absolute loyalty, while shedding some dim light on the subtle etiquette within which gestures of trust and betrayal were buried. Episodes of court life, and some military accounts, animate the dim background to the archaeological echoes of social competition in tombs and luxurious objects.

Outside the bounds of domestic etiquette and formal banqueting, there were two dynamic and dangerous fields in which the status of the Persian aristocracy was challenged: the hunt and battle. The two kinds of activity were intimately linked. In the cavalry-dominated Persian military tradition, hunting (of lions, boar and other big game) was active training for mounted fighting. But the chase did not merely offer practical training, it was loaded with social significance for those who took part. Within all the older monarchies of the Near East, hunting had been the sport of kings. For the neo-Assyrian monarchs in particular, it was elevated to a performance of royal virtue, in which the king demonstrated his power over chaos by his ability to subdue wild beasts. The Achaemenid kings developed aspects of this ideology. An image of the king holding up and stabbing a lion, once used on Assyrian reliefs and the royal seal, had been transformed into an Achaemenid motif both in seals and in the over-lifesize reliefs guarding the shady doorways of two halls at Persepolis. Large 'paradises', or enclosed hunting grounds, were reported at key satrapal capitals across the empire, from the Hellespont to Sogdiana (fig. 3.19).[30] A means of controlling natural landscape on a large scale, they were arenas for the forging of social bonds between those hunting there. There is anecdotal evidence to suggest that members of the king's entourage could improve their position by proving

4.18 'I am a good horseman. As a bowman I am a good bowman ... As a spearman I am a good spearman ...' Darius I's royal virtues, inscribed on his tomb at Naqsh-i Rustam, were ideals for the Persian elite. The hunting image on this gilded disk or boss pairs spear and bow in a deer hunt.

their bravery in the hunt. This bravery could not infringe too much on the king's excellence in the fray, however, which should, naturally, be unparalleled.[31] The ideal of a harmonious band of mounted hunters translated well in societies across the empire. Isolated motifs of the horseman at full stretch in mid-pursuit were popular on seals and weaponry. Group hunts were a particularly popular tomb decoration in the west of the empire, frozen images of the fraternity in power.

Similar thematic currents appear in comments on the battle. One of the features of battle accounts involving the Persian army is the spotlighting of brave individuals who proved their merit beyond doubt in the midst of the slaughter. During the battle of Cunaxa in 401 BCE, King Artaxerxes II lost his horse underneath him. A Persian monarch without a horse would be a sorry and ignoble thing, so the noble Tiribazus is said to have provided him with a replacement mount, saying as he did so, 'Remember this day, your highness, for it should not be forgotten'.[32] Reputations and careers could be made and lost in battle, as well as lives.[33] A further characteristic of battle accounts, such as Cunaxa, is the narration of particular exchanges of blows between high-profile participants – the usurper and the king's right-hand man, for example. Such epic presentations were perhaps tweaked into dramatic shape in retrospect, rather than being accurate war reports. The frequent, personal confrontations of Darius III and Alexander at close quarters in battle, in historians' accounts, in vase paintings and, ultimately, in the Alexander mosaic, typify this kind of story (fig. 6.4).[34] Descriptions of pitched battles separated by seventy years and the reigns of four kings often share common themes.

COMPETITION AND POWER – THE FIFTH TO FOURTH CENTURIES

The available sources make it quite difficult to write a history of the Achaemenid politics of the late fifth and fourth centuries. The accounts of Persian military activity on the western fringe of the empire featuring (sometimes very briefly) in the works of Thucydides, Diodorus and Xenophon are only partly balanced by scanty epigraphic and documentary evidence in other languages. Xenophon's lively, adventuring *Anabasis* in particular is a fully coloured careerist memoir suffused with exploratory and military ideology, rather than a logistical guide to the Persian empire. Other reports of political machinations, particularly those relating to Cyrus the Younger, brother of Artaxerxes II, are presented entirely in the terms of the personal experience of involved foreigners, such as Xenophon, Lysander or Ctesias. In evaluating such sources, on the one hand, the suggestion of primary, contemporary report by an eye witness might appear attractive. On the other, personal involvement naturally brought with it all the baggage of self-justification and advancement in the competitive context of imperial government. To some extent, even leaders in the major positions of imperial administration – satraps or subject kings and dynasts – seem to have taken some opportunities to jockey for position within the margin allowed by their status. They owed absolute loyalty to the Great King, but not, perhaps, to each other. Disturbances in the west during the fifth and fourth centuries required the intervention of the king and his representatives in the business of settling and supporting one or other claim on power, with money, armies or both. Where spurious kingships were claimed, they were usually based on local thrones. Only very occasionally did this rivalry begin to infringe on the central power of the Persian king directly. The real rivals for the throne, until 334 BCE, were those within the same Achaemenid family.

Brief campaign references in Xenophon and Diodorus record Artaxerxes I's efforts to reassert control over Egypt after its rebellion during or after his accession in 465 BCE. A force led by his brother Achaemenes against the rebel Libyan king Inaros reportedly came to a sticky end, besieged by the Nile. Inaros had recruited a mercenary army and in 459, the support of the Athenian fleet, still campaigning in the eastern Mediterranean after military successes in Pisidia and possibly in Cyprus, and exerted most control over the Delta, the gateway to the rest of the satrapy.[35] In response, Artaxerxes at first attempted a piece of diplomacy that was to work well in the future: he gave money to the Spartans to invade against the Athenians.[36] But finding no success on this occasion, he raised a fresh army and allied fleet, commanded by Artabazus and Megabyxus (both nobles with historic and close family relationships with the king).[37] This campaign turned the tables on Inaros and the Athenians: under a concerted assault this alliance crumbled and the Greeks, cornered on an island in the Delta, had to retreat without many of their ships.[38] With the opening up of communication routes between Memphis and the sea, the rebellion was seen as solved. Inaros' rebellion had lasted for nearly ten years, but it was concentrated in the Delta, where there was a tradition of local domains.[39] Inaros, despite claiming descent from the Egyptian dynasty of Psammetichus, was not recognized as pharaoh elsewhere in Egypt. Four years after its likely beginning, an inscription from Wadi Hammamat was dated in the fifth year of the king, 'Lord of the Double Country, Artaxerxes'.[40] The satrap, 'Sarsamas', who reportedly was appointed in the wake of the rebellion is likely to be the very same Arsames whose administration is documented there over twenty years later.[41] The uprising was significant, but driven by a faction rather than the entire province.

Comparable details of rebellion and military action are completely lacking for Bactria, where a Persian satrap seems to have tried his luck at seizing more power at around the time of Artaxerxes I's accession.[42] By the end of the century, historical references in Xenophon and Ctesias suggest that Bactrians were seen as stalwarts of the king.[43] The province was governed by satraps closely linked to the king and, barring fraternal dissatisfaction, seems to have been a long-term bastion of the dynasty. A rebellion there was potentially far more damaging than the secession of upper Egypt, but we have no further details of the severity of the disloyalty from the beginning of Artaxerxes' reign – it seems to have been quelled.

This kind of lop-sided picture of the empire in the sources unfortunately persists until Alexander's invasion. There is very little other very coherent or deep context for territorial or dynastic problems during Artaxerxes I's long reign. The Athenian commander Cimon made a short-lived attack on Cyprus in 451, while an embassy from Athens travelled to Susa in 448 in order to reach some kind of diplomatic agreement on territorial influence around the Aegean coast. The exact terms of a treaty, by which the Greek cities of Asia retained 'autonomy', are reported only much later, in the fourth century, so the agreement of the mid fifth century must remain debatable.

Within the empire, Megabyzus, one of the commanders of the victorious force in Egypt, may have overreached his position in Syria and come into conflict with a royal army, but the story as it is told by Ctesias is a heroic romance.[44] Several prominent members of the court from the fifth and fourth centuries have this kind of tradition attached to them. The political reality lying behind the tales of adventure and exile is difficult to recover. Artaxerxes I may have undertaken some reform within the court, but whether this impinged directly on the status of the encircling family of nobles is hard to tell.[45] He certainly followed his predecessors' technique of emphasizing his right to the throne and the continuity of dynastic rule, by building and inscribing a substantial palace near the terrace wall at Persepolis.[46]

After forty years on the throne, Artaxerxes I died some time in December 424 or the beginning of January 423.[47] The empire stayed firmly in Achaemenid hands, that is to say three pairs, since the king's sons Darius (also known as Ochus), Xerxes and Sogdianus all seem to have laid claim to the kingship on their father's death. Documents from Babylonia show a smooth acceptance of Darius II as king in their dating formulae. But Xerxes may have been recognized as king elsewhere, as a memory of his status as king is recorded by Ctesias.[48] The third brother, Sogdianus, quickly disposed of Xerxes, but could not make headway against the existing strong support for Darius among the aristocracy, particularly in the region of Babylon, where he mustered his army. After Sogdianus' execution, a further challenge by a fourth brother, Arsites, makes it clear that there was still a faction in the governing class who thought that another candidate had more to offer them.[49] The preceding long reign had perhaps allowed a competitive court to develop under the aegis of loyalty to one individual; with the uniting figure gone, the rivalries within a very close set of families were played out.[50]

As for the Aegean frontier, where the micro-focus of the Greek authors fell, continuing instability drew or tempted the satraps of the neighbouring provinces into tortuous diplomacy with the Greek cities. The satraps' independent initiative was perhaps driven by the hope of territory or tribute, as well as dividing potential enemies, and leading to greater favour with the king. A governor of Sardis, Pissouthnes, actually used his connection with Athens to rebel temporarily.[51] His son Amorges, who was more persistent, was finally captured by a Spartan force working for his replacement in Sardis, Tissaphernes.[52] But this alliance with the Spartans, brokered in Lycia, collapsed for lack of support.[53] Tissaphernes' fellow satrap in Phrygia, Pharnabazus, recruited first Sparta, then Athens, as a regional ally.[54] Into this mind-boggling series of foreign policy initiatives intruded the king's son, Cyrus, who in 407 was given special authority over the entirety of western Asia Minor, perhaps in the hope of eliminating the competing interests of the previous satraps.[55] After his arrival, the alliance with Sparta was adhered to consistently.[56]

References to specific events in government across the rest of the empire are sparse; surviving documentary sources in the shape of Babylonian business archives indicate a continuity in the practice of local administration by both civic and satrapal authorities.[57] It is difficult to assess events in the west in proportion, without knowledge of the complex goings on across the vast majority of Persian territory. Darius II may have had to deal with a rebellion in Media in 407 BCE, an event perhaps also related to ambition in the ruling class rather than disaffection in the general population.[58] Other short hints could be expanded into revolts or campaigns, but our attempts to rationalize some can be misleading. For example, in Darius' reign there occurs the first of several scattered references in Greek sources to a people called the Cadusians, who were perceived to be a troublesome or fierce group living in harsh territory on the edge of Media.[59] The temptation is to read a plausible long-term drive for independence into the gaps between these short lines.[60] Yet the references are all rather anecdotal or folkloric: later in the fourth century, Artaxerxes II was to stride heroically up hillsides in Cadusia while his army lived off the land (although, apparently, at no point coming to blows with an enemy), and, as a young man, Darius III proved his bravery in a duel against a Cadusian chieftain.[61]

These episodes, as well as tales involving Scythians and Bactrians, suggest that there was a kind of stereotyping applied to different peoples within the empire. Achaemenid ideology emphasized subjects' distinct contributions to the king's power according to their ethnic group; both Greek and Persian sources allude to an array of roles as key to Persian strength, including the ideal of hardy virility. Tales of fierce and warlike tribes seem superficially to hint at instability. They have contributed to the persistent questions about the consistency of Persian control across the empire.[62] Further questions need to be asked about the nature of relationships between the king and diverse communities. Some of the same belligerent groups appear frequently to take their place in line in the king's army. Their impact on the enemy was bolstered by their fearsome reputations.[63] Like wild lions corralled in a satrapal paradise, their controlled savagery enhanced Persian power rather than undermining it.

Darius II died in 405, and by spring 404 his son, Arses, was firmly identified as King Artaxerxes II in the dating formulae of Babylonian documents.[64] The succession, unlike his father's, seems to have been smooth at first. Measures may have been taken before Darius' death to formalize it more securely, with the first report of an initiation ceremony at Pasargadae dated to this reign.[65] But Artaxerxes' brother Cyrus harboured his own ambitions, and mustered a mixed satrapal and mercenary force there: 'his brother, he said, was too effeminate and cowardly either to sit his horse in a hunt or his throne in a time of peril'.[66] A central historiographic source for this dramatic family struggle is a later biography of Artaxerxes written by Plutarch. Plutarch drew on two memoirs by Greeks employed in the two opposing entourages. Ctesias attended Artaxerxes as a doctor and part-time Greek diplomat. Xenophon was impelled, he says, to join Cyrus' army by recommendation and the king's reputation for great fairness and generosity in rewarding service.[67] The early phases of Xenophon's *Anabasis* suggest that Cyrus collected his army under false pretensions of regional security. It is possible that, had he revealed his intentions earlier, he would have been held back by local lack of co-operation.

4.19 In the surface of a stamp seal, a combat between the heroic king and a fantastical beast is delicately carved. This hero is clearly crowned. The theme of a crowned but generic king overpowering one or two beasts was particularly popular. Such seals testify to the easy and wide dissemination of adapted but recognizably Achaemenid images throughout the empire, driven by the engine of personal seal commissioning and aspirational luxury collecting.

The brothers met in battle at Cunaxa, in Babylonia, in 401. The rival accounts of the battle, umpired and sifted by Plutarch, are riddled with the claims of individual participants creating their own epics out of a significant historic moment.[68] Xenophon's central picture of a spirited and generous Cyrus shows us a model of an ideal candidate for kingship. He charges with abandon through the midst of the battle towards his foe, mounted on a spirited and almost uncontrollable horse. Xenophon's portrait of the prince's virtues on his death in battle represents a perfect mirror of the qualities of a good king. He was an excellent horseman, archer and spearsman. He took risks in the hunt, but rewarded those who helped him as they hunted alongside. Similarly in battle, he offered meritocratic rewards for excellence. As a diplomat he kept his word and rewarded men according to their good deeds or bad, exhibiting extreme generosity and justice. Xenophon's summary is a propagandistic set of ethics originating in the tactics used to win over support at the expense of the real king; it is an updated version of the qualities claimed by Darius I in his tomb inscription.[69] Yet all hung in the balance in battle, with a few well-placed blows enough to remove the danger. Cyrus' death could not remove all questions over Artaxerxes' authority, however. Numerous lieutenants claimed a hand in the death of the prince.[70] Technically, this gave them some of the king's power, having saved his claim to the throne. The aftermath of the battle probably saw an extensive round of reward and punishment according to the faithfulness or future risk expected from each individual.

Artaxerxes must have spent some time in the early decades of his reign settling the network of empire-wide loyalty around him.[71] His building programme, the most extensive since the reign of Darius I, included a new palace at Susa and the extensive development of Hamadan, as well as a full Achaemenid-style extension to the neo-Babylonian palace in Babylon. At Susa, his inscription claims that he restored the *apadana* after a fire: 'This palace Darius my great-great-grandfather built; later under Artaxerxes my grandfather it was burned; by the favour of Ahuramazda, Anahita and Mithras, this palace I built' (A_2ASa).[72] The inscription, whether it records the real history of the building or not, mentions the two longest reigning kings to precede Artaxerxes. This choice illustrates his desire to emphasize the long-term continuity of power over recently fractured trust. Again, for the first time since the early texts of Darius I, the entire semi-legendary genealogy of the Achaemenid family is rolled out in building inscriptions at Susa and Persepolis.[73] A new emphasis on the roots of power in the past suffuses sources of the period. The inscription above reveals another innovation of Artaxerxes' reign, the inclusion of three Iranian gods as the protective deities of the Achaemenid kingship.[74] The innovation may have something to do with strenghening Artaxerxes' connection with traditionally Persian gods and may have been connected with greater definition of Persian religion across the empire.[75]

Traditions were a significant tool in political combat elsewhere. In Egypt, a king named Amyrtaeus seized the opportunity of the change of kings to claim the throne there, linking himself to the native dynasty that had been defeated by Cambyses and to subsequent rebels. The rebellion seems to have had an impact across the province only by 401, when the first documents in Elephantine begin to be dated by the regnal years of Amyrtaeus.[76] This success was perhaps a result of Artaxerxes' concentration in Babylonia on defeating his brother in the same year. The opportunities offered by Egyptian independence were the focus of great competition by prominent families of the Delta. Amyrtaeus' short reign was followed by that of Nepherites I, from Mendes, whose seven years in power introduced a twenty-ninth dynasty into the Egyptian royal tally.[77] A possible relative, Achoris, won a confused and disputed succession, managing to hold out for thirteen years.[78] But after his death, another family group from Sebennytus took power. The successful founder of this thirtieth dynasty, Nectanebo I, lasted nineteen years and passed the throne on to his son Tachos, who had ruled with him for his last three years in power.[79] Tachos' attempt to campaign against Persia in the Levant was undermined by his brother and his son, who became Nectanebo II in 359/8. The exiled King Tachos, ironically, sought refuge in the Achaemenid court, demonstrating how Egypt, once independent, settled into the same contradictory network of competing interests into which Persia tapped in the rest of the Mediterranean.[80]

Like Inaros sixty years earlier, these kings relied heavily on privately raised, mercenary forces to secure their positions. Particularly prominent was Sparta, whose kings enthusiastically joined in anti-Persian activity throughout the fourth century. Yet, ideologically, they revived a strong image of Egyptian nationalism, all claiming descent from the twenty-sixth dynasty. Epithets and iconography were sourced from that period to create an image of canonical pharaonic rule.[81] Although temples had continued to be maintained well throughout the Achaemenid period, the new Egyptian rulers raised the profile of certain cults and complexes through selective building projects, particularly in Thebes. A surviving sarcophagus carved, but perhaps never used, for the last king, Nectanebo II, is adorned with texts from the Book of the Underworld. It was found in Alexandria, to where it was probably transferred in an effort to build a convincing historical environment for the new Ptolemaic dynasty, only thirty years later.

The lack of an immediate response to the Egyptian rebellion from Persia is quite surprising, but perhaps due first to Artaxerxes' need to secure his position after Cunaxa, and then to the lack of availability of a fully co-ordinated large fleet. After a diplomatic breakthrough in 386 (known as the 'King's Peace', by which the Persian control was confirmed over the cities of Asia Minor 'liberated' in the Persian wars), Artaxerxes II sent force against the Egyptians in the Levant in 385; unfortunately the only contemporary references to this episode survive in the highly anti-Persian rhetoric of a speech by Isocrates called the *Panegyricus*. He implies, along with several apocalyptic predictions about Persian strength, that the campaign was a disaster.[82] Artaxerxes waited until 274/3 to send a further invasion force directly against Nectanebo I in Egypt.[83] Commanded by the satrap Pharnabazus and the Greek general Iphicrates, it failed to break through Egyptian defences. After the failure of that expedition, Egypt was left to its own devices until the reign of Artaxerxes III. Ideologically, Egypt was still considered part of the empire, never leaving the list of subject peoples.[84] It is also clear that diplomatic and trade contact

4.20 Once assumed to belong to Alexander of Macedon (and found in a mosque, used as a basin), this sarcophagus is attributed by its hieroglyphic inscription to Nectanebo II, the last pharaoh of independent Egypt in the fourth century BCE. The dynasty drew on the iconography of pre-Persian pharaohs in an active temple-building programme which asserted their ancient Egyptian identity.

was still possible throughout the period of independence. Underneath the strong rhetoric of nationalism, we do not need to assume that secession turned the entire province away from its links with Persia.

Running in parallel to Egypt's dynastic activity was turmoil in Cyprus. The ambitious king, Evagoras I, cultivated a local, lively court in Salamis after seizing power from the previous incumbent.[85] The multi-ethnic cities of Cyprus were governed separately by hereditary kings, who led their fleets together in the cause of the Great King, when summoned. Evagoras, after taking Salamis, believed that he could improve his position further and invaded several of his neighbours. Support from Athens and associated anti-barbarian, philhellene propaganda combined to cast this episode in the guise of a rebellion from the Great King.[86] Yet the outcome, after he was curbed in 380 BCE, was a slight improvement in his status, but within more controlled territorial limits.[87] Two generations of his descendants ruled after him until Evagoras II was ejected by a rival during the reign of Artaxerxes III. The episode is an illustration of how such ambitions, dramatized to the highest degree as a danger to the Persian king, could on a larger scale be seen merely as regional disputes requiring mediation from the Great King, backed up by force.

Accounts of events in Asia Minor are again comparatively extensive for the reign of Artaxerxes II. The satraps Pharnabazus and Tissaphernes, just two of the multiple governors with whom the king dealt throughout his reign, were crucial and powerful figures to the Spartan and Athenian contingents who attacked or sought alliance with them. From a Greek viewpoint on the shore of the Aegean, they dominate the historical horizon. The Spartans, tarnished by an association with Cyrus' attempt against the king, continued to pursue a policy of harassment along the Aegean seaboard. Pursuing a weakness in regional security, the Spartan King Agesilaus embarked on an expedition along the fringe of Asia Minor and won a battle outside Sardis, although he failed to take the city.[88] Having allowed the satrapal capital to become vulnerable to an outside force, Tissaphernes was abruptly removed from office.[89] Agesilaus did not proceed much further, eventually being recalled to his own city.[90]

From around 370 onwards, we again come across accounts of the daring and transgressive careers of individual satraps, such as Megabyzus in the mid fifth century, in the west of the empire. Because these come in a cluster from c.370 to c.360, they have become known in historical accounts as the great 'Satraps' Revolt', although this gives the events the illusion of unity that they probably did not possess.[91] The difficulty of using these biographical incidents to construct a military and political account is underlined by the later attempt by the Sicilian historian Diodorus to put them all in a rational order.[92] Although he is the main source for this period, his chronology is shaky and indefinite, and events do not relate to each other clearly. It is best to regard the stories he used as dramatic nobles' biographies reflecting their individual ambition.

First there is the so-called revolt of Datames, an account of whose life is available to us in Latin, written by Cornelius Nepos.[93] His talent reached the attention of the king when Datames, in disguise, brought a captive rebel right into the Persian camp. He was given direction of the war against Egypt. However, Datames' success aroused envy: 'He incurred the dislike of the courtiers, because they saw that he on his own was more valued than all of them together … on this account they all conspired to ruin him.'[94] In response, Datames made alliances reinforcing his position in Paphlagonia and Cappadocia, and at some point came to blows with his neighbours, while being abandoned by members of his family. The king's deputy, Autophradates, was sent against him with an army (it is not clear whether he directly rebelled or infringed on disputed territory), but they reached a truce.[95] The rest of his troubles consist of mysterious series of double-crosses by fellow satraps, in the course of the last of which he was slain.[96] The brief information about his military activity is embedded in a conventional biography very like those of other skilled courtiers in the Persian empire.

Another satrap who is implicated in Datames' story is Ariobarzanes, the satrap of Hellespontine Phrygia, who is talked of as also revolting against the king.[97] Autophradates and Mausolus of Caria fought him and his Spartan and Athenian allies near Adramyttium (modern Edremit). The Spartan contingent were allegedly bribed to leave by the two commanders, but what kind of diplomatic planning was in motion is anyone's guess. Both of these commanders appear later to have also decided to rebel. By the 360s, a new character had entered the fray. Orontes, a half-Bactrian satrap married to the king's daughter, had cultivated support in Athens.[98] Although several of the participants (Tachos the exiled Egyptian king, Agesilaus again and Orontes) are reported as moving armies to the south-east, they seem not to have got further than the upper Euphrates before any concerted intention to attack the king disappeared (if there in the first place).[99] On occasion, it is not entirely clear from the sources who is in rebellion against the king and who is not.[100] It is possible that this remained vague on occasion because the satraps were fighting locally against each other, rather than campaigning directly against the king (as Cyrus had done). In the aftermath of these events, there was a gradual reordering of territorial status in Asia Minor. The power of Caria, for example, extended to include the satrapy of Lycia, which had previously been under the supervision of Autophradates.[101]

The fervent rivalry to which the evidence so patchily attests seems to have been born of an aristocratic culture of ambitious competition. The substantial local fiefdoms of each king or satrap, such as Evagoras or Mausolus, were built up and celebrated by their activities. Mausolus' massive tomb, one of the later seven wonders of the world, was begun in 367, a striking symbol of his ambition for his dynasty and his personal memory.[102] Although sampling recognizable features of aristocratic mixed, local Persian and Mediterranean culture, these leaders were constructing an image different from that of Achaemenid kingship. The direct benefits they could gain on the ground by jostling for position set off frequent disturbances. That Artaxerxes II's successor, Artaxerxes III (also known as Ochus), thought these processes could be damaging is suggested by his order that the mercenary armies of the satraps should be disbanded.[103] Apparently his father had not felt so threatened, despite the fact that events had required his frequent indirect intervention.

In Plutarch's biography, Artaxerxes II's old age and death are surrounded by a melancholy foreboding as to the quality of his successor.[104] The king's long reign, like that of his grandfather Artaxerxes I, seems to have allowed closely packed court factions to flourish. Another brilliant noble, Tiribazus (who made *his* reputation during Artaxerxes' epic march through Cadusia), resentful that he had not been given the hand of his preferred royal daughter, Amestris, apparently incited the crown prince Darius to rebel against his father.[105] We see the entire intrigue through the thick, distorting lens of a stereotypical court tale, in which all resentment is based on the king's appropriation of too many women and the plot is energized by obligatory gifts and accommodating but turncoat eunuchs. After an attempt on the king's life, Tiribazus fell in a struggle and Darius was put to death after being tried by a collective noble jury. Plutarch (drawing on the history of Dinon) attributes the deaths of two further eligible princes to Ochus (who became Artaxerxes III), one of whom was driven to suicide, the other killed by Tiribazus' son.

The nature of the necessary steps taken by Artaxerxes III to secure the empire during his reign does not help his reputation. Tennes, the governor of Sidon, the important naval base, rebelled and destroyed the satrapal paradise, but failed to hold out once besieged by the Great King.[106] The city as a whole was punished severely; the Babylonian Chronicle mentions the deportation of (possibly high-status) Sidonian prisoners to Babylon in 345 BCE.[107] Artaxerxes' comprehensive and violent reconquest of Egypt brought negative judgements down on his head, from those whom he had displaced; this negativity permeates the later sources, as similar stories had influenced Herodotus' account of Cambyses.[108] Although some official inscriptions indicate that there was a continuity of personnel in power, who accommodated the restoration of Persian rule, the later Demotic chronicle lamented the invasion as a disaster for Egypt: 'the Medes will bring them to ruination.'[109] One action by Artaxerxes III was to have long-term consequences for Persia's fortunes. He defended Perinthus against the attack of Philip II of Macedon, in the process casting himself as an obstacle to Macedonian expansion.[110] It was this opposition that was to prompt Philip to declare an allied assault on Persian power. Philip's resolution gave his son, Alexander III, one of his initial justifications for his fateful invasion of the empire.[111]

Artaxerxes III and his family fell to a comprehensive court-based coup in 338. Our sources attribute the intrigue to a eunuch, Bagoas, who raised the king's son, Arses/Artaxerxes IV, to the throne, but only two years later murdered him.[112] A more distant member of the Achaemenid clan, Artashata, took the throne himself, with the throne name Darius III, and disposed of Bagoas. Artaxerxes IV had certainly been recognized as the legitimate king, according to contemporary records.[113] Whether the conveniently short-lived and stereotypical interference of Bagoas is really historical or not must remain an open question. Darius III was, at least in the first few years of his reign, successful in establishing his authority.[114] The high degree of competition within the Persian ruling class to which political events testify kept a degree of flexibility in the Achaemenid monarchy. Darius III is given a background rather comparable to the high-flying satrapal aristocracy who made their presence felt in Greek sources for the fourth century. His success is an illustration of how close to kingship the satellite members of the royal family could see themselves to be. Their ambitious jostling gave Persian rule a substantial safety net of personnel who had a great investment in the empire, and who could step into a breach when the whole superstructure was threatened.

4.21 A larger-than-lifesize sculpture of a Carian man, although once identified with Mausolus himself, was one of a series of figures adorning his massive dynastic tomb at Halicarnassus. Although he continued to be a vassal of the Persian king, he was a winner in the local competitive turmoil of the mid fourth century, a success manifested in his family's new stepped 'wonder of the world'.

5 PEOPLES, COMMUNICATION AND RELIGION

5.1 'When in Egypt …' – Darius I, his cartouche visible above, is represented worshipping Anubis (with Isis behind) on a wooden shrine door inlaid with coloured glass. Whether officially or independently commissioned, the representation of Darius in a fully Egyptian setting illustrates the degree to which Achaemenid rule could be cast in existing monarchic traditions in different regions of the empire. Achaemenid ideology emphasised the distinctive differences and characteristics of each subject people. The Persian king's patronage of diverse religious and cultural groups gave each one an individual investment in his power.

When the Achaemenid kings talked of the extent of their kingdom, they listed and showed ranks of peoples, rather than geographical limits. The organization of these lists in the royal inscriptions, moving from centre to peripheries, suggests that the peoples were thought of in a spatial sense, giving them a meaning very close to 'countries'.[1] The overall lists of the inscriptions, like the serried ranks of throne supporters that were the visual equivalent, were very much a sweeping, ideological presentation of the king's subjects. By no means do they preserve all the names of ethnic groups within the empire, nor can we assume they always represent fully the ethnic group in which subjects would place themselves. During the reign of Darius, the number of peoples varied in different inscriptions, as he worked to establish anew a territorial claim to the Persian empire. After his death, the preservation of a more stable list of thirty to thirty-one peoples or lands became part of a consistent message of order and legitimate rule in Achaemenid inscriptions and reliefs.[2] The ethnic subdivisions of the Achaemenid army related to this ideological overview.

The administrative picture was more variable. Other written evidence shows that the empire was divided up into provinces for the convenience of government, but these do not exactly correspond with the names of peoples. Xenophon attributed a fully formed system of administrative regions to the wise state-building of Cyrus the Great, but administrative roles may have developed slowly during his and his successors' reigns.[3] Some of the definitions of regions that were absorbed by the Achaemenid empire were adapted from those in use under the neo-Assyrian and Babylonian empires, such as Ebir-Nari 'Beyond the River' for the territory from the Euphrates to the Levant coast. But the definition of different administrative regions changed during Achaemenid rule according to local circumstances, including, for instance, local fiefdoms and city states that could be controlled most conveniently by the locally preferred government. For some provinces, particularly to the north and east of the empire, we have virtually no definite contemporary information about their precise limits and evolution as a separate administrative entity.

Our use of the word 'satrapy' for these administrative provinces is traditional, but is only attested directly in Greek. Commanders and deputies of the king who assisted in his rule were given the Old Persian title 'protector of the kingdom' or *xšaçapavan*; in the Bisitun inscription, Darius used this title for two Persian nobles in the provinces of Bactria and Arachosia who fought on his behalf in the struggle for the throne.[4] The word was adapted into both *satrapeia* and *xatrapes* in Greek, the former describing the subdivided territories of the king, the latter his deputies.

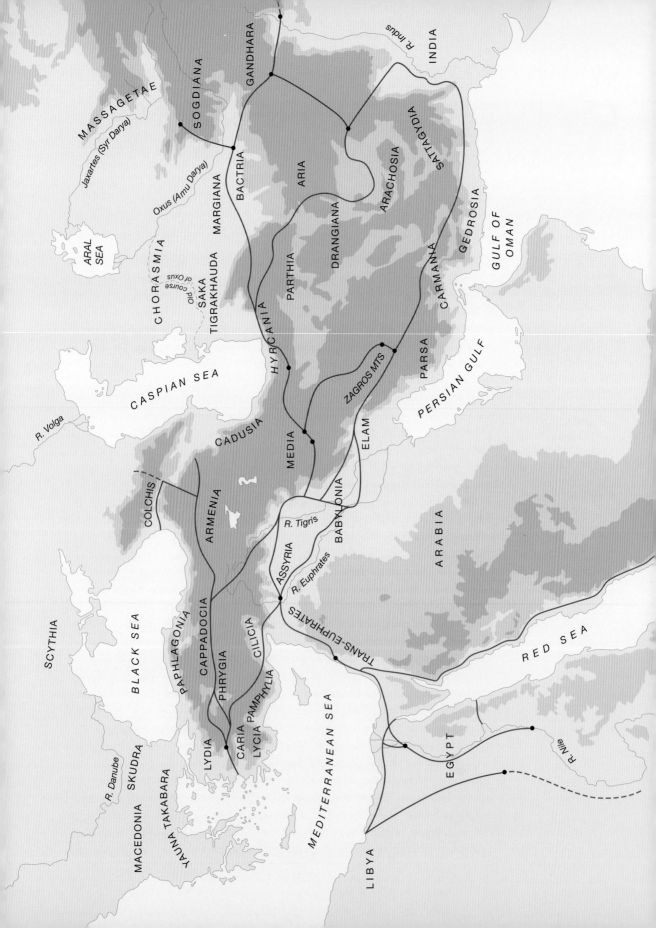

MASSAGETAE

Jaxartes (Syr Darya)

SOGDIANA

GANDHARA

R. Indus

INDIA

Oxus (Amu Darya)

CHORASMIA

ARAL
SEA

SAKA
TIGRAKHAUDA

Old course of Oxus

MARGIANA

BACTRIA

ARIA

DRANGIANA

ARACHOSIA

SATTAGYDIA

GEDROSIA

GULF
OF
OMAN

PARTHIA

HYRCANIA

CARMANA

CASPIAN SEA

R. Volga

CADUSIA

ZAGROS MTS

PARSA

PERSIAN GULF

MEDIA

ELAM

COLCHIS

ARMENIA

R. Tigris

BABYLONIA

ASSYRIA

ARABIA

R. Euphrates

SCYTHIA

BLACK SEA

PAPHLAGONIA

CAPPADOCIA

CILICIA

TRANS-EUPHRATES

RED SEA

PHRYGIA

CARIA

PAMPHYLIA

LYDIA

LYCIA

MEDITERRANEAN SEA

EGYPT

R. Nile

R. Danube

SKUDRA

MACEDONIA

YAUNA TAKABARA

LIBYA

5.2 Peoples and
Communication.
A simplified schematic
representation of land
communication routes
across and beyond
Achaemenid territory, set
over regions and peoples.
Significant connections by
water existed throughout
the eastern Mediterranean,
between Egypt and the
Levant, Greece and Egypt,
the Indus valley and the
Persian Gulf, throughout the
Black Sea, and between the
Transcaucasus, Chorasmia
and Central Asia, around the
Caspian or along the banks
of the Amu Darya. It is
unclear how functional the
Red Sea canal of Darius I
became, but other routes led
to the Nile valley from the
Red Sea.

This does not mean that any provincial leader was always called a *xatrapes* or *xšaça-pavan*, since rulers of provinces in the empire are also referred to as governors and (in the case of local dynasts) kings. Generals in command of Persian armies who may not have had a permanent territory assigned to them are also occasionally called 'satraps' in Greek sources.[5]

From the Greek perspective, the military responsibilities of satraps were foremost; their duty to maintain garrisons and raise armies in support of the king was certainly central. But surviving letters illustrate a range of responsibilities, including the protection of imperial revenue and arbitration in property transactions and in administrative disputes of all kinds. The satraps, who remained almost exclusively Persian throughout the empire's history, dominate our concept of how the empire was governed, but subject peoples could liaise with central power through a great variety of local systems of government. Greek authors use a variety of terms for local leaders, while both Babylonian and Egyptian documents show several levels of staff interacting in the administration of land and communities.[6] Subject peoples or cities could aspire to having their own representative in the royal court itself, or could establish their communication with the king as he moved between capitals or went on campaign.[7] The court and domain of each satrap could contain people, either Persians or foreigners, who might establish their own channel of communication with the king. The extent of satraps' autonomy within particular regions is uncertain. Xenophon visualizes their realms as capsule royal domains, yet they were not totally autonomous and were likely to be constantly accountable to the king. Moreover, satraps in specific regions did not constitute the only level of supervisory government within the empire; the king occasionally appointed commanders, usually members of the royal family, with wider regional powers over several provinces and their governors.[8]

The vast extent of the empire, and the patchiness of present evidence, means that a comprehensive understanding of its everyday workings is elusive. There exist several tantalizing and detailed groups of evidence. A very few sets of archives, together with scattered texts, offer written records of administration and communication. These processes were documented not just in words but also in images, which suffuse the surviving evidence. The two groups interrelate, since texts were often accompanied by an image in the shape of a seal impression on a seal fastening or, in the case of tablets, the text itself (fig. 5.4).[9] Both combine to give a glimpse of complex systems and the people who ran them.

At Persepolis, two groups of thousands of clay tablets were excavated in the 1930s. One was an archive containing documents dating to the years 509–494 (from the thirteenth to the twenty-eighth year of Darius I's reign) deposited in administrative quarters on the edge of the royal platform. The fragile mud-brick cells in which they were housed were built against the terrace fortifications, from which the name 'Persepolis Fortification Tablets' is always applied to them.[10] They relate largely to arrangements for the movement and distribution of commodities in the immediate area of the palace, to local bands of male and female workers, travellers and religious personnel. Although the transactions are local, the recipients

5.3 The low walls and column foundations in the foreground of this view show the Persepolis Treasury in its final incarnation, having developed storage and administrative cells around enclosed courts and porticoes. Nestling behind the *hadesh* palace of Xerxes I (later popularly known as the 'Harem', and restored as the museum) and the Hundred-Columned Hall, the Treasury was largely self-contained, with restricted access.

display connections reaching to the edge of the empire, either through their ethnic origin (a band of Cappadocian workers, for instance) or through their travel plans, which could reach from Sardis to India. Across the platform in the Treasury was unearthed a smaller group of tablets dating from a longer period of time, from the end of Darius' reign to Artaxerxes I's seventh year on the throne (492–458).[11] They are very similar to the Fortification Tablets in format and function, but relate mainly to the distribution of silver in payment to people in the vicinity of Persepolis.

The Persepolis tablets are impressed with cuneiform Elamite writing, but are occasionally labelled in ink in Aramaic (and, on one example, in Greek); the texts occasionally refer to 'writers on skins'. These ink notes were a way of making the organization and location of archived tablets easier. Cursive ink writing was in much wider use on rolls of skin or papyrus, a technology that had begun to be used extensively in the neo-Assyrian period. Ink-written Aramaic on more perishable materials largely replaced cuneiform on clay by the late fifth century, leaving us with only scanty finds of surviving contemporary documents. Prepared skins and papyrus possibly held a greater variety of texts in the Achaemenid court than the accounts and receipts in clay. Surviving letters can include more circumstantial detail about imperial communication and concerns, although evidence for their non-administrative use is scarce.[12]

ORINST, P 57459 PERSEPOLIS, IRA
IMPRESSIONS OF STAMP SEALS ON A

5.4 Administrative images cover a clay *bulla* from the Persepolis Treasury. A label like this might have marked the string-fastening of goods or rolled papyrus documents, recording the variety of individuals responsible for the transaction in question. Images could be impressed using the faces of coins, bevel rings, stamp seals and rolled cylinder seals.

5.5 A blue chalcedony cylinder seal displays a segment of its carved scene, featuring a date palm and winged disk – both typical elements in Achaemenid cylinder seals. Cylinder seals, enjoying a small renaissance in the early Achaemenid period, could be fully rolled or briefly impressed on clay, producing a full scene or a selective glimpse.

While clay tablets were verified, checked and annotated with seal impressions made alongside the text, seal images accompanied papyrus or leather documents pressed on small lumps of clay called *bullae*. *Bullae* could be pressed between the fingers and pressed on to the rolled document directly, or on a string tie holding it closed. Since this was a common way to seal commodities in baskets, bags or vessels, when we find *bullae* that show the impression of a lost string, we have little way of telling whether they travelled with words, wine or silver. Clusters of *bullae* have been found at a few locations across the empire, either fully excavated, as at Daskyleion in Turkey, or through small and piecemeal finds. The many collections of letters, marriage contracts or loan agreements that they must have sealed have disappeared. Egypt's climate provides us also with a precious trail of documents extending through the whole Achaemenid period, including a batch of papyri in two languages from the garrison community at Elephantine.[13]

The type of information to be gleaned from all this material varies. Detailed analysis of the personnel who were mentioned in or whose seals cover a large number of Persepolis tablets, for example, can build up a picture of how resources were controlled and by whom.[14] The tablet archive of a Babylonian family business reveals, through minutiae of loans, land-use and revenue, economic and social developments over many years.[15] Administrative letters, on the other hand, often encapsulate individual problems or situations in one document. Letters were a dominant form of written communication throughout the empire. A surviving group of letters written in Aramaic, in ink on leather, was discovered in an unknown location in Egypt. Presumed to originate in a local governmental archive dating to the reign of Darius II (some may have been duplicate copies of sent letters), they were found inside a leather pouch, sealed with clay *bullae*. The written word was sent across the empire via swift couriers carrying other such pouches. With the address line and subject summary written on the exterior ('From 'Aršam to Nehtihur, the officer, the comptroller and his colleagues the accountants, who are in Egypt'), each letter includes a polite greeting and launches into a recap of its subject. Many close with an annotation giving the names of the official and scribe involved in dispatching the letter. 'Aršam, who was satrap of Egypt in the later fifth century, may have sent most of the surviving administrative letters to Egypt from Babylonia, where he had significant rural estates.

The letters show a close association of what appears to be both official and personal business. 'Aršam's title in the letters is 'son of the house', which may indicate his blood relationship to the royal family, but seems likely to have also been an official identity. The satrap takes care of personal appeals from other Persians for the enforcement of estate-inheritance and revenue, he authorizes the supplies for the journey of his deputy to Mesopotamia and back and finally, from a distance, makes arrangements for a sculptor from whom he has commissioned several works to be taken to Egypt. The use of letters to the Persian authorities for specific personal appeals and orders extended to civil and judicial situations in the evidence from

5.6 Elephantine, lying in the Nile across from the city of Aswan/Syene, was the site of a military garrison staffed with personnel from Judah. Founded as a colony with its own governor in the southernmost administrative district of Egypt by the beginning of the fifth century, the community was supported by official rations and plots of land which were allocated to colonists. Syene had a separate garrison with its own Persian commander.

Elephantine, far up the Nile. There, an Egyptian community at Aswan played host to a Persian commander, while a Judaean military garrison lived on Elephantine island with the local *frataraka* or governor. Administration was conducted in two languages, Demotic and Aramaic. The documents show the participation of both local governors and the satrap of Egypt in local religious, judicial and civic decisions. For example, the governors' co-operation with a local network of judges and civil law enforcers is precisely requested in a letter dating to the reign of Darius II, in the matter of a religious conflict.

The social, religious and economic appeals and decisions contained in these letters made them valuable documents. Letters not only worked as tools for immediate appeals but, once accepted, could stand for generations as documents establishing a precedent. Letters from the king himself had the impact of disembodied orders.[16] Similarly, the text of royal proclamations could reflect a letter structure, even if they were designed to be read out or passed on orally. Royal letters granting rights to a community could be enshrined and transformed through oral or written tradition in local histories, since their format could be very easy to remember and reproduce. For example, a later Greek inscription carved on a *stela* set up to reinforce a sanctuary's right to its resources claims to have been sent by Darius I to his deputy Gadatas in Magnesia on the Meander. The inscription was valuable locally for preserving the privileges of the sanctuary by direct appeal over the local governor's head.[17] This administration via authoritative written words was characterized, ironically, in contemporary Greek literature as a world in which the despot's verbal power circumscribed freedom.[18]

Both a letter of 'Aršam and documents from Persepolis show how the mobile administration of letters and permits made possible official long-distance travel. The Egyptian satrap sent a passport with his deputy Nehtihor, returning from Babylonia to Egypt, in which all the commanders he would encounter in his travel stages were named and requested to supply provisions.[19] An allowance was given to Nehtihor himself (five measures of different grains, two measures of wine or beer,

5,7 A wide range of images and styles coursed through the documentation of personal and business transactions in the Achaemenid period. This selection of sealings came from a grave at Ur, southern Iraq, for whose occupant they may have formed a design resource for gem-carving or other miniature arts. The two hundred images were impressed by coins, ring-bezels, cylinders, and conoid stamp seals. Illustrated here are brief glimpses of motifs originating in Greek art (top, second left, second right and bottom left), Mesopotamian myth (top, centre), Assyrian religion (bottom right) and Achaemenid court imagery (bottom middle).

and a sheep) – some of this generous provision could have been exchanged privately for other types of food. Specific provision was also made for an entourage of ten servants and three colleagues in the satrap's employment. Nehtihor was kept on his toes (and the supplies of the local way stations preserved) by the qualification that no stage could provide him with more than one day's resources. Documents such as this are our only evidence for the number and location of administrative districts and way stations in the empire. Some of the day stages leading west on the road from Persepolis and Ecbatana have been identified. Some, such as Bisitun, the site of a later large caravanserai, were also set in cultivated paradises, where the supply of provisions was connected with surrounding estates.[20]

A large number of the Persepolis Fortification Tablets are concerned with the distribution of food rations from such estates, and from warehoused resources, some of these specifically dealing with travellers.[21] Very occasional scattered finds of Elamite tablets elsewhere (in Susa and Kandahar) suggest that the Persepolis system for dealing with these demands was used in other imperial and regional capitals.[22] In the Levant, similar administrative notes were written out on broken ceramic fragments, or *ostraca*, one of the most common forms of disposable receipt in the Mediterranean region.[23] The tablets archived at Persepolis themselves seem to have originated in way stations across the province.[24] The travellers whose daily requirements were authorized on clay in the Persepolis region were travelling to

India, Sogdiana, Arachosia and Bactria in the east and Babylon, Sardis and Egypt in the west. The records give the recipient's basic job title or social status – 'messenger', 'escort' (leading foreign groups), 'express courier', 'worker', 'boys'.[25] Many appear to travel on foot, although rations for post horses, which could cover thirty-odd kilometres between way stations in less than a day, are included in the provisions for express couriers.[26] Members of the royal household were provisioned using this administration, as well as other levels of officials. In late winter 499, the daughter of the king, Artozostre, journeyed with three other women and Gobryas, the king's spearbearer, between Susa and Persepolis; all these travellers drew large rations according to their high rank.[27] The terse language of the tablets unfortunately does not fill out the context for such journeys. Often, the traveller's official authorization, like Nehtihor's permit, is the only justification cited: 'he carried a sealed document of the king'. In some cases, long-distance missions coincide tantalizingly with historical events, as in the case of Datiya, who leaves a document trail on his way to Sardis, from visiting the king at Persepolis in winter 494. This is usually taken to be Datis, the Persian general whom Herodotus named as leader of the punitive expedition against Eretria and Athens in 490. Here, he may have been reporting to the king on the situation along the Asia Minor coast.[28]

Many of the travel tablets give the destinations of a stream of officials converging on the king to report and request instructions. They allow us to map the movements of the royal court between capitals for the period they cover.[29] They do not give many clues to the time taken to make trips across the empire, nor do they identify many of the stages, beyond regional capitals and the local centres of Parsa. However, a vivid overview of the road system is given by Herodotus who was extremely impressed by the connected personnel and way stations.[30] Herodotus estimates the distance of the royal road from Susa to Sardis, the best known route to the Greeks, at a distance of 450 parasangs, a parasang being equal to just less than five and a half kilometres.[31] He does not mention the empire's other central routes, such as the road from Babylon to Ecbatana and the north-eastern or upper satrapies. One of the few sites where ancient road construction has noticeably survived is a hillside near Pasargadae, where a road 1.7 m wide cut into the rock gave a durable approach to the royal capital. Unfortunately the most detailed survey of routes all the way from Ephesus to India, the *stathmoi* or 'stages' written by Ctesias, has not survived.[32]

Most of the ancient routes remained central to the structures of successive, later empires in the Middle East over the following centuries. In Greek, they are referred to as substantial chariot tracks that must have taken extensive caravan trade traffic as well as official parties.[33] Workers could be employed to maintain the roads (as a few documents from Persepolis show), but, since most were unpaved, passage could still become difficult during winter seasons.[34] Large-scale route clearance and maintenance was one of the tasks associated with military campaigns.[35] The king's role as a pioneering route-finder, directing his army into new roads in conquered territory, was one of the traditional ideological virtues of Near Eastern kings. Water transport is not as prominent in the ancient sources (although the dramatic acts of fording and bridging rivers are).[36] Apart from the ease of travel from the major ports of the Mediterranean, such as Tarsus and Sidon, it is likely that embarkation on the Persian Gulf coast could at certain times allow swifter travel to the south-eastern satrapies than the tough desert route. The Tigris and Euphrates were useful as routes for the transportation of goods, while the Oxus and Caspian Sea enabled connections reaching across the northern edge of the empire.[37]

Herodotus estimated that the journey from the Mediterranean coast to Susa would take three months.[38] For official diplomatic parties, hosted and hampered by hospitality along the way, it could take much longer. Aside from the supernatural swiftness of the king's couriers, journey times can be estimated from references to the more effortful movements of armies across the central routes. Between the capitals, for example, approximately three weeks would be enough to move from Babylon to Susa, or from Ecbatana to Persepolis. The main route from Susa to Ecbatana (through Babylonia) could take over five weeks, although a stiffer route through the mountains might be taken in under ten days. The Fortification travel texts attest to approximately twenty way stations on the route from Persepolis to Susa, suggesting a possible travel time of between three and five weeks, according to the type of party making the journey. The scope of the Persepolis documents indicates that travellers could plan routes direct from the royal capitals to almost any part of the empire; when Xenophon evoked the accessibility of the four corners of the king's territory from his capital in Persia, he seems to have been referring to a practical possibility.[39]

The storehouses that provided the means for this empire-wide communication were husbanded carefully by a local bureaucracy. The resources they contained were marshalled locally, but formed part of a vast system of contributions that kept the empire logistically afloat. Persian control of the resources of subject lands worked through two main mechanisms: obligatory contribution of tribute and semi-obligatory gifts and the management of Persian-owned estates and businesses. The emphasis placed by royal inscriptions on the resources offered to the king by his subjects, and by Greek authors on the enormous wealth stored up in the royal palace treasuries, have a fundamental administrative basis. Court stories and letters of appeal focus on the rewards and advantages which the king could bestow on individual subjects and interest groups from his exclusive resources. The generalized idea of an exchange of benefits (stability in return for tribute) was possibly one of the major engines driving subjects' investment in the monarchy. The practical mechanics involved in the building of the empire's resources for the purpose of supporting peace, military commitments and social hierarchies, are more difficult to recover on a large scale.

The primary evidence, for example receipts and accounts, for contributions from subject provinces comes from tablets found in Persepolis and Babylonia.[40] Secondary surveys of how the empire's resources were gathered are available also in both contemporary and later Greek authors. The primary texts deal with local systems which we may try to extrapolate into a general system; the secondary sources frequently present pictures which occasionally cloak regional variation in philosophical neatness, or fail to match in all their details with what we know from other evidence.

5.8 A gold daric of the late fifth or fourth century BCE shows a generalized image of the Achaemenid king wielding the weapons in which the Persian elite traditionally claimed excellence, the bow and spear. Unlike the combined images of local motifs (such as battlements and ships) featured on western city coinages, darics and *sigloi*, also minted in Asia Minor, traditionally carried plain punchmarks on their reverse. Dating is usually established by stylistic assessment of the royal figures on the obverse.

An ideological overview of the concept of tribute is present in the inscriptions of Darius I.[41] The Old Persian word used there for what subject peoples owe to the king is *bāji*. By analogy with the Akkadian and Elamite words used in the parallel texts, this word is usually translated as 'tribute'. It is listed with other obligations to the king (for example, obedience) and is not accompanied by any kind of economic details that would help us define it. The word in fact seems to be an umbrella concept for a spectrum of material goods and services due to the king.[42]

In Parsa itself, the Fortification Tablets record a series of contributions from individuals and communities of the region to the king.[43] These local obligations, some called *bāziš*, were a form of levy or tax since they may have been generated as a share of produce from land that was permanently associated with the king, perhaps as owner or protector.[44] That the people of Parsa actually had a special status in relation to the king was perceived by outsiders, such as Herodotus, who understood it as simple privilege and exemption from tax.[45]

Other provinces apparently contributed assessed tribute in weighed silver, as well as goods in kind, such as horses and other livestock; payments in kind could also be sold on at a market rate.[46] Although some Persepolis texts record the transfer and transport of portions of silver, our only statements of the amounts recovered from peoples and satrapies on a large scale occur in Greek authors.[47] Their terminology distinguishing gifts from tribute (which is not clear in any Near Eastern texts) may have been the result of diplomatic rhetoric dictated by the local politics of the contributing source. The boundaries between the concepts of land-obligations or tithes, tribute and gifts were very likely to be fluid (while tribute could appear to be given freely, gifts might also appear to be given under necessity).

The authorities could take a customs charge from material traded through the Nile, a slice of the money generated from slave sales in Babylon, or income from market tariffs in Caria. These local, flexible sources of income were mirrored in the practical obligations required for the king. Statutory labour on behalf of both civic authorities and the military forces of the king could be enforced via several mechanisms. Communities from across the empire were maintained in garrisons as mobile manpower in both peace and war. Workers, whether free or enslaved, were kept on rations in Parsa in order to perform work for the royal administration. In Babylonia, portions of land were distributed from large estates in exchange for compulsory military service. Classified as 'chariot-land' or 'bow-land' according to the kind of draft attached, these land grants were tracked over many generations, through multiple loans and tenancies; in times of peace these obligations could transform into a payment of silver.[48]

Silver was the universal measure by which most of these requirements could be valued. The metal was weighed and transported in traditional shekel weights. Within the royal treasuries, quantities of wealth would have been weighed in shekel values, but took many forms of raw and worked metal, including jewellery and vessels.[49] Although everything could have a silver value, it did not need to be an active stage of every transaction. The Persepolis Fortification Tablets illustrate how the value of a variety of commodities could be easily translated directly in comparison to each

5.9 The eroded surface of a conoid stamp seal made from cast glass made this impression of a three-figure combat. Although not appearing in monumental form at the palace centres, this heroic image of the king controlling wild animals was one of the most popular Achaemenid-style motifs reproduced in miniature across the empire. The unprovenanced seal may have been manufactured in the Levant.

5.10 The image of the Persian elite hunt, shown here drilled and cut into a gem designed to be carried on a ring, bracelet or string, was adapted widely across Achaemenid territory. A leaping horse with a rider aiming spear or arrow was a desirable image on seals, inlaid jewellery, metal vessels and weaponry and even sarcophagi.

other.[50] Although some forms of inscribed, marked or coined money are found across the empire by the end of Achaemenid rule, large quantities of coinage did not circulate beyond the western edge of the empire. Silver and electrum coinage had begun to be struck in western Asia Minor before the Persian conquest. It was apparently after Darius' initial campaigns in Europe that gold and silver coins were minted in Sardis under Persian authority. The gold coins were commonly known in Greek as 'archers' (from the image of the king with bow stamped on them) or darics (after 'Darius' or the Persian word for gold) (fig. 5.8).[51]

The innovation of minting coins carrying the image of the king in conquered territory probably had some ideological meaning for Darius. But the act of striking exclusive royal coinage never became a totally controlled propaganda system in the way we might expect from later empires.[52] Coinage was more useful in the empire as a regional economic and political tool; independently formulated types (on the shekel weight standard) were struck by dynasts and satraps in the western provinces. There was a particular boom in city coinages in the fourth century, when mobile armies, Mediterranean diplomacy and satrapal activities in the region increasingly required ready cash of the kind recognizable to the workforces of the Mediterranean.

City and satrapal coinages carried a mixture of images evoking both authority and distinctiveness. Several, such as those of Cilicia, Cyprus and Samaria, borrow strikingly Achaemenid motifs, even for very small denomination coins. At the same time, these images were used in a specific context with local interpretations.[53] The two-figure combat between Persian king and lion and the winged disk also appeared on Samarian and Cilician issues, echoing images in use locally on stamp seals (fig. 5.9). The coinage of satraps and dynasts frequently used male heads which, if they represent the local source of authority, appear to be the beginning of the portrait genre on coinage.[54] Achaemenid iconography ultimately may have been incorporated in coin images as part of a free-for-all use of trustworthy or

religious motifs in which the Persian administration could also engage. For example, when Artaxerxes III began to coin money for the reconquered province of Egypt in the mid fourth century, it carried the highly recognizable image of the owl of Athena, used on Attic coinage.[55]

The absence of coinage as a major economic tool in large swathes of the empire in no way hampered the development of complex financial enterprises. One of the best known private businesses of the Achaemenid period is the Babylonian Murašu family firm, known from hundreds of documents recovered from the city of Nippur. During the neo-Babylonian and Achaemenid period, the cities of southern Mesopotamia had become particularly prosperous and cosmopolitan. Iranians and other ethnic groups settled in the cities and countryside. The comparative density of legal and financial documents found there offers information largely about real estate and agricultural business. The Akkadian documents indicate a hybrid administration, peppered with Iranian official titles and Aramaic notations. Nobles from the highest levels of the Achaemenid ruling class were substantial landowners in the area; estate ownership in this area was closely linked to the political changes within the court.[56] The Murašu family profited at this interface of imperial administration and provincial business, handling the proceeds of leased land grants, rented assets and loans. They acted as agricultural agents, providing proprietors with the tools to exploit their small holdings (with the land itself given as security, the Murašus accumulated substantial estates of their own).[57] Business was not always apolitical, as the interests of the late fifth-century governor Belšunu (Belesys in Greek sources) show. Documents from the Kasr archive at Babylon show that he was involved in commercial leasing and loans; his business status may have caused his recruitment into government, or it may have been built on this political role.[58] His roots in the region are an illustration of the substantial investment held by administrators of the empire in the continuity of stable Achaemenid rule. Xenophon's account of Cyrus the Younger's assault on Babylonia includes the observation that Belesys' estates were ravaged in retaliation for his loyalty to Artaxerxes II, a loyalty that was rewarded after Cyrus' isolated challenge failed.[59]

RELIGIONS IN THE EMPIRE

PERSIA AND THE GODS

The ever watchful Ahuramazda dominates the royal inscriptions as the patron of the king. Darius' tomb inscription describes how the god actively gave him the wisdom and ability to enable him to rule.[60] The iconography of the rock relief carved over every royal tomb showed the king raising his hand towards a winged figure hovering over a fire altar; this may have been designed to show a divine relationship between king and god (fig. 2.7). The god's favour was associated strongly with the king's strength.[61] This kind of link gave the guardian god of the Achaemenids a very active role in bolstering their legitimacy. It is possible that his position as 'the greatest of the gods, who created heaven and earth' was given greater prominence and definition as a result.[62] Despite his high profile, Ahura-

5.11 The production of currency and coinage was governed largely by regional factors in the Achaemenid empire, but both motifs and individual coins could travel widely. These two examples are silver coinage of the Kabul region (early fourth century BCE).

Top: local 'bent-bar' coin. The characteristic curved shape was produced by punching the same circular geometric symbol at either end of the face.

Above: this coin is struck in the same way as the main Achaemenid coinage, but appears to have been produced by a local administration, with novel geometric designs on both sides.

mazda did not have a monopoly on Persian religion, nor even on the royal inscriptions. Darius' texts also implicate other 'gods of the royal house' with whom Ahuramazda would protect the country of Parsa. Other unidentified gods are referred to collectively in several other royal inscriptions.[63]

Artaxerxes II went so far as to name two more gods alongside Ahuramazda as his primary divine sponsors, Anahita and Mithras; both were related to Indo-Iranian religious traditions.[64] Artaxerxes may have been refreshing a connection between the monarchy and these Persian gods, or he may have been reacting to their particular popularity in cult practice at the time. A very brief reference contained in a later Christian commentator suggests that Artaxerxes II also instituted an innovative step of setting up temples and statues to Anahita and Mithra in regional centres including Sardis and Jerusalem.[65] Potentially, this was a policy of beneficence to growing local communities of worshippers. Alternatively, this gesture could be seen as a semi-political sponsorship of Persian religion aimed at uniting the scattered population of the Iranian diaspora around a religious focus.

Our knowledge of gods involved in royal patronage before the reign of Darius is almost non-existent.[66] The alleged imposter Bardiya/Smerdis was known as a Magus (a particular type of priest) by Herodotus, and as an impious destroyer of

5.12 An Akkadian cuneiform tablet from Babylonia testifies to a convergence of Achaemenid and Babylonian temple administration. The text alludes to lay personnel of the temple of Bel who held 'bow lands', the land grants through which individuals were obligated to contribute to the drafted army. The great estates of some of the Babylonian temples became linked with the Achaemenid system.

religious sanctuaries in the Bisitun inscription. What relationship either allegation had to do with existing royal religious practice is hard to pin down. Herodotus' magian plot fits in a class of court stories about historical enmity against a particular religious or ethnic faction; similar purges on grounds of religion and betrayal are reported being enacted against other ethnic groups.[67] In the case of Bardiya/Smerdis, Darius' allegation of impiety is a conventional accusation of inadequate behaviour against a defeated predecessor. It is difficult to analyse further the isolation of the Magus as a villain on this occasion, since the word was used generically by Greek authors as a term for many different varieties of Iranian priests.

Two enigmatic monuments at Pasargadae may have been the site of early dynastic religious ritual. The tower building now colloquially known as the Zendan-i

5.13 Two limestone blocks standing at over 2 m high at Pasargadae appear to be an open-air sanctuary. The steps on the farther platform may have allowed a priest to stand facing a focus of worship on the nearer one, in a similar position to the king represented on the royal tomb façades.

5.14 The remaining façade of the tower building at Pasargadae, showing the remains of a stairway leading to a narrow window or opening on high. Designed, like the altars (above) for high visibility, the building has been interpreted as the location for a religious or royal ceremony, such as the king's investiture. This structure was copied in the slightly later model which faces the royal tombs at Naqsh-i Rustam.

Suleiman (prison of Solomon), standing between the pavilion halls of the plain and the walls of the *takht*, dates to the early development of the site. Both this structure and the slightly later replica of it at Naqsh-i Rustam have been in the past interpreted as either temples or specialized housings for a kingship ritual, such as coronation.[68] With no surviving reference to their construction or use, nor consistent archaeological information such as artefact finds or even surroundings, the buildings' function remains open to question. Perhaps rather more promising are two massive hollowed and carved limestone blocks set in an artificially enhanced natural shallow amphitheatre near the river on the edge of the Pasargadae site. One has a set of carved steps beside it, turning it into a highly visible platform for one focus of attention. The other block has no stairs, but also no signs of adaptation to one use or another (they have been broken open by past treasure-seekers). The blocks have been compared in their arrangement (if not in construction) to the combination of low podium and fire altar marking the relationship of king and (probably) Ahuramazda on the Achaemenid rock-cut tomb reliefs. Herodotus' ethnological description of the Persians includes the statement that the Persians sacrificed in sanctuaries open to the air, not in closed temple buildings; this information *could* be taken to reinforce the context for a ritual use of this area.[69] The fact remains, however, that both iconographic and archaeological evidence takes us only a very short distance towards any conclusions about ritual use of this site.

One major connection between later cult and religious ritual surrounding Cyrus and Cambyses is the commemoration of dead kings. Right at the end of Achaemenid rule, a Macedonian visitor passed on the story that sacrifices had been carried on by Magi at the tomb of Cyrus since the time of his death.[70] Whether exactly the same ceremonies were in use unchanged for two hundred years is unknown, but the Persepolis Fortification Tablets testify to officially supported cult sacrifices throughout the region during the early fifth century.[71] Certainly the royal tombs as a whole were clearly designed to have a massive impact on memory. The signs are that an active system of commemoration was kept alive around them.[72] Fragments of Ctesias convey a few extra details about royal burial. His information suggests the importance seen in conveying the bodies of members of the royal family back to Parsa for burial.[73] The importance of cult in Parsa was closely tied to the land itself.

The Persepolis Fortification Tablets record the distribution of rations for the purpose of maintaining sacrifices and cults in the immediate region. Like the travel texts, they relate to several locations, but were ultimately archived at the palace. We might expect to see an elevation of an official cult involving the king, but in fact this is very difficult to see with any certainty. The documents record the maintenance of cults of many different gods, including Elamite gods and deities of places. They specify the use of wine, foodstuffs and livestock in the maintenance of sacrifices. These materials were either dedicated directly to the god or used to purchase or support the production of artefacts used in worship. These records do not often distinguish the kinds of rites they are supporting, nor the precise structure of personnel performing them. Instead, a general class of priests are named in Elamite the *šatin*, while a smaller group, going by the name *makuš* or *magus*, performs the rite known as the *lan* ceremony.[74] The narrow administrative and chronological focus of the tablets does not offer a full panorama of ritual over time; despite coming from a royal palace, they cannot be seen as necessarily representing the full scope of religious activities involving the king.[75]

The Persian kings lived in a world of omens and divine favour conveyed by forces beyond human perception. If in doubt, a traditional Near Eastern response to the diversity of religious traditions was to cover all bases. Particular groups of religious personnel may have been foremost in advising the king of the divine signs surrounding him or intruding his dreams. Herodotus suggests that the king's religious world was made up with Persian magi dealing only with traditional Persian worship of Ahuramazda and other deities. But substantial documentary evidence from Babylonia, in the shape of the Astronomical Diaries, shows the active continuity of local systems of belief which also claimed insight into the king's welfare. It is highly likely that these scholars co-existed with priests from Iran in the Persian court, and perhaps mutually influenced as well as competed with each other. Civic sanctuaries and regional pantheons, when relevant and convenient, could be cultivated and drafted into a recognition of Achaemenid rule.

5.15 Two different glyptic scenes are impressed by a single agate cylinder seal. On the left is a scene of the worship of the god Marduk, with the crescent symbol of the god Sin overhead. Typical of earlier neo-Babylonian stamp and cylinder seals, it continued to be used during the Achaemenid period. Balancing it is a compact Achaemenid three-figure combat featuring a king and two lions. It is possible that the owner deliberately commissioned a combination of Persian and Babylonian motifs from the seal carver, perhaps to represent his own hybrid culture or interests.

RELIGIONS AND COMMUNITIES

Although the Persian kings strongly associated themselves with certain gods, there is no sign that a state religion was used as a tool for drawing all kinds of subjects into a ritual relationship with the monarch. Despite implications of overweening ideas about divinity suggested by some Greek authors, the Persian kings were not perceived as divine in their own milieu (the mantle of divinity descended only where regional kingship traditions, as in Egypt, required it). Herodotus mentions that loyal subjects were expected to pray for the health of the king when sacrificing.[76] However much this was enforceable, it was clearly adaptable to all sorts of cults and could be rationalized as (or even just made equivalent to) a basic hope for peace and prosperity. Since the king was the natural prime provider of these, a prayer for one was a prayer for both. The recognition of the king as a benefactor to cults and temples was a traditional, advantageous relationship. The monarch was set in a role which gave him legitimacy while the religious institution might gain from royal patronage of buildings and sacrifices. The traditions from Cyrus' reign associate him with the restoration of temples in Babylon and Jerusalem, while Darius' construction at the el-Kharga oasis in Egypt still stands: 'He has made this monument for his father Amun-Re … renovating his temple as it had been originally'.[77]

5.16 The squat Egyptian god Bes occupies a vertical band in a cornelian cylinder seal. Although originating in a foreign pantheon, Bes-like figures and faces became a popular motif, perhaps a protective symbol, in Achaemenid artefacts of the sixth to fifth centuries, an illustration of the eclecticism of religious culture during this period. He adorned seals, jewellery, appliqués and perhaps larger equipment, as the Bes face visible on the face of the Oxus chariot suggests.

Participation in the maintenance of temples and cults inserted each king into a traditional, sustainable partnership with regional populations. Conversely, Xerxes and Artaxerxes III were characterized negatively in local traditions for their alleged violence against sanctuaries in the wake of regional unrest or rebellions. While revolt might result in a sanctuary's loss of privileges, accusations of impious sacrilege were a highly stereotypical method of attempting to smear royal reputations. The evidence suggests that Achaemenid policy was to foster a positive but removed relationship with the diverse religions of co-operative communities.

The cult practice of a particular region or sector of society was another individualized interest which fed into the king's role as enforcer of stability and 'rights'. The letter of Gadatas and the book of Ezra illustrate how local populations could expect a long-term relationship of beneficence exchanged for loyalty and support. Sanctuaries of rebellious areas might suffer, but the language of ideology would always cast this as the restoration of correct worship after deviation from piety. The smooth functioning of religious administration was closely connected to territorial control and economic prosperity. The closeness of governmental interests to the business of sanctuary maintenance appears in documents relating to Babylonian temples (fig. 5.12). These were complex centres of production and land ownership and were subject to patronage and overall supervision by the Achaemenids, as they had been by previous powers. Temple lands were used in the military land grants that supplied the king's armies. The temple systems that administered them became part of state bureaucracy and, as in Parsa, were centrally maintained and monitored as such.

Evidence for the popular perception of royal involvement in local religious activity is usually lacking. Ostensibly religious iconography, such as the winged

5.17 The habitual symmetry of much Achaemenid design is illustrated by the balanced beasts and figures of this seal and 5.18. The winged disk, which possibly represents Ahuramazda (as the king's divine sponsor), appears centred protectively over a whole variety of scenes, including these opposing horned and winged lions.

disk or an enthroned king or god, was adapted in numerous contexts, such as coinage or glyptic, in which it represented specific regional identities, whether individual or city-wide. The presence of Achaemenid style or elements appears to show a mixing of Persian and regional religious elements. But the meanings of motifs in local sacred contexts are almost impossible to pin down; conclusions about what they could symbolize remain open-ended. However, there are two written traditions that offer some insight into how the Great King could be incorporated into a religious group's history and self-definition. Both have been to a large extent transformed in the hindsight of successive later relationships with imperial powers.

The more famous in the Western tradition is the relationship between the Judaean communities and kings Cyrus, Darius and Xerxes or Artaxerxes. Equally influential in the historical perspective on the Achaemenids in the Eastern tradition are the sacred books of the Zoroastrian religion. Both need to be measured and filtered through evidence for their context in order to assess their impact of both on our knowledge of Achaemenid-period political and religious practice. For the Jewish tradition, we have parallel contemporary documents from a Judaean community based in upper Egypt, in which concerns about their religious and property rights are aired. A series of letters were exchanged with the governor of the province of Judah, who, in the absence of the satrap Arsames who was in Babylonia, was the community's next stage of appeal to a higher authority. The community's appeal concerns the desecration of 'the temple of Yahu' by local officials. The concerns of these letters can be compared to the theme of the larger Jewish community's relationships with the Persian authorities underlying the books of Esther, Daniel, Ezra and Nehemiah.[78] The survival of actual letters enables us to compare constructively the edited officialese attached to the later accounts of Nehemiah's administrative missions. There is also a densely studied body of early fragmentary literature, such as the Dead Sea Scrolls, which places the development of the novelistic Biblical stories in a literary genre, and in some archaeologically dated contexts. This evidence means that the development of the representation of the Achaemenid court in Jewish texts is at least partially visible. As a result, aspects of the Biblical texts can still illuminate ancient regional perspectives on Achaemenid rule.

The written evidence relating to Zoroastrian religion is somewhat different. The

5.18 Here, the winged disk overhangs a more specifically religious scene on a stamp seal. Two figures in Achaemenid court dress (perhaps crowned) hold up a bowl and a blossom towards a stepped fire altar. Variants of this scene are found on other seals and funeral monuments. The fire altar seems to have been the focus of prayers or sacrifice to a number of different gods. Drawing after Cox (Moorey 1988).

Avesta, the texts which preserve the ritual and cosmological traditions of Zoroastrianism, appear linguistically early; the part of the Avesta called the *Gathas* is written in a particularly archaic dialect, the imperfectly understood Old Avestan. But they are known almost exclusively from manuscript copies of the medieval period. The texts themselves may only have been written down during the Sasanian period, surviving in the meantime in the form of an archaic oral tradition. The Avesta and other works preserve stories about the history of the Zoroastrian religion which date its revelation in the court of a mythologized king named Gushtasp or Vishtasp. The religious enlightenment of this king and the authorship of the *Gathas* are both attributed to the prophet Zarathushtra, or Zoroaster. The latter (Greek) form of the prophet's name is used to talk about a sage or magus in historical fragments of the fifth century BCE. The magus Zoroaster continued to be the subject of discussion in the fourth century, when Aristotle discussed his 'teachings'.

Zoroaster was a magnet to whom overlapping traditions, anecdotes and scholarly works were attributed. The degree to which they represent the career of a real, historical figure is a matter of faith rather than evidence. A traditional date in the sixth century associated Zoroaster with the beginnings of Persian rule and the Achaemenid dynasty. An alternative dating of *c*.1000 BCE or before has been proposed on the basis of the internal philological evidence about the linguistic evolution of the Avesta.[79] Linguistic analysis of the texts potentially sheds light on both their preservation and their evolution as the authoritatively ancient core of religious practice. But the relationship of the prophet and his works to the traditional religious beliefs of Persian kings and priests, as reported by Herodotus and others, is unclear.

Apart from the royal inscriptions, there are no surviving contemporary texts in which an overall affiliation to a specific religious *doctrine* rather than a *god* is asserted by the Achaemenid kings. Instead, we are reduced to comparing Zoroastrian ideas with the royal ideology of the Achaemenid inscriptions; the minutiae of religious practice, which are partially attested in the Persepolis Fortification Tablets and reported in Herodotus can also be compared with those that later became canonical in the fully established Zoroastrian religion. The Achaemenid opposition to the chaotic 'Lie' and worshippers of false gods seems to correlate with the more extensive binary opposition between the positive value *asha*, encompassing virtue, truth and purity, and the negative value *drugh*, a word related to *drauga*, the Lie of the false Bardiya. The royal elevation of Ahuramazda as principal patron god coincides with the Zoroastrian doctrine that Ahuramazda was the sole creator god, with whom the whole world, including lesser divinities, originated. The revelations of Zoroaster also describe the existence of an opposing evil spirit, Angramainya; the two opposite forces embody the contrast between *asha* and *drugh*.[80]

However, among the religious multiplicity of Parsa in the Achaemenid period, there is little evidence for a systematized hierarchy of gods based on the Zoroastrian doctrine, while the presence of Angramainya as a prominent religious concept is not attested. Nevertheless, the practices of Zoroastrian ritual can be seen to have some similarities to religious worship in the Achaemenid period. The imagery of

5.19 The Achaemenid winged disk in its most elaborate form on a door jamb of the Hundred-Columned Hall, featuring a human form clad in a Persian robe and a crown, holding a ring. Surviving paint traces on the less exposed examples revealed full colouring in red, blue, green and gold paint. Just below the winged disk, the more abstract version is visible engraved in the representation of the cloth canopy shading the king. Related to the motif used to represent both Egyptian and Assyrian gods, the Achaemenid winged disk is usually found hovering protectively over scenes in seals and sculpture. The symbol is most widely interpreted as showing the Achaemenid's divine sponsor, the god Ahuramazda. In later Persian tradition, it was increasingly seen as representing a divine quality of the king himself, the *khvarna* or charisma, an idea that perhaps reflected the original close association of king and protective god.

Achaemenid ritual, in which fire altars are used to burn a sacred flame as a focus of worship in the worship of a deity, or in the use of certain ritual equipment, such as the *barsom* or bundle of sticks held in worshippers' hands, is shared in common with some practices of later Zoroastrians (fig. 5.20).[81] While there are remains of enclosed fire temples dating to the late Hellenistic, Parthian and Sasanian periods across Iran and the southern Caucasus, no dedicated temple building has been securely identified for the Achaemenid period, and Herodotus' assertion that the Persians worshipped only in the open air seems to stand. The evidence for an orthodoxy of Zoroastrian practice is simply not present in the Achaemenid period; its suggested antiquity can only be viewed through the filter of its Sasanian-period adoption as an official state religion, in which Achaemenid-influenced imagery played a part. Some of the priests who surrounded the king could perhaps have held beliefs similar to Zoroastrian doctrine, but the religious context of the court and dynasty as a whole may have been the wider Indo-Iranian tradition on which Zoroatrianism drew. The majority of our primary evidence, for the official Achaemenid use of festivals, rituals and inscriptions, is a world away from showing the private, exclusive adherence of the royal family to a single doctrine.

The subsequent history of the Zoroastrian and Jewish religions had an influence on the formation and preservation of their literature. Jewish communities' difficulties in the Hellenistic and Roman world somewhat reinforced the importance of their archetypal brave representatives in the Persian court. The young girl chosen as the king's bride, Esther, conceals her religion until she is able to claim a favour from her husband to ensure her people's safety. Daniel foretells and outlives the

5.20 A thin gold plaque is embossed with a figure wearing Iranian riding costume of a sleeved tunic over trousers with a soft headdress. The gold sheet, 15 cm high, is often suggested to be an *ex-voto*-like religious object, since it is one of about fifty small plaques impressed with a variety of figures which form part of the Oxus Treasure. The bundle of grasses or twigs grasped in the man's right hand are paralleled in other images from seals and funerary reliefs showing figures in Persian or Median dress standing by fire altars clutching blossoms or sticks. These have become the *barsom* used by priests in Zoroastrian ritual, but this does not imply that the figure represented here has a specific religious role. The plaques from this group show a variety of levels of workmanship; although some are dated to the fifth to fourth century, others could have been manufactured later.

demise of the Babylonian regime that oppressed him and proves his talent under pressure in the following Persian monarchy. The Sasanian kings' adoption of Zoroastrianism as their official state religion was possibly the motivation for the writing down of the ritual words of the Avesta. Zoroastrianism fell from power, along with its sponsors, to the Arab invasion, and its beliefs and texts had a difficult subsequent struggle for survival.

Saviours, survival, judgement and justification were central historical themes in both religions' literature. Cyrus was granted the title 'the anointed' or *messiah*, in the Bible, for guaranteeing the return of a small exile community from Babylonia, and the restoration of their temple. As such, he was a saviour of the community. Yet the quite generic diplomatic character of his actions can be compared to his evocation of Marduk in the Cyrus Cylinder, or Darius' renovation of 'his father's' temple at el-Kharga. All worked to put the king and a particular ethnic, urban or religious community on a good and positive footing. This does not mean, of course, that neither Cyrus and Darius could deport any other troublesome group in the empire, perhaps in the process depriving them of their ancestral place of worship. Persian religious tolerance was a result of an inclusive imperial ideology, but it was a tactic of domination and could still work well for some, harshly for others.

There are some interesting parallels between the presentation of these religions' relationship with the ruling power. In the tales accumulated around their prophets, Daniel and Zoroaster, great importance is placed on the Great King's recognition of the importance and reality of their God. In both cases, this is set against a competitive backdrop of other religious experts clustered around the king, all of whom claimed to be able to interpret omens according to their own beliefs; the Persian *Denkard* preserves a particularly disdainful reference to the 'primitive learned of Bapel'. In the Bible, the king's recognition of the god of Daniel and Esther is the prelude to protection for their community, both in exile and in the province of Judah. In the *Denkard*'s account of Zoroaster's life, the prophet was able to instruct the king in the correct religion, after his success in court. In both cases, the king's approval is taken to be a long-term, prestigious stage in the recognition of the rights of both a religious practice and a community. Although both religions to some extent claimed the Persian king for themselves, as saviour or faithful patron, he was merely a stage in the development of their individual histories. The immersion of the Achaemenid empire in these very focused histories shows how the rule of the Great Kings could have been seen as important or relevant to any one of the thousands of ethnicities and communities inhabiting his territory. His status enhanced by his distance, but with a sense of contact created by court representatives and appeals by letter, the king became a powerful, crucial mediator in an increasingly mixed, multi-ethnic environment.

6 ALEXANDER AND THE END OF EMPIRE

Persepolis was the capital of the Persian kingdom, Alexander described it to the Macedonians as the most hateful of the cities of Asia. It was the richest city under the sun … The Macedonians raced into it … plundering the residences … the enormous palaces famed throughout the whole civilized world, fell victim to insult and utter destruction.

Diodorus Siculus, 6.7.4

The sack and devastation of the royal palaces at Persepolis in 330 BCE is one of the most dramatic acts of Alexander the Great's invasion of Persian territory.[1] He reached Persepolis four years after crossing from Europe into Asia in 334 at Abydos, where Xerxes had shackled two continents. Apart from the brutality inflicted on the city, the royal treasure was destroyed or looted and the rich interiors of several palaces eviscerated. The invaders' systematic vandalism of the most distinctively Persian of the four royal capitals, where the last Achaemenid kings had been buried, undermined the foundations of the monarchy's identity. In later Western tradition, the ruins of Persepolis became the ultimate symbol of Alexander's inevitable supremacy over a stereotypically failing dynasty. In reality, the burning of the royal palaces was a short-term political tactic that punctuated a gruelling ten-year campaign. The legendary picture of a cataclysmic struggle between East and West is offset by the reality of the vast and complex world over which Alexander had to assert his power.

Alexander III succeeded to the throne of Macedon after his father's death in 336. After campaigns in the Balkans and the crushing of a rebellion in Thebes, in central Greece, he acted on his father's declaration of war against Persia. He led across the Hellespont a force of up to five and a half thousand cavalry and around thirty thousand infantry made up of Macedonian troops, forces levied from the Corinthian League and mercenaries.[2] The first major military engagement came around late spring at the Granicus river, where the Macedonians met the local satrapal cavalry and infantry in a closely fought battle.[3] The Persians, who lost several prominent figures in the fighting, did not fully organize an immediate counterattack, and the cities of Sardis, Ephesus and Magnesia diplomatically accepted Alexander's advance.[4] Miletus, holding out at the hope of being defensible with the help of the strong Persian fleet, surrendered to aggressive siege tactics. This was a wise decision, as the fate of other coastal cities was to show.[5] Alexander sidestepped a direct encounter with the formidable Persian navy, hampering instead their ability to land and fight at strategic points along the coast. At Halicarnassus, fierce and desperate fighting at the walls left the city open, but the Persian forces

133

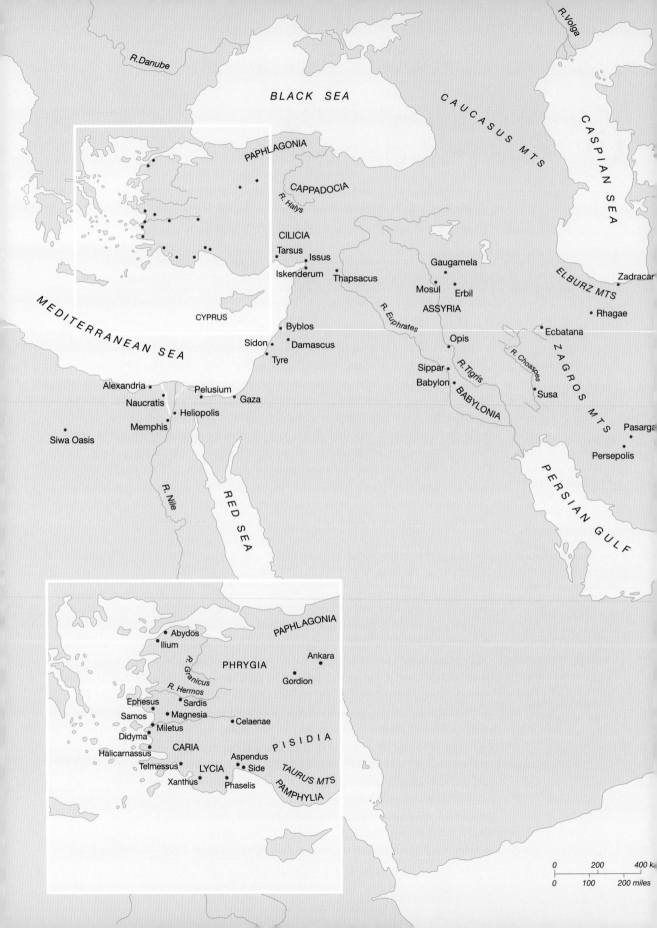

R.Volga

R.Danube

BLACK SEA

CAUCASUS MTS

CASPIAN SEA

PAPHLAGONIA

CAPPADOCIA

R. Halys

ELBURZ MTS

Zadracar

CILICIA

Tarsus

Iskenderum

Issus

Thapsacus

Gaugamela

Mosul

Erbil

ASSYRIA

Rhagae

R. Euphrates

Ecbatana

MEDITERRANEAN SEA

CYPRUS

Byblos

Sidon

Damascus

Tyre

Opis

R. Tigris

R. Choaspes

ZAGROS MTS

Sippar

Babylon

BABYLONIA

Susa

Alexandria

Pelusium

Gaza

Naucratis

Heliopolis

Memphis

Siwa Oasis

R. Nile

RED SEA

Pasarga

Persepolis

PERSIAN GULF

PAPHLAGONIA

Abydos

Ilium

R. Granicus

PHRYGIA

Ankara

Gordion

R. Hermos

Ephesus

Sardis

Samos

Magnesia

Miletus

Celaenae

Didyma

CARIA

PISIDIA

Halicarnassus

Aspendus

Telmessus

LYCIA

Side

TAURUS MTS

Xanthus

Phaselis

PAMPHYLIA

0   200   400 k
0   100   200 miles

6.2 The central and western parts of the Achaemenid empire. The western segment of the Persian empire, to central Iran, was conquered by Alexander between 334 and 330 BCE. The defeat in battle of a satrap at the Granicus river, and of the Great King and his western army at Issus, left cities and satrapies in Anatolia and the Levant open to invasion. In the face of implacable siege tactics in Tyre and Gaza, the centres of power in lower Egypt took the politic decision to 'welcome' Alexander.

remained intact in two well-defended citadels, keeping a crucial strategic base on the Aegean coast.[6]

Even given Alexander's initial successes and the size of his army, it is possible that the Achaemenid hierarchy did not expect his territorial ambitions to extend much further; his predecessors in anti-Persian adventuring had never pressed further eastwards, despite, in Isocrates' words, aiming to dominate 'all of Asia'. The heartlands of the empire had not seen a battle since Cyrus the younger's campaign three generations earlier. As far as we know, the province of Pars and the upper satrapies had been largely undisturbed since the accession of Darius I. None of these disturbances came from outside the royal family, let alone from a foreigner. However formidable Alexander's forces appeared, it was a stretch of imagination to see the leader of a remote former client kingdom aspiring to the position of Great King.[7]

Taking a leaf out of the Persian diplomacy book, Alexander installed a rival member of the satrapal Hecatomnid dynasty as an amenable governor of Caria before moving inland for the winter of 334. Sending forces into Phrygia, in central Anatolia, and Pamphylia, to the south, Alexander for the first time moved to secure large tracts of territory inland. By winter, after pausing at Phaselis on the Lycian coast, he moved eastwards along the Pamphylian coast, occupying cities along the way (Aspendus and Sillyum reluctantly). A campaign northwards in early 333 left Pisidia bruised but fractious and Alexander occupied the satrapal palace at Celaenae after a brief siege. Leaving his general Antigonus in charge, he moved north to Gordion in central Anatolia. Meanwhile in the Aegean, the Persian fleet campaigned successfully under the Rhodian general Memnon, undoing much of Alexander's work by reclaiming the loyalty of many of the coastal cities.[8] Both sides prepared to engage the successful portions of the enemy forces; Alexander commissioned a larger fleet, while Darius mustered a full, drafted army at Babylon.

Before heading south again, Alexander received the nominal submission of the Paphlagonians of northern Anatolia, but their allegiance was in practice questionable. Apart from a small-scale campaign in the following year, this mountainous region, like much of eastern Anatolia, Armenia and the rich transcaucasian kingdoms, remained largely untouched by the invader.[9] In early summer 333, Alexander occupied the capital of Cilicia, Tarsus, at the edge of fertile and strategic plains at the geographical hinge between Anatolia and the Levantine coast. The satrap, Arsames, had retreated to Syria, possibly at the orders of Darius, who planned his next big confrontation in its defence. Alexander spent the summer in Cilicia, halted by illness while the Great King brought his army from Babylon. The Greek sources suggest there was dissent about Persian strategy among the king's advisers, and it is entirely likely that divergent ideas were aired. Darius decided to meet Alexander on the Cilician plain in a decisive battle with the full force of his army. His expedition was mounted with the full trappings of the mobile court. As well as a huge baggage train (which lodged partially at Damascus) the King was accompanied by a substantial portion of treasure and the royal women. Darius did not campaign alone, but amidst the entire royal house.[10]

Alexander moved his army to a defensive position south of modern Iskenderum.

But towards the end of the year, when the Persians made their move, they took an unexpected approach through the north-eastern pass around Mount Amanus, effectively isolating their enemy on the coastal plain. The Macedonians swiftly returned north and, for the second time, apparently made their first attack on the Persians across a river. Accounts of the battle present the violent charge of Alexander's central cavalry directly against Darius in his chariot and his guard as the most successful move of the battle, forcing the Great King to retreat precipitately and causing the rest of his forces to flee, despite their initial successes. The unexpectedness of the retreat and the difficult surrounding terrain led to a dispersal of the Persian forces, a drastic weakening of their position which left the entire coast open to Alexander. The retreat seems to have set off something of a domino effect of disconnection, with different mercenary forces and segments of the fleet detaching to look after their own interests. Just as disastrously, the Macedonians captured the royal entourage and three thousand talents' worth of royal treasure, both of which were core elements of a successful mobile court and campaign. For the first time, Alexander had in his hands some of the substance of Achaemenid kingship. Not only could he reward his troops and defectors from the Persian side with substantial bullion, but Alexander also gained some ideologically important authority over his enemy's extended family. He responded positively to this situation by guaranteeing the safety and privileges of the royal women, naming the queen mother, Stateira, his own mother. He apparently took as concubine a noblewoman called Barsine, daughter of the former satrap Artabazus, who himself had spent several years in exile in Macedon. The woman, although never given the legitimacy of a marriage alliance, was a personal link to the world of the Persian elite.[11] Although it is disputed to what extent Alexander saw himself taking on the mantle of the Achaemenid dynasty, his appropriation of the household and treasure was a way of getting under the skin of the ruling system he intended to dominate.

After the obliteration at Issus of any hope of defence from Persian forces, the nearby cities of Byblos and Sidon swiftly submitted to Alexander. At Sidon, as elsewhere, Alexander's arrival and the disruption of Persian patronage was an opportunity for local power to be taken away from one group and bestowed on another.[12] The prosperous merchant city of Tyre, further south, also first looked as if it would freely acknowledge the power of the invaders, but negotiations with Alexander quickly hit a diplomatic snag. Alexander wanted to sacrifice to the city god Melqart at the island's main sanctuary during the god's festival. The Tyrians baulked at allowing him such a royal privilege and proposed that they would take a neutral position instead, allowing neither Persians nor Macedonians near the prestigious city festivities. This compromise was essentially a denial of Alexander's claim to kingship in Asia, since it denied him a king's role as religious patron. In retaliation, Tyre was subjected to a gruelling seven-month siege, during which both sides used stupendous waterborne weapons, such as floating siege towers and fireships, in the struggle to possess the city. With the help of newly turned Cypriot ships, Tyre was isolated and the walls breached. Thousands of its inhabitants were massacred and the majority of the survivors were enslaved. Alexander finally sacrificed to Melqart and held victory games.[13] At Gaza to the south, the city governor (bravely, in the circumstances) held out for a two-month siege. After the city walls were destroyed, the male population was slaughtered and the women enslaved. The governor Batis was reputedly given a Homeric execution, dragged to death behind a chariot by his heels.[14]

The exemplary annihilations of Tyre and Gaza towards the end of 332 were strategically crucial to the annexation of Egypt. No doubt aghast at such total destruction and merciless punishment for neutrality as well as resistence, the recently appointed Egyptian satrap, Mazaces, negotiated at a distance to ensure that the port Pelusium and the capital Memphis would not suffer similar punishment.[15] Alexander's arrival was handled diplomatically in a tried and tested Near Eastern method for pacifying conquerors. In both cities, a civic welcome pageant was staged, in which Alexander was treated as a liberator. At Memphis, he was quickly offered the treasury and palace furnishings.[16] This was the only way to convince the invader that, unlike Tyre, the satrapy of Egypt really perceived him as king. In return, Alexander began to perform the required kingly duties. He sacrificed to the gods, including the Apis bull. The resulting mantle of divine approval is evoked in the sources' accounts of his mission to the pilgrimage shrine of the Libyan god Ammon, at the Siwa oasis in the western desert.[17] The oracular signs at the temple there were apparently favourable to the conqueror, who was addressed as the son of Ammon, a title bestowing divine endorsement on his rule in Egypt. Most later believed that, on his return from the oasis, Alexander made a further gesture of royal authority by initiating the first of his city foundations, Alexandria.

In the spring of 331, Alexander led his rested army northwards out of Egypt and put down a revolt in Samaria, where the Macedonian governor had been disposed of. Holding court in Tyre, or en route to the Euphrates, Alexander may have received diplomatic proposals from Darius. The precise terms are unclear in the sources, but Darius may have decided to buy time and leverage by granting Alexander the rule of part of the conquered territory, across the Euphrates and in western Asia Minor. A proposed marriage alliance with the Great King's daughter may have grown out of later tradition to make Alexander's seizure of the empire legitimate.[18] But if it originates in a real suggestion, marriage might have been intended to draw Macedon into a further web of obligations within the Achaemenid royal family, as had happened with several Western leaders before. Such concessions would have provoked much debate among Alexander's advisers at the time; in retrospect his decision to refuse the diplomatic solution was presented as a natural result of his heroic ambition. His perseverance was also practical; for the whole time, Darius III was gathering the massed troops of the central and eastern empire in Babylon.[19]

In summer 331, Alexander moved north-east to cross the Euphrates at Thapsacus (defended until the last minute by a cavalry force with the satrap Mazaeus), following a route along the fertile foothills at the border between Assyria and Armenia. Darius III had led his army northwards to a strategic position on the plains by the Tigris, north of Erbil and north-east of Mosul, called Gaugamela in the sources. Giving Darius good cavalry terrain, the choice drew the military conflict away from the major capitals of Babylon and Susa, preventing the battle turning into a destructive city siege. The Greek sources agree that Darius' army outnumbered

Comme alixander paſſa leſ
fiuereſ de tigriſ et deuffrateſ à
tout ſon oſt alait … lo roy dure

et teſte multitude . voulat …
et ſon entencion fiſt aſſamb…
… oſt … nt …

6.3 Quintus Curtius Rufus'
account of Alexander's
logistical triumph over the
rivers Euphrates and Tigris
inspired a fifteenth-century
French illustrator to depict
his army marching through
a miniature Mesopotamia.
The defeat of rivers, through
a successful crossing, was a
demonstration of power
over enemy territories.

Alexander's, but their massive exaggerations obscure our view of the real picture
before the battle. As for the action, as in other royal battles, we are given glimpses
of the rival kings facing each other through clouds of dust and over wheeling
horses. Secondary reconstructions of the course of the fighting suggest that
Alexander and his companions drove through a chink in the line left by cavalry on
the Persian left wing (by one account, commanded by the royal kinsman Bessus).[20]
As this left Darius vulnerable, he turned to flee; while there was still an empire to
defend, the legitimate king was best surviving rather than dying in battle. The
weakness of Bessus might have grown in the telling, as he later became Alexander's
principal opponent.[21] It is clear that other segments of the Persian army made serious headway with their opponents, including the armoured Saca and Bactrian

divisions, and Mazaeus' cavalry, who broke through battle lines to raid the Mace-donian camp. If the accounts are right in placing Darius' flight long before the end of the fighting, the rest of the Persian army must have begun to retreat in response to their leader's departure.

The Roman-period author Quintus Curtius Rufus makes dramatic capital out of Darius' precipitate retreat into the Zagros mountains towards Ecbatana; in his account of the battle of Gaugamela, he evokes the cries of inhabitants along the route of the king's desperate flight who 'were calling on Darius as if he were still

6.4 The Alexander Mosaic from the 'House of the Fauns', a Hellenistic villa preserved under the lava covering Pompeii, appears, from its style and content, to be a copy of an earlier wall painting probably dating to the third century BCE. The battle is generalized, and presents a concentrated, symbolic view of the confrontation between Alexander and Darius III.

king'.[22] His timing maximizes the poignancy of the cry, since it really was in the aftermath of Gaugamela that the Great King's power began to disintegrate permanently. Contemporary records from Babylon show that, following his victory at Gaugamela, it was Alexander who was referred to as 'king of the world', while Darius was merely 'king'.[23] The king and satraps apparently did not contemplate an apocalyptic last stand either at this sophisticated city or at the other Mesopotamian capital, Susa, despite the presence of some intact forces. The balance of status had shifted across the centre of the empire, with the hope for a Persian counterattack resting on organized resistance on the Iranian plateau and Central Asia.

With Darius intending to form a new army at Ecbatana, Mazaeus, the satrap of Babylon, acted to preserve the city, like Mazaces in Memphis, by staging a ceremonial welcome for Alexander and his troops.[24] A fragmentary cuneiform tablet records a sequence of Alexander's assurances to the Babylonians, issued by proclamation throughout October 331 (fig. 6.5). He guaranteed that citizens' homes would not be invaded and that the city's premier sanctuary, the Esagila, would be restored, offering also the sacrifice of a bull before finally entering the city with a full military entourage, escorted by Mazaeus and his cavalry.[25] Alexander was treated as a conquering king, presented with gifts and enveloped in aromatic incense. The picture of him gladly welcomed as a liberator is a strikingly similar piece of public relations to that concocted by Cyrus II over two hundred years

6.5 The writers of the Astronomical Diaries recorded announcements made in the vicinity of Babylon, including Alexander's proclamations to citizens prior to his takeover of the city in 331 BCE. Asserting his respect for their private property and his responsibility for the city's main religious sanctuary, the assurances illustrate the kind of diplomatic manoeuvring that preceded any peaceful and victorious entry into an ancient Near Eastern city.

before. As both Cyrus and Assyrian kings had done long before him, the Macedonian moved straight to the palace to take possession of the royal furnishings and the bullion of the royal treasury.

While Alexander and his troops fully enjoyed the comforts of Babylon, Abulites, the governor at Susa, apparently made the same diplomatic calculation as Mazaeus about the city in his charge. A Macedonian envoy had completed the negotiation; the sources suggest that a splendid procession had been prepared in advance, meeting Alexander outside the city by the river Choaspes.[26] The exotic parade of elephants, camels and other assorted livestock was a public exhibition of the king's new possessions in the city, perhaps like the similar display frozen in stone at Persepolis. Aside from the ideological capital Alexander gained by at last being treated as a legitimate monarch in these most authentic of settings, the resources of Babylon and the massive 49,000 talents of bullion and coined gold from the imperial treasury at Susa gave him part of the economic supremacy that had previously been held entirely by Darius. The boost coincided with the arrival of large numbers of reinforcements from Macedon.

At the end of 331, Alexander pressed eastwards, deciding to follow the passes through the Zagros despite the winter weather.[27] He faced two points of severe resistance from the inhabitants of the mountains, the Uxians; the first organized by the satrap Medates and the second arising from the upland villages of the same people, who were severely punished for their defiance.[28] Alexander took the more

6.6 A modern road runs through gate-like cliffs in the Zagros mountains, forming a pass on to the Iranian plateau from Elam (modern Khuzistan). The satrap of Parsa used such landscape to mount a damaging defence against the army of Alexander in 331; this action was probably the cause of savage retribution against the residents of his city.

mobile element of his army via a mountainous route towards Persepolis, which was defended at the point of a narrow gorge by Ariobarzanes, the city's satrap. The damage that could be inflicted from the steep narrow sides of these 'Persian gates' was too much for the attackers and they retreated. After interrogating prisoners of war, they found an alternative route and Alexander split his forces, catching the defenders' camp in a pincer attack. Ariobarzanes escaped, only to fall on the plain before the city in a final battle. It seems that the garrison commander, Tiridates, tried to hedge his bets and attempted to preserve the city itself by not taking responsibility for the satrap's defence of its approaches.[29] While this meant that the palaces themselves were initially preserved, the surrounding settled population were treated as savagely as the citizens of Tyre, as if they had defended the city in a siege and sacrificed their right to protection. The loot from this prosperous and privileged region went to the army. Alexander stayed in the ancestral capital of the Persians for four months. The royal treasury, estimated by some authors at the massive amount of 120,000 talents, was completely removed, significantly neutralizing the capital's role as a monetary and ideological resource.

The decisions taken at Persepolis reflect the scale of the task of conquest still ahead. As the Macedonians crested the edge of the Iranian plateau, the horizon ahead of them expanded perhaps beyond their expectations. In terms of area, the free territory ahead was as great as that already covered, and far less familiar. To the north, the legitimate Persian king still had access to fearsome forces, his one remaining royal capital and the riches of the eastern satrapies. The mechanisms of the empire behind them had essentially been left in place, and could adapt to a return of Persian power just as, if not more smoothly, than they had to the invader. The army itself had changed in character since it had first crossed into Asia; it was now padded with campaign marriages and troops, both Greek and Asian, who had previously served Darius. The sense of cultural vertigo induced in the invaders by this panorama must have been great.

The eventual destruction of the palaces of Persepolis was rationalized in the Greek reports as a retaliation for Xerxes' sack of the temples on the Acropolis at Athens, and as the ultimate dinner party finale, when drunken high spirits led

6.7 The destruction of Persepolis, as visualized using contemporary travellers' sketches of the ruins in 1693. This illustration to the dramatic account of Quintus Curtius Rufus shows an almost ghostly gang of Macedonian ruffians firing already skeletal palaces.

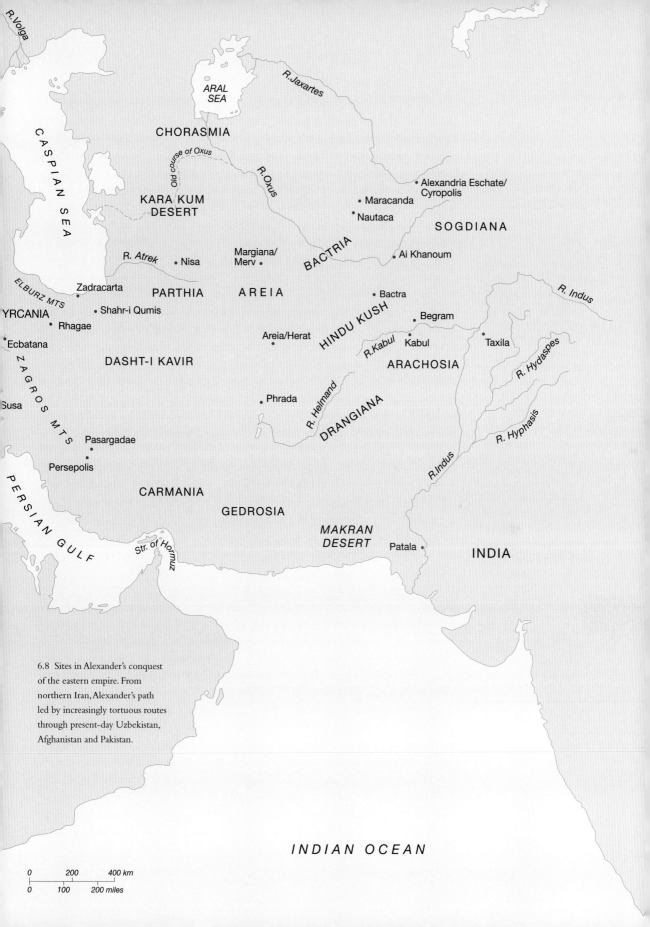

R. Volga

CASPIAN SEA

ARAL SEA

R. Jaxartes

CHORASMIA

Old course of Oxus

R. Oxus

KARA KUM DESERT

• Alexandria Eschate/ Cyropolis
• Maracanda
• Nautaca

SOGDIANA

BACTRIA

• Ai Khanoum

R. Atrek   • Nisa

Margiana/ Merv •

ELBURZ MTS

Zadracarta

PARTHIA   AREIA

• Bactra

HINDU KUSH   • Begram

YRCANIA   • Shahr-i Qumis

Areia/Herat •   R. Kabul   Kabul

R. Indus

• Rhagae

ARACHOSIA

• Taxila

• Ecbatana

DASHT-I KAVIR

R. Hydaspes

ZAGROS MTS

• Phrada

R. Helmand

DRANGIANA

• Susa

Pasargadae •

R. Indus

R. Hyphasis

• Persepolis

CARMANIA

PERSIAN GULF

GEDROSIA

MAKRAN DESERT

Str. of Hormuz

Patala •

INDIA

6.8 Sites in Alexander's conquest
of the eastern empire. From
northern Iran, Alexander's path
led by increasingly tortuous routes
through present-day Uzbekistan,
Afghanistan and Pakistan.

INDIAN OCEAN

0   200   400 km
0   100   200 miles

directly to the firing of rafters. Modern discussions of the archaeological clues to the burning conclude that Xerxes' palace did indeed suffer from a more intense conflagration than elsewhere. But the excavations also showed that the fires were not first concentrated within the building structures but sprang from heaps of the furnishings within the rooms. The mobile property within the palace was as important as the buildings themselves: an incoming conqueror entered the palaces to take possession of the *basilikata* or the royal furnishings and paraphernalia, as well as the treasure. If the whole splendid, visual array of Persepolis were left untouched, it would have been a ready-dressed stage on to which another suitable Achaemenid relation could step, ready to be hailed as king.[30]

After the cedar rafters of the Hundred-Columned Hall and *apadana* had been transformed into smoking cinders, Alexander moved north towards Ecbatana. Darius' intention to rally opposition there had been seriously damaged by the failure to prevent the invaders reaching Parsa; Ecbatana became an outpost rather than a bastion. The Persian king took the contents of the royal treasury and moved swiftly eastwards along the southern edge of the Elburz mountains. Alexander, realizing that, to confirm his position as king of Asia, the previous incumbent needed to be eliminated, followed swiftly, leaving the takeover of Ecbatana to his general Parmenion. Among Darius' supporters, his new, exclusive reliance on the power of the eastern satrapies seems to have caused tensions about his suitability as leader. The satraps of Bactria, Aria and Drangiana who accompanied him perhaps felt they would command more loyalty in the east than Darius, who was no longer a figure uniting the different halves of the empire. In an obscure and subsequently highly romanticized episode, some of the highest ranking nobles confined and killed their king on the road east of Rhagae (Rayy).[31] The story told in the Greek authors makes the incident very difficult to decipher in Achaemenid terms. Responsibility for the killing seems to have been shared between several very highly placed nobles, or, alternatively, blamed mainly on Bessus. He, the satrap of Bactria, subsequently became king, taking the throne name Artaxerxes (V).[32] The killing left a window of legitimacy for Alexander, spurred to greater speed by news of the betrayal, allowing his discovery of the dead or dying king to be interpreted as a symbolic handover of power. The fugitive killers were characterized later (after they offered further opposition to Alexander) as traitors and usurpers.

The killing of Darius, whatever strategic or symbolic measure was intended, proved to have an even more divisive effect on the Persian leadership, scattering his closest courtiers; Nabarzanes went north into Hyrcania, Bessus, Barsaentes and Satibarzanes eastward, and other members of the royal family, no longer bound by loyalty to the king, melted into the entourage of Alexander. The nature of Alexander's campaign changed too, with this overwhelmingly symbolic (if not practically complete) victory marking the end of the road for several Greek contingents who had originally been mobilized for the war against Darius. After pausing at Hecatompylos (Shahr-i Qumis), Alexander pursued remnants of Darius' entourage into Hyrcania, whose satrap, Phrataphernes, surrendered.[33] At Zadracarta, the satrap of Tapuria, Autophradates, also surrendered, along with Artabazus and his family,

6.9 'Iskander tending to the dying Dārā', a famous episode in some versions of Alexander's history which became central to later reception of the invasion in Eastern languages. This painting is a fifteenth-century illustration to the episode in Nizami's *Iskandernama*, in which Dārā is portrayed as Iskander's half-brother. The hints of a somewhat ritualized killing (involving arrest and imprisonment) became secondary in the sources to the legitimacy that Alexander drew from Darius III's death. Reports of his donation of a cloak to the dead or dying king simultaneously showed his superiority and respect. In some versions, Darius managed to pledge both his empire and his daughter's hand to his successor with his last breath. Saving Alexander from the sour taint of regicide, Darius' death allowed him to crush further opposition under the mantle of justice.

and Nabarzanes.[34] As Alexander moved into Aria, the satrap Satibarzanes peacefully submitted, but his co-operation was to prove illusory. Bessus' elevation to the kingship prompted the Macedonian to head straight towards Bactria, leaving Satibarzanes to revolt almost immediately in favour of his fellow satrap and new king.[35]

Backtracking to deal with this uprising, Alexander fired Satibarzanes' stronghold, but only after the rebel had fled eastwards. The neighbouring satrapy to the south, the capital of Drangiana, Phrada, was the next target. There the Macedonian army and leadership were distracted by a foiled plot against Alexander and a series of purges followed. The army was rested, while the persistent Satibarzanes returned to reclaim Aria.[36] His move was part of the beginnings of a campaign co-ordinated by Bessus/Artaxerxes V, who also sent new forces west to recover Parthia. The counterattack involved recently turned Persian governors such as Phrataphernes in conflict against their former colleagues. Satibarzanes was killed in a formalized duel with a Macedonian commander, but unrest in the region continued for two more years.[37] Alexander moved on to Arachosia with reinforcements but in spring 329 was delayed in the Kabul valley by snow to the north. When he eventually made the difficult journey through the Hindu Kush into Bactria, however, Alexander's foe, Bessus/Artaxerxes, had retreated with his comparatively small forces across the Oxus river to Sogdiana and Chorasmia.[38] After crossing the Oxus, Alexander received word that the arrest of the rival king Artaxerxes V had been accomplished for him by two Sogdian nobles. The obstinate 'Artaxerxes' was transformed back into the ordinary traitor Bessus when he was stripped of his royal garb. In the satrapal capital Bactra he suffered the traditional punishment for disloyalty, the mutilation of his nose and ears; according to some reports, he was sent all the way back to Ecbatana to die, in an echo of the executions of pretenders past.[39]

After the deaths of Darius and Bessus and the dissolution of bonds of loyalty to them, the boundaries between enemy and ally, defector and rebel, became increasingly blurred. According to one mysterious story, en route to Sogdia, Alexander's army fell upon a town of transplanted Greeks, the Branchidae, from the region of Miletus, in punishment for an alleged past sin.[40] Alexander and his army reached Marakanda (Samarkand) in early summer. Although Alexander marked his reaching of a symbolic limit of the empire, the Jaxartes river (Syr Darya), with another city foundation, Alexandria Eschate ('the furthest'), Bactria and Sogdiana again erupted in rebellion around him, the active aggression spreading even to the Saka across the Jaxartes. A series of fortresses were besieged and sacked, while the Saka, who had some success against the Macedonians, were apparently beaten back to the point of concluding a peaceful truce. An expeditionary force failed against the fresh cavalry forces of Spitamenes, a Sogdian leader who had obligingly taken a part in the arrest of Bessus, and subsequently, less obligingly, attacked Marakanda. In the face of a mobile and elusive enemy, Alexander took to the second-best expedient of massacring the local population as collaborators.[41] After they wintered in Bactra, spring 328 saw the invaders again tackling unrest in Sogdiana, this time using further city foundations as a more permanent tool of control. As Alexander returned to a further spell of residence at Marakanda, opposition around him persisted. Mobile raids

6.10 The huge dimpled mound of Afrasiab covers the early medieval and ancient remains of Samarkand/Marakanda, an Achaemenid centre. Alexander based his operations here for many months. View taken and tinted by Prokudin-Gorsky, 1911.

were co-ordinated by Spitamenes, and local commanders in formidable fortresses, such as Sisimathres at Nautaca, had to be besieged one by one. Spitamenes eventually fell victim to the wavering loyalties of his own allies, who decided, perhaps in the face of continuing slaughter in Sogdiana, that their better interests lay in concluding a peace.[42] Alexander eventually put something of a cosmetic seal on the subjection of the north-eastern satrapies (although some rebellions continued after the marriage) by marrying into the local nobility. Roxana, the daughter of the noble Oxyartes, whom Alexander had captured in 328, carried the same name as several of the women of the Achaemenid family before her and was part of the local ruling elite.[43] Our Greek informants suggest that this alliance, embedding Alexander in local hierarchies, caused an increase in dissatisfaction and active intrigue among his Macedonian supporters. Their growing disapproval of his 'oriental' ways is a significant theme in the Western accounts of the invasion.

After the great problems encountered in the subjection of the north-eastern satrapies, Alexander was being drawn in to the local politics of the south-east, India. The rulers of these provinces, now without any recourse to a greater political authority like Darius III or even Bessus, may have begun to communicate with Alexander in

147

6.11 Modern ruins near the city of Bagram, Afghanistan. Alexander chose this strategic site, renamed Alexandria-under-the-Caucasus, as one of a series of city foundations made in an assertion of control over the rebellious eastern satrapies.

the hope of securing or bettering their positions.[44] Nevertheless, when the invading army came to make its way towards the Indus river in spring 327, after recrossing the Hindu Kush, the amount of resistance encountered prompted extremely bloody retribution in places. Cities along the way either held out for a siege, attempted diplomacy or were evacuated to mountain fastnesses such as the rock of Aornos, which itself was besieged with gruesome results.[45] On crossing the Indus, Alexander was welcomed into the probable satrapal capital of Taxila by the petty prince Omphis, who was to be his bridge to the negotiation of further capitulations. Further to the east in the Punjab, the Indian King Porus failed to reply diplomatically and became the next target of the expedition. An army including a detachment of elephants failed to make headway against the Macedonian cavalry, and Porus was forced to surrender (as a result surviving to rule again), a defeat later celebrated in a famous series of coins minted at Babylon (fig. 6.12). In an unexpected U-turn, Porus became Alexander's ally, assisting him in further campaigns against his neighbours.[46]

This perpetually lengthening domino trail of local wars could have kept several satraps occupied for years, and the value of Alexander's pursuit of nominal control to the east was now seriously questioned by his army. Most of our evidence for wars in and on the fringes of the Persian empire before the Macedonian invasion concerns the Great King's militarily enforced settlement of territorial and status disputes. Alexander's campaign in the Punjab was in danger of becoming the catalyst for a never-ending round of these. In monsoon season, this was not an attractive prospect for the ordinary soldiers. In the face of their determined obstinacy, unfavourable divine omens conveniently discouraged their leader from proceeding further. Instead, in autumn 326, at two new city foundations on the Hydaspes river, Alexander ordered the construction of a new fleet to carry the army down to the Indian ocean under the authority of the Cretan Nearchus. The journey entailed further brutal campaigns in hostile territory along the river route, during which Alexander was seriously injured.

At Patala, in the summer of 325, serious preparations for a return journey west were begun.[47] A land expedition under Alexander departed weeks before the fleet, which made a premature getaway in early autumn, in the face of local hostility. As both contingents made their way along the coast of Baluchistan, their massive provisioning requirements entailed further military action against the inhabitants they encountered, whose harvests were requisitioned by force. The terrain ahead in Gedrosia was also extremely harsh, but scattered with inland settlements which, along with consignments from Drangiana, provided the army (willingly or not) with the support to continue.[48] Carmania, by the strait of Hormuz, in contrast, presented a much more hospitable environment with abundant supplies. But with the plenty came a flood of dissatisfaction and festering rebellion as Alexander was reconnected with the network of satraps he had left behind in the central plateau.[49]

6.12 On the obverse of this five-shekel coin, a heroic horseman tilts at a war elephant while a standing figure holding a thunderbolt, a divine attribute, adorns the reverse. Possibly produced by an eastern mint, such as Babylon, the images seem to celebrate Alexander's victories in India. The figure with the thunderbolt has been interpreted as being Alexander; but whether it was he or one of his successors who decided to add the divine aspect is unclear. Said to have been found near Bokhara.

The turmoil resulted in several executions, as several Macedonian deputies who had travelled down from Media were punished for misdeeds that perhaps amounted to near-usurpation of Alexander's authority there. It is unclear to what extent their excesses had been prompted by continuing opposition in Iran; Media had produced at least one ill-fated claimant to the Persian throne. Certainly, the first foreign casualties were followed by widespread purges of Iranian satraps, no longer needed as place-holders during Alexander's absence. These measures, including a move to disband local mercenary forces in favour of bolstering the central army, may have been aimed primarily at preventing regional rebellions and independent challengers to Alexander's rule.[50] By 324, an atmosphere of paranoia seems to have infected many levels of administration throughout the empire. At the beginning of the year, Alexander rejoined his fleet at Hormuz before returning to Parsa. He found a member of the Achaemenid family, Orxines, inhabiting the royal residence of Cyrus at Pasargadae, claiming descent from the Great Kings and disbursing royal gifts from the remnants of the ancestral treasure there. Whether Orxines was seriously aiming to challenge Alexander's position or was merely hoping to found rule of his home province on the foundations of Achaemenid legitimacy, his use of royal prerogatives was threatening, and he was executed. Alexander took the opportunity to prove his superior generosity and connection to the monarchy's roots by 'restoring' the tomb of Cyrus and, with great condescension, donating his own cloak to the corpse of his predecessor. As

6.13 Alexander visiting the tomb of Cyrus (before restoring it), as visualized in 1796 by de Valenciennes. Seventeenth- and eighteenth-century drawings of Persepolis are here merged with Egyptian architecture to create a complete ancient setting. A *stela* displaying cuneiform letters is an attempt to show the inscription described by ancient authors as identifying the tomb. Alexander is aghast at the damage, while a priest is apprehended in the background. The restoration of Cyrus' tomb gave Alexander the opportunity to become the patron of his predecessor.

reverently as he acted, his marking of the tomb entrance with his own seal (so that no one could re-enter to access the sovereignty-imbued clothing) had an air of finality about it.[51]

After leaving Pasargadae and Persepolis, Alexander and his army once again reached Susa in spring 324. In a measure equally loaded with positive propaganda and precautionary pragmatism, he and over ninety Macedonian nobles married women from the Persian aristocracy in a massive celebration at the palace there. The marriages had the joint benefit of diffusing the exclusivity and integrity of the Persian families surrounding the kingship, clans who might otherwise produce well-born pretenders like Orxines, while linking the foreigners themselves with the same inherited status.[52] Reports suggest that Alexander and his courtiers by now had adopted significant elements of clothing from Achaemenid court practice, visually displaying their status in a way that both foreigners and former Persian subjects could understand. Accounts of Alexander's behaviour in Mesopotamia become increasingly comprehensible according to the terms of traditional royal virtues in the region. His exploratory expedition to the mouth of the Tigris, his clearance of dams in the same river and the repair of canals on the Euphrates, the large-scale banquet for Macedonians and Persians at Opis and, later, authoritarian campaigning in the mountains of Media, all echoed the actions of conquering

Assyrian kings of the past, while catering practically to his need to maintain control.[53] Alexander began to follow the leisurely route of seasonal court migration, travelling to Ecbatana via the paradise at Bisitun in the autumn. The stay was marred by the death of Hephaestion, which was apparently the occasion of further skewed appropriation of Persian practice: the empire-wide mourning usually offered to a king was offered to his close companion in power.[54] At the beginning of 323, the court returned to Babylon, where Alexander, like his Persian, Babylonian and Assyrian predecessors, was subject to the cautionary advice of court scholars.[55] The world of potential within Alexander's grasp was signalled by the myriad peoples represented by envoys seeking audience with him.[56] But at the point of victory, Alexander fell fatally ill in the summer heat, an affliction blamed on heavy drinking (although much ink has been spilled on the possibility of foul play).[57] His premature death foiled not only a planned expedition into Arabia, but any hope for a swift return of stability in the fractured empire. The scrupulous compilers of the daily observation of omens in Babylon, continuing the work accomplished for the neo-Babylonian and Persian kings, on 19 June 322 noted the positions of Mercury, Mars and Saturn, and the fact that 'the king died'; the day was overcast.

SOURCES AND PERSPECTIVES

The simplified account given above represents only a narrow trail through the maze of problematic evidence for Alexander's conquest. All of the roughly complete surviving accounts in classical languages were written more than three hundred years after the events they recount. Two histories of the Roman period, Arrian in Greek and the more colourful Quintus Curtius Rufus in Latin, were entirely dedicated to Alexander's reign. The universal history of Diodorus Siculus and the geography of Strabo incorporated parallel information about Alexander's crossing into Asia, using some of the same primary sources. Plutarch included the Macedonian king in his series of paired biographies of famous men written in the second century CE (Alexander was paired with Julius Caesar, a comparison to which the Roman general himself had aspired). These authors used several accounts written soon after the conquest for their source material. Several of these were written by close associates of Alexander: Ptolemy, who was to rule Egypt, Nearchus the admiral and the courtiers Callisthenes, Aristoboulus and Cleitarchus. Like Xenophon's memoir of his time in Cyrus' service, all were skewed to glorify their king and bolster the author's own role in his success.[58] Anecdotal tales from less well known characters in Alexander's entourage such as Chares of Mytilene were mined for gems of scandal and extravagance by Athenaeus.[59] Modern historians, sifting for factual insights through the secondary accounts, find innumerable contradictions, mysteries and omissions. For those interested specifically in the Persian side of events, the distortions of the victor's perspective and cultural misunderstanding are added to the mix. Despite these problems, the stories of Alexander's invasion are valuable because they widen our visible horizon to encompass the entire breadth of Persian territory for the first time since the reign of Darius I.

6.14 The Astronomical Diary for June 322 BCE records the conditions surrounding the death of the king. Circumstantial historical evidence suggests that Alexander had been heeding scholars' advice about unlucky omens in the preceding months.

6.15 A detail of painted relief from the carved side of the so-called 'Alexander sarcophagus' from the royal necropolis of Sidon (and which instead belonged to a ruler of the city who died *c*.310 BCE). The melting pot from which the occupant's status emerged is portrayed on the sides – a pitched battle between Persians and Macedonians, including Alexander.

There are no surviving contemporary narratives of Alexander's invasion written from the Achaemenid perspective. But there are two types of extant contemporary written sources for events and reactions during the campaign. First, a small collection of Aramaic letters and accounts recently bought from the open market concern satrapal business in the region of Bactra during the fourth century BCE. On two leather documents are written provision lists; one is dated to the month *Kislev* in first year of the reign of a King Artaxerxes, the second to the month *Sivan* in the seventh year of the reign of King Alexander (9 June, 324 BCE). The documents are tiny fragments of the ongoing Achaemenid administration, which continued in the face of the Macedonian invasion. The first document in fact records the passing of provisions to a *Bys*, whom the editors interpret as ★*Bayasa* or Bessos, the 'Artaxerxes' in question, moving eastwards in December 330, in preparation for his final stand.[60]

Far more plentiful and better known, are cuneiform documents from Meso-potamia, written on clay. As mentioned above, both the Astronomical Diaries and the Babylonian Chronicle reflect events with a focus on Babylon and its environs: omens before the battle of Gaugamela, Alexander's change in status after the same battle, the diplomacy leading up to Alexander's first entry into the city and his death.[61] Some of the records also give a narrow window on an alternative cultural perspective on the invasion. In the Babylonian of the Chronicle and a text known as the Dynastic Prophecy, the Macedonians are called 'Hannaeans', an ethnic name first used in the mid second millennium for a troublesome (and rather uncivilized) group who attacked Babylonia. The traditional ethnic term maps the newcomers on to an exist-ing Mesopotamian world-view, giving them an identity comprehensible in tradi-tional terms. The Dynastic Prophecy was an attempt to embed the new rulers in a comprehensible Babylonian history. Written as if the events were foreseen by a Baby-lonian astrologer from the neo-Assyrian court, it included the 'Hannaeans' as one of a series of future regimes foreseen as destined to rule Babylon.[62]

Greek accounts of Alexander's second sojourn in Babylon also suggest that the new king was integrated into traditional court systems. It is clear that, as he approached the city, omen scholars advised him that it was not propitious for him to enter immediately, or perhaps that it would be better to enter via a different gate, later. The Greek reports misunderstand the context for this advice (suspecting the priests only of dissimulation), as they also only partially represent a ritual performed in Babylon in order to protect the king. From the neo-Assyrian period onwards, we have ample evidence for the practice of 'substitute kingship'. If omens suggested that the king was in mortal danger, he would be removed from the throne and sent into hiding (administrative letters sent to the Assyrian king in this kind of retreat were addressed to 'the farmer'). Meanwhile, a condemned criminal, or someone perceived to be a madman, was treated as king in his place. After this disposable 'king' was killed at the end of the danger period, the real king returned, safe from the fatal omens. The changes to the practice of substitute kingship during the Achaemenid period are difficult to trace, but signs of the practice re-emerge in the wake of Alexander's inva-sion.[63] Arrian and Diodorus report that a condemned man took it upon himself to sit on the throne instead of Alexander, provoking signs of grief among his attendants. Their sources were aware that the incident was somehow customary, but did not understand that it was designed to safeguard the life of the king; in their respective accounts the Alexander historians use the episode instead to foreshadow his death.[64]

Alexander may or may not have understood the full complexity of the court mechanisms surrounding him, but perhaps was shrewd enough to seek some bene-fit in them. For example, the accuracy of the Babylonians' long-accumulated knowledge of the links between cosmic omens and worldly effect had been under-lined recently; Darius' defeat at Gaugamela followed eleven days after a deeply unlucky total lunar eclipse. Alexander's partial adoption of Persian dress and cus-toms was interpreted in terms of indulgence and alienation in the Greek authors. But decisions such as that to introduce Persian forms of address and etiquette in the court and to visit and 'restore' the tomb of Cyrus in Parsa were strategic rather than acts of hubris. They coincided with occasions when Alexander benefited from emphasizing his royal status in contrast to challengers such as Bessus/Artaxerxes V and Orxines. Other pragmatic measures, such as the burning of Persepolis, or the training of young Persian nobles in Macedonian army detachments, radically dislocated Alexander's rule from the traditions of Achaemenid dynastic rule.[65]

The question of how far Alexander absorbed the Achaemenid ruling mentality of his conquered territory is the subject of continuing debate. Existing administrative and religious practice inevitably continued, but, after Alexander's return to Parsa and Mesopotamia, almost exclusively under Macedonian direction. The possible coin portrait of Alexander produced in the empire towards the end of his reign projects a ruler image utterly different in style, pose and dress from the Achaemenid monarch (fig. 6.12). Yet the obverse of the same coin continues a recognizable theme of military heroism found in earlier seals and jewellery. Similarly, some of the more dramatic or elaborated episodes of the Alexander historians sound curious echoes of older kings. Alexander, like neo-Assyrian kings before him, campaigned in the mountains of Lebanon, sourcing the prized cedars for his fleet.[66] The vivid account attributed to Chares of Mytilene talks of him forging ahead in the rough terrain on foot, facing extreme hardship with great fortitude and ingenuity. His rivalry with predecessors was promoted in Alexander's desert treks across the Libyan desert and Gedrosia. He was in competition not just with the founder of the Persian empire, Cyrus, but also with semi-legendary monarchs of the past, such as the queen Semiramis, a neo-Assyrian queen who had been transformed into a world-conquering harpy in stories of the fifth and fourth centuries.[67] The glory of surviving extreme deprivation on campaign was one of the key themes in histories of the deeds of wandering conquerors of the Near East.[68]

Ultimately, Alexander finally toured the empire in a fashion that perhaps very clearly evoked traditions of the Great Kings for the observing inhabitants. His funeral procession took the form of a covered wagon ornamented with painted panels, some of which may have been covered with pictures echoing Achaemenid as well as Graeco-Macedonian originals: Alexander surrounded by his court, enthroned in a chariot, hunting with his companions.[69] His burial in Alexandria was used by his general Ptolemy as the foundation of his own sphere of influence in the old satrapy of Egypt. Without a single figure who could unite the interests of the competing Macedonian generals, the former satrapies of the Persian empire were broken up into a patchwork of competing kingdoms. The Seleucids governed the lion's share of the old Iranian heartland, stretching into Central Asia; but the furthest provinces, including India, soon took a more independent route. The regions to the north of Anatolia and the Caucasus, relatively untouched by the violence of the invasion, eventually formed into independent dynasties that drew on their Achaemenid heritage.

Alexander's invasion was traditionally seen in European historiography as the moment when Hellenic civilization swept over the East. In fact, aspects of Greek style, language and material culture already played a part in the society of the empire and had done so since the sixth century: Greek diplomats and exiles lived in the court, the king and satraps supplemented their forces with Greek mercenaries, Greek speakers worked at Persepolis, elites in Anatolia, Libya and Colchis could showcase Attic pottery in their grave goods as well as Achaemenid bowls.

The long-term influence of Seleucid rule and increased Greek settlement brought about a gradual transformation of styles in sculpture and ceramics. A Greek-style high-relief sculpture of Herakles was carved in the side of Mount. Bisitun by the road below Darius' relief. Greek forms of architecture and ideas about civic space influenced the refoundation or adornment of existing sites such as Babylon (which acquired a theatre) and Ai Khanoum in Bactria, which was transformed into a colonnaded urban centre. Nevertheless, the forms of administration of the Achaemenid period, such as the satrapal divisions, continued. Aramaic continued in use as a popular *lingua franca* in Mesopotamia and the Levant, and as an authoritative written script in the eastern provinces, although Greek was increasingly used in official and epigraphic contexts. In the third century, Aramaic was chosen as a parallel epigraphic language for the inscriptions of Ashoka, and the form of the script influenced the development of Indian alphabets.

One of the most powerful and long-lived cultural bequests left by Alexander's invasion was the epic story of his life itself. In the later tradition that permeated both Western and Eastern literature, Alexander's brutal conquest of the empire was transformed into a wondrous journey of discovery. The so-called Alexander Romance tradition played up the philosophical, personal and folkloric aspects of his journey into the East. Alexander's exploration of the new world became the legendary frame for lengthy speculations about rulership and the wonders of strange lands. In modern scholarship, the Alexander Romance is used and contextualized quite differently from the Alexander historians, because of its obvious fantastical embellishments. Yet it too seems to have originated at least in part in ancient sources and some of its more fanciful elements nevertheless recall episodes in Quintus Curtius Rufus and Plutarch.

All versions of the Alexander Romance are supposed to have derived from the work of one author, called Pseudo-Callisthenes. This text purported to be the work of the great nephew of Aristotle who joined Alexander's as the official historian of his campaign. The history of the real Callisthenes is only known in fragments, but the Romance story is likely to be a compilation of the Hellenistic period, which mixed fictional epistolary collections with a colourful narrative account.[70] The compiled letters include terms of address that, like the compiled letters of the Bible, echo the epistolary style of Achaemenid administrative letters between satraps and king. The earliest surviving passage, possibly excerpted from an existing work, appears in a Greek papyrus dated to the first century BCE. In the third and fourth centuries CE, the complete work began to be translated into in the languages covering the Mediterranean and Near East: Middle Persian, Syriac, Latin, Armenian, Hebrew and Arabic.[71] From these branches, versions of the Romance spread throughout the late antique and early medieval world, through translation into French, English, German, Spanish (from the Arabic) and even Ethiopian. Alexander became an icon of heroic kingship and courtly idealism in the Western manuscript tradition, a role that gradually dislocated him from the Near Eastern context for his story.

Nevertheless, the dissemination of the Macedonian's deeds and adventures as 'Iskander' was equally widespread in the literary traditions of the Near East. The earliest Syriac texts of the Romance may be translations of the Greek pseudo-Callisthenes, though an intermediate stage of transmission through a Middle Persian text is also plausible. The Eastern traditions about Alexander are extraordinarily rich and varied, and may have drawn on many more sources, produced by the empire-wide responses to his invasion. An epistolary novel or novels, which fed into the Pseudo-Callisthenes compilation, dealing with Alexander's philosophical investigations into kingship with the help of the world's sages, has parallels in Demotic and Aramaic literature, as well as Greek. Many of the stories in later Arab and Persian works, concerning Iskander's wondrous discoveries and exploratory missions, have parallels with earlier stories about Cyrus II, Darius I and even Gilgamesh, suggesting that the ingredients used in both Pseudo-Callisthenes and later versions of the Eastern Alexander Romance drew substantially on traditional narratives circulating in Mesopotamia and Iran.[72]

Perspectives on Alexander/Iskander changed according to the religious or nationalistic interest of each author. Early Zoroastrian and medieval historians highlighted Iskander's anti-Persian, impious destructiveness, such as a renowned and much-condemned order for the destruction of Persian books, which overshadowed or replaced his destruction of Persepolis/Istakhr in most accounts. By contrast, under Islamic rule, Iskander became identified with the prophet Zu al-Qarnain, 'the two-horned' in the Qur'an and his invasion was seen as an enlightened forerunner of the Arab conquest of greater Iran and Central Asia. According to early Arab historians such as al-Dinawari and Tabari (ninth to tenth centuries CE), Dārā, like the Median Astyages, had become an oppressive tyrant and Iskander, like Cyrus II, led a war of liberation against him. The war between them originated in Iskander's principalled refusal to continue paying a tribute of golden eggs to Dārā, as his father Philip (al-Filqus) had done. Moreover, Iskander was in fact the elder half-brother of Dārā, from a short-lived marriage between a daughter of Philip and the elder Dārā (this father of Dārā/Darius III was a composite of the later Achaemenid kings). This relationship turned the foreign invasion into a more common and perhaps palatable tale of warring siblings, similar to (and perhaps influenced by) the tale of Cyrus the Younger's assault against his brother Artaxerxes II. This blood relationship differed from a second secret royal origin alleged for Alexander in the Pseudo-Callisthenes tradition, that he was the son of the last Egyptian King Nectanebo. The common point of both traditional 'lost royal offspring' stories was to link Alexander firmly to the last king of the previous authentic regime.

This material, when it was sourced by later authors writing in Persian, was further embellished in order to transform Iskander fully into a civilizing hero of the Persian nationalist tradition. The poets Firdowsi (eleventh century CE) and Nizami (twelfth to thirteenth century CE) both wrote elaborate histories of Iskander; the first as part of a magisterial, epic succession of Persian dynasties, the *Shahnama* or 'Book of Kings' and the second in a dedicated trio of books known together as the

Iskandernama, the 'Book of Iskander'.[73] Nizami's poem in particular transforms the violent invader, Iskander of Rum, into a positive, civilizing power. His adventures are wide-ranging, and although Nizami was significantly influenced by Firdowsi's earlier account, he claims his authority from intense and extensive research:

> The deeds of that monarch, world-wandering, I saw not written in one book.
> Speeches that were like stuffed treasure were scattered in every work. I took up
> materials from every book; I bound on them the ornaments of verse. More than new
> histories: Jewish, Christian, and Pahlavi.
>
> Nizami, Iskandernama 13, l.15 ff.

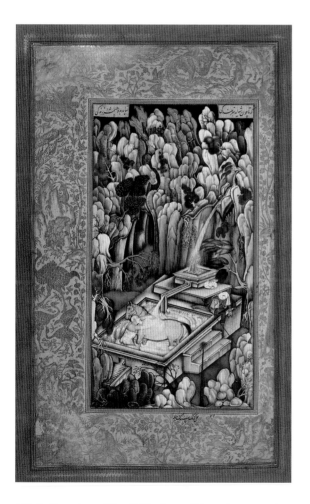

6.16 An illustration to Nizami's *Iskandernama* (thirteenth century CE) connects the fame of his horse, Bucephalus, with Alexander's doomed search for the waters of eternal life, a fable that echoes the journey of the legendary Mesopotamian hero Gilgamesh. The king's mount is bathed in the waters of eternity, while the monarch's destiny requires him to remain mortal.

According to Nizami, Iskander began the coining of gold and the gilding of silver in the East, preserved the law of his predecessors ('the great kings of Kay'), translated Persian books of wisdom into Greek, measured the earth, 'raised a city in every land and clime', gained early insight into the Islamic religion by making a pilgrimage to Mecca and even journeyed like Gilgamesh into the 'Land of Darkness' in search of eternal life. Each stage of Iskander's journey was a discrete campaign of liberation against a different enemy: against the Zangi in Egypt, Dārā in Persia, the Russians in Central Asia and the submissive kings of India and China (who visits Iskander in disguise in his camp). In Iran, Iskander respectfully recognizes and accepts the burden of Persian culture and kingship tradition from his predecessors, a process exemplified in the romanticized scene of the death of Dārā, his brother:

> When he reached Dārā's special guard,
> He saw none of the moving body-guard:
> He beheld the body of the lord of the marches in
>   dust and blood:
> The royal head reversed …
> The spring of Firidun and the rose-bed of Jamshid
> Became, by the autumn wind, the prey of grief:
> The recorded lineage of the empire of Kaykubad
> Carried, leaf by leaf, by every wind.
> Iskander alighted from the back of his bay horse;
> He came to the head-place of that powerful one.
> [They converse, Dārā bestows the kingship on Iskander
>   on condition that he looks after the royal household
>   and marries his daughter, Roxana (Rowshanak)]
> Over that king of auspicious lineage – Sikander
> Wept in the night-time, till the morning.

Iskander's respect for Dārā, to the point of giving him a glorious burial, begins his initiation into the legitimate rule of Iran. Enthroned at Istakhr/Persepolis, Nizami says Iskander was fully schooled in the traditions of Iran by an anonymous sage (as the Egyptian priest Udjahorresnet had claimed to advise Cambyses) and gathered the seven wisest sages around him as his advisers. His wise and considered government echoes the ideals of wisdom and civilization aspired to by monarchs from the time 'before the Flood' in the words of Assurbanipal, to the Arab and Turkic rulers of the Muslim world in the late first and early second millennia CE. More so than the disputed tales of Alexander's Persianizing and the practical persistence of established administration, the Persian literary tradition transforms Alexander into the last of the Achaemenids; an historical cusp, in whom the national and religious ideals of the past and future kings of Iran are indissolubly united.

6.17 In many Islamic period histories of Alexander, traditional Persian hostility to the 'accursed' destroyer of their culture is played down. Instead, Alexander becomes a pioneering philosopher king who prefigures the Muslim conquests of the East. This illumination to a late fifteenth-century manuscript shows Iskander (Alexander) surrounded and being counselled by sages. Alexander's curiosity about Eastern wisdom became a central theme of these more positive literary portraits. The association of the king with famous wise advisers has a long history in Sumerian and Babylonian literature as well as in texts of the Achaemenid period.

232

7 LEGENDS, LANGUAGE AND ARCHAEOLOGICAL DISCOVERY

The rule of Soloman has run its span;
The world is here, but where is Soloman?
How much could Sam and Soloman retain
Of countless gold and glitter of their reign?
Earth's sojourners are now in dust's disguise:
How knows the earth, beneath its dust, what lies?[1]

The Persian original of this poem, laboriously but elegantly carved on the glassy inner walls of Darius' palace at Persepolis in the fifteenth century CE, is characteristic of historically tinged meditations of the Islamic period on Iran's ancient monuments. The Persian literary tradition, epic and folkloric, persists in both European and Eastern imaginings of ancient Iran. Soloman, a king with divine connections in Muslim, Jewish and Christian religious history, is a significant character in the landscape of Fars.[2] His role, most evident in the net of names covering the ancient site of Pasargadae, could be compared to that of the magical King Arthur in the topographical mythology of England and Wales. As prehistoric and Roman ruins in the British landscape became the work of the magician Merlin or supernatural giants, so were the massive platform and columns of Persepolis attributed to djinns commanded by the powerful kings Soloman or Jamshid.

LOST DYNASTIES AND RUINED THRONES

Persepolis was formally known in Farsi as Takht-i Jamshid or the Throne of Jamshid from at least the early nineteenth century (and perhaps for far longer). It represents an influential link with one of many story strands about Iran's ancient history which have developed over the past two millennia. They are important not because we may think they preserve flawless gems of truth about the Achaemenids but because they show the changing light in which the period and its material remains have been seen over the centuries. As the royal cities of the Achaemenid world disappeared from view, through reuse, demolition or decay, the guises in which they were remembered or re-imagined were transformed too.

As sources such as Herodotus show, even during the lifespan of the Persian empire, stories of the past were constantly adapted to changing contemporary circumstances; they evolved through the retelling by a succession of authors, bridging languages along with generations. In the fourth century BCE, something like an instinct to cloak places in an greater aura of age populated Bisitun, Hamadan and

7.1 The south-eastern bull guardian of the gate of Xerxes at Persepolis. One of a series of views of Persepolis taken by Antoin Sevreguin c.1900. Sevreguin, born in Tbilisi, ran a photographic studio in Tehran. Friedrich Sarre and Ernst Herzfeld commissioned him to produce the plates for their publication of Iranian rock reliefs in 1910. Sevreguin also independently took archaeological views of Persepolis between 1900 and 1908.

The figure on the left may be Sevreguin himself; his signature is carved, alongside those of other famous travellers, on the inner flank of the bull guardian shown here. An archive of his surviving work is now held in Washington.

Persepolis with the ghosts of archaic monarchs such as Semiramis, 'Ninus' and Cyrus. The deep dynastic and literary history of the states preceding the Achaemenid empire seeped into the past imagined for the Persian monarchs. A Persian-period poetic apology for Cyrus' conquest of Babylon recast Nabonidus as an impious madman wandering in the wilderness, a tradition that was also influential in Biblical presentations of the neo-Babylonian empire. Assurbanipal and the last neo-Assyrian kings were transformed into decadent, effeminate opponents failing against the challenges of Median or early Persian heroes, giving a plausible historical parentage to the idea of Persia's inevitable rise.[3] As earlier empires had been attached to legitimizing stories in the Persian period, so were the Achaemenids enmeshed in the definition of later stages and groups. The settings of the Biblical books of Esther and Daniel draw on an Achaemenid setting to give powerful stories of origin which historically define the Jewish community (then, as later, amidst the pressures of powerful imperial governments). These books, probably reaching their concrete form in the late Hellenistic period, presented the image of a glamorous but impressionable Persian court, full of wealth and intrigue. Names and stories from the Persian empire, most notably those of Cyrus II, Darius I and Xerxes, also entered Western literature via Herodotus and Xenophon, divorced from much of their wider historical or archaeological context.[4] Such accounts were to have a significant influence on European ideas about kings and empires of the East for millennia.

As for Eastern traditions, most surviving texts purporting to contain pre-Islamic history derive from medieval manuscript copies of histories written in the Islamic period. While not preserving unchanging memories of Iran's ancient history, they are also a further development of those memories, from the perspective of successive later societies and states.[5] For the intervening nine hundred years from 330 BCE, there are occasional material signs of some response to Achaemenid remains within the territory of Iran. At both Persepolis and Susa, large fragments of decorative stone masonry were moved to prominent positions on the sites and reconstructed on shallow foundations. The 'Donjon' at Susa and Palace H, perched on the southern fortification wall at Persepolis, were both constructed in post-Achaemenid times, but whether immediately or long after Alexander's conquest it is hard to tell. They speak of some effort to appropriate the architecture of an obsolete empire to lend authority to a new order.[6]

The local governors, who ruled in provinces of the old Achaemenid empire during the Seleucid (312 to c.129) and Parthian (c.174 BCE to 224 CE) periods of domination drew on ancient remains close to hand in the images they used to define themselves on coins and rock reliefs. In Fars, Achaemenid visuals still exerted an influence on coin designs and rock reliefs;[7] as with the Persian use of Assyrian motifs in palace imagery, elements from the past monarchy became incorporated in the promotion of a new one. The monumental impact of Persepolis continued to be exploited by local dynasts, the Fratarakas, who built on the remains of an Achaemenid structure in the plain to the north-west of the platform.[8] While these local rulers are very likely to have had their own ideas about the monarchy on whose foundations they stood, we have little knowledge of how views of the Achaemenid period within Persian history developed, even when Iran began to be recovered by a local dynasty, starting in Khorassan in the first half of the second century BCE. The Arsacid dynasty gained power over territory reaching from the Euphrates to Central Asia, which they retained for nearly four hundred years, and this Parthian empire (named after the home province of the ruling family) became a formidable opponent of Rome. During this period new religious and ethnic mixes developed throughout an empire rooted in a network of influential diplomatic and mercantile relationships reaching from China to the Mediterranean. However, when the last Parthian king died in battle in 224 CE, the new ruling dynasty, who claimed descent from a legendary ancestor called Sasan, was again historically linked to south-west Fars.

These Sasanian kings had expanded their power from a relatively small satrapal domain centred on the city of Istakhr in the Marv Dasht plain. Istakhr today is an expanse of sherd-littered mounds lying between two flanks of the mountains fringing Marv Dasht, where the river Pulvar flows into the plain towards Shiraz. The open site is punctuated by walls of eroding mud brick and a few blocks of masonry from the Achaemenid and later periods. The Sasanian city lies beneath and to the west of the principal surface remains, which date to the Islamic period. Some of the Achaemenid fragments, moved several times over hundreds of years, may have originated from the area of Istakhr, but others were moved from Persepolis, less than 3 km to the south. At the terrace itself, fine drawings of the knight-like outlines of Sasanian horsemen can be found between two windows of Xerxes' *hadesh* palace, now reconstructed as the site's museum. On a windowframe of the same building, faint Aramaic inscriptions may testify to some clearing or reconstruction early in the Sasanian period.[9] In the fourth century CE, two more high-profile texts in Pahlavi were added to the northern doorway into the main hall of the palace of Darius. One dates to the beginning of the reign of Shahpur II and records a ceremonial progress from 'Stakhr' to *Sat Stune* ('One Hundred Columns') in order to perform a religious ritual. The Sasanian dynasty's Zoroastrian faith was linked to an ancient past in coin images of worshippers at stepped fire altars like those on Achaemenid seals and royal tombs. At Naqsh-i Rustam, Shahpur inscribed a lengthy account of his achievements as king on the Kaba'i Zardusht, including his successful campaigns on the western frontier with Rome. The whole local environment was turned to the purpose of rooting Persian power in memory, as had happened under the Achaemenids over six hundred years before.[10]

The Sasanian inscriptions and reliefs, most of which are dated to the earlier kings of the dynasty, identified the new Persian empire with the powerful symbols of

7.2 A view of Istakhr from 1,250 feet in 1935, taken from the 'Friend of Iran', the aeroplane of the Chicago Aerial Survey expedition (an airborn offshoot of the Oriental Institute team directing excavations at Persepolis). The sunken outlines of the medieval walls and caravanserai, at the entrance to the Marv Dasht, are clearly visible. The major Islamic monuments have been investigated, but only limited soundings made of deeper levels.

7.3 Achaemenid doorways
and reliefs from the
medieval structure at Qasr-i
Abu Nasr, near Shiraz,
drawn by the surveyor,
writer and artist
Muhammad Mirza Hosayni.
His fully illustrated work
The Monuments of Persia was
published under his pen
name of Fursat Shirazi in
Bombay in 1896. The book
documents his antiquarian
interests in ancient ruins,
shrines and mosques in and
around Fars, providing a
record of local histories and
memories.

now semi-mythical ancient kings. After the Arab invasion ended Sasanian rule in
Iran in 642 CE, the incoming rulers had the advantage neither of geographical
origin nor of religious history to justify their legitimacy. Both the presence of
Achaemenid ruins in Fars and the active Sasanian use of them showed them to be
a valuable resource for fledgling monarchies. In Istakhr, some of the Achaemenid-
like architectural fragments come from the site of a later mosque. It is possible that
the mosque was a very early foundation, a symbol of power and civic beneficence
constructed by an Arab governor of the city in the mid seventh century CE following a rebellion there.[11] Likewise, Achaemenid doorways used to be prominent at a
fortified site now on the eastern outskirts of Shiraz, known as Qasr-i Abu Nasr,
dated to the late Sasanian and early Islamic periods. The remains of this structure,
once known as Madar-i Suleiman, were dismantled in the 1970s when the Persepolis restoration team established that they had been taken from the palace of
Darius.[12]

Contact with the past was still sought in the following centuries. Again in the
palace of Darius, near the two Sasanian Pahlavi inscriptions, the ruler 'Adud al-
Dawla, of the Buyid dynasty (945–c.1055 CE), had two Arabic texts carved, documenting his stays at Persepolis during a military campaign in 344 AH (955 CE). The
stop there was neither routine nor casual; both inscriptions boast that he sum-

7.4 A Persian poem is inscribed below an inscription of Xerxes I on the west pilaster of the south portico of the palace of Darius. Designed to accompany a prose proclamation of Ibrahim Sultan's power 'in this lofty site and eminent place', it contains meditations on the transience of worldly power and legendary kings: 'Who did not lose his throne and rule at last, Deposed and overthrown by fate's strong blast?'

moned a local priest, Mar Sa'and, who could read the fourth-century Pahlavi inscriptions out to him.[13] Such a performance and its record were gestures not just of connection but also of cultural domination, parallel to his military success; 'Adud al-Dawla was visiting Persepolis on his return from the conquest of Esfahan. The ruin became a stage for rulers to proclaim their powers, while conscientiously meditating on the mortality of their predecessors.

The habit of inscribing memorializing messages on the walls of ruins was not confined to passing dynasts but was taken up by several others with the leisure and determination to commemorate their visit (nor was Persepolis the only site to stimulate this kind of activity).[14] Many of the verses to which travellers were inspired evoke the ghosts of legendary or semi-legendary kings such as Solomon, Jamshid and Khusraw. They hint at the rich historiographical background into which the ruins were set by visitors from the Islamic world. Source material drawn from Sasanian literature in Middle Persian was recast by historians who expressed new Muslim perspectives on the past of Iran. Medieval texts, first in Arabic and later in Persian, transmitted a compendium of the succession of Persian dynasties.

The accounts contained in the prose work of the tenth-century Tabari, or the eleventh-century Persian epic poet Firdowsi, reached back over thousands of years. Their span easily exceeded our chronological structure of attested historical kings in Iran, partly owing to the immensely long lifespans assigned to the most famous rulers. These authors did not seek historical truth by gleaning scant 'facts' from the traces of ancient writing and cities available to them. They were more concerned with creating a coherent, but impressively deeply rooted, story which made sense according to contemporary values and ethnic identities. History began with the archaic dynasties of the Pishdadians and the Kayānids; the first monarch, Gayomard, founded Istakhr (Persepolis, because of the proximity and the reputation of its Sasanian neighbour, became known as the most ancient sector of Istakhr); Jamshid, a later heroic Pishdadian king, built up its walls and palaces and instituted the new year ritual there.[15] The prophet Zoroaster appeared first in the court of the Kayānid king Gushtasp. Several kings of this dynasty (Bahman, Dārā and his son of the same name) are traditionally equated in secondary literature with individual Achaemenid monarchs. But since they are generic legendary figures with merged and overlapping histories, they are best compared to the unspecific 'Ahasuerus' of the Bible. The victory of Iskander over Dārā, a struggle recognizably derived from Alexander of Macedon's defeat of

Darius III, came after the Kayānids and the long reign of Queen Homay (who, according to some, also built at Istakhr); there followed a confused era of 'petty kings' or the rule of the Ashkanis, after which the glory of Iran was restored by rulers of the Sasanian dynasty, beginning with Ardashir I. Middle Persian literature, and the medieval Persian and Arabic writers who sourced it for their own purposes, developed the past into a vividly realized pageant of heroes, wise men and the occasional supernaturally evil villain.[16]

As with the other historical traditions which we sift for information on the Achaemenids, memories were transformed into material which illuminated the identity of its writers and their patrons. The influence of the Sasanian period (224 to c.650 CE) on this structure of history is betrayed by this characterization of the dynasty as saviours of Iran, in contrast to the chaos that prevailed under their immediate predecessors, the Ashkanis. In the Sasanian world, where religious affiliation was strongly identified with the dynasty, the revelations of the prophet Zoroaster were assigned to the distant reign of Gushtasp. The vast territories ruled over by the Kayānids and their battles against the non-Iranian barbarians of Turan parallel Sasanian struggles on their western and eastern borders. When Persian histories came to be written under the patronage of Seljuq Turk invaders, the space devoted to the enmity of Turan was reduced tactfully. The story of Iskander's invasion became either a flattering showpiece of royal ideology or was condemned as an act of barbarous violence against Iranian culture. The latter characterization would have been potent in the first two centuries of Arab rule, where religion, language and even alphabet had been superseded along with the ruling class.

Where such historical tales are applied to archaeological remains, Iranian and Islamic themes become intermingled. Persepolis, because of the size and prominence of its remains, is the focus of most surviving literature concerned with sites. The first Islamic-period account of the ruins in Persian formed part of an eleventh-century dynastic history about the province of Fars by a writer known as Ibn al-Balkhi.[17] His account emerges from Iranian dynastic history, including a treatment of Iskander's struggle against Dārā that incorporated apocryphal letters exchanged between Aristotle and his pupil. His description of the site itself hints also at the more diverse supernatural qualities attributed to the ruins:

> Jamshid built a palace at the foot of the hill, the equal of which was not to be found in the whole world ... At the foot of the hill Jamshid laid out a platform of solid stone that was black in colour, the platform being four-sided, one against the hill foot and the other three sides towards the plain ... upon the platform he erected columns of solid blocks in white stone so finely worked that even in wood it might be impossible to make the like by turner's art or by carving; and these columns were very tall ... among the rest there were two pillars which stood before the threshold ... Nowhere else in all the province of Fars is any stone like this to be found, and no one knows from where these blocks were brought ...
>
> ... There is to be seen here the figure of Boraq [the mount of Muhammad] ... Now all these columns had borne originally upper storeys erected on their summits ... Round and about lie mounds of clay ... [in which local people dig for special eye medicine] ...

Everywhere and about may be seen the sculptured portrait of Jamshid, as a powerful man with a well-grown beard, a handsome face, and curly hair … On the upper part of the hill are many great tomb-chambers, to which the people have given the name of the Prison of the Wind.

Ibn al-Balkhi's extensive description gives some idea of the continuing importance of the ruins to the contemporary prestige of Iran, and Fars in particular. This eleventh-century text touches on several themes that were to recur in later Persian, Arabic and European accounts: the seemingly impossible architectural feat of raising the columns, the supernatural character of the gateway guardians and the mysterious breezes of the site's tombs and underground passages.[18]

The same kind of Iranian guided tour probably lies behind the first lengthy account of Persepolis published in a European language written by the Venetian ambassador, Josapho Barbaro, in 1474. His account focuses on the character common to both his and Persian culture, Soloman, a name which he heard from his Iranian companions.[19] For the first time, he transliterates the popular Persian name for the ruins, Cilminar or Chehelminar, 'Forty Columns': 'there is a mightie stone of one peece, on which arr many ymages of men graven as great as gyaunts'. Barbaro described the royal image he saw carved above the tombs in the mountain as Soloman, rather than Jamshid. Since both were named as builders of the palace, the confusion is natural; it may also be a sign of a deeper merging of the identities of the two civilizing kings. The Muslim rulers and aspiring kings who visited ancient ruins wanted through them to be associated with their wisest predecessors. The grandson of Timur (Tamburlaine), imagining the Sasanian era, asked plaintively at Persepolis:

Where are the first great monarchs, called Khosro?

Their stores of treasure gone – themselves also.

Such inscriptions were not part of a search for the reality of the past, but emphasized the transience of earthly power. They exploited powerful images of ancient kingship, while retaining the moral high ground of pious believers looking sadly back on unfortunate heathens. The rich dynastic tradition built around such ruins in Iran remained their dominant cultural definition for hundreds of years and, once foreigners embarked on the struggle to understand ancient Persian on their own terms, continually resurfaced as a strong influence in their conclusions.

MERCHANT ADVENTURERS AND THE MEETING OF TWO HISTORIES

In their researches in Asia, Western travellers and European scholars had until this point searched for real locations to correspond to significant places from the Bible, such as the Garden of Eden and the Tower of Babel. Over the late fifteenth and sixteenth centuries, European historical interest grew in the Eastern courts glimpsed through Greek sources. Simultaneously, the expanding mercantile economies of Portugal, England and the Netherlands led greater numbers than ever before of literate, conscientiously observant commercial travellers further into the Levant, Anatolia, Iran and beyond into Central and South-East Asia. Diplomatic negotiation in securing concessions and safe trade routes became essential, bringing with it a renewed interest in explaining both the ancient and the recent history of Asian states (particularly the often hostile relations between the Ottoman and Persian kingdoms). Expertise in Persian increased, and publications on miscellaneous customs, characteristics and historical events multiplied.

The increased accessibility of Iran beyond the area of the Persian Gulf was the direct result of an active policy of the Safavid kings (the dynasty ruled Iran from 1501 to 1722). Shah Tahmasp granted foreigners access to markets within Iran, and Shah Abbas, who came to power in 1571, invested in the roads and caravanserais across Iranian territory. Newly formed British merchant companies were seeking such opportunities to reach new markets (in competition with the established trading posts of the Portuguese). In what was perhaps an early attempt to prod the English king towards political patronage of the mercantile exploration of Iran, the account of Josepho Barbaro was translated into English in an elegantly bound manuscript copy presented to Edward IV in 1551 (the extract above is from this translation). But it was a positive diplomatic relationship between Elizabeth I and Ivan the Terrible which allowed substantial missions such as those of the London Muscovy Company to make their way into northern and central Iran.

The necessity of travelling overland from Hormuz on the Gulf coast to Esfahan, or from the Caucasus or Caspian into the bazaars of southern Iran, brought foreigners along the main road past the most notable remains of Chilminar. Between the years of 1589 and *c*.1614, the ruins became widely identified as a site associated with Cyrus, Darius and Artaxerxes, as well as Jamshid and Soloman. The first sparks of recognition are difficult to isolate. Back in London, literary enthusiasm for Eastern historical settings ran closely alongside published 'eyewitness' reports; the first hazy claims to have sighted the actual 'Persepolis' came in the wake of popular performances of Christopher Marlowe's *Tamburlaine*, in which the ancient city was a prominent setting.[20] Merchant Geoffrey Ducket (of the Muscovy Company) and travelling clergyman-scholar John Cartwright (who possibly was employed by the rival Levant Company) both claimed to have visited Persepolis (in 1569 and 1602–3 respectively), describing a site that perhaps encompassed Naqsh-i Rustam and the later ruins of Istakhr, as well as the Persepolis platform. The background to the realization that Chilminar was Persepolis may have been the Iranian conviction that Shiraz, Istakhr and Chilminar could be collectively identified as the same capital in successively shifting locations. Iranian companions and locals might have explained to their foreign charges that Iskander once destroyed Istakhr in his wars against Dārā, whose name was still attached to the much-inscribed Palace of Darius. The similarity of the names and history to Alexander and Darius could have been the key that unlocked the door between the two traditions in European minds.[21]

By the time of the visit of the Spanish ambassador Don Garcias da Silva e Figueroa in 1618, he was well aware of the suggested identification of Chilminar as Persepolis. After a melancholy introduction lamenting his alienation in a foreign land during his mission to the Shah, Figueroa's 'Letter Concerning Persian Matters' launches immediately into a discussion of the site. He credits the classical authors of his own familiar education with describing exactly where Persepolis was and claims that Diodorus' passage on the city, in particular, still accurately described the ruins. He notes the difficulty of guessing the language of the inscriptions in an unknown script, or even deciding what mode of architecture the ancient Persians used, in comparison to Greek and Roman models.[22] This kind of Classics-influenced outlook was already evident in Cartwright's account, and dominated subsequent travellers' books.

As visitors to Iran multiplied in the seventeenth and eighteenth centuries, debate about the date and function of monuments continued to be highly speculative, because the cuneiform texts inscribed at Persepolis, at Pasargadae and at Bisitun could not yet be read. Although Pasargadae was seen to be an ancient site at about the same time as the first accounts of Persepolis, it was not connected to descriptions of the capital of Cyrus until the early nineteenth century; its identity as a Muslim shrine of the mother of Solomon overrode anything else. This association was understood to have protected the tomb, despite the reuse of architecture around it to construct a mosque courtyard; even in the twelfth century Ibn al-Balkhi commented that no one entered the tomb for fear of being blinded by a spell, although interior carvings show that it had once been used for prayer. Nevertheless, James Morier, of a British diplomatic embassy, tentatively drew a parallel between Greek descriptions of the tomb of Cyrus and the shrine in 1812; the scholar Grotefend made a definite identification after beginning to decipher the inscriptions on the palaces of Persepolis and Pasargadae from 1802.

7.5 Cyrus' tomb was known until the early nineteenth century as the shrine of the mother of Solomon. Barbaro first mentioned the monument, 'with a church on top', in 1474. This artist's approximation of the strange building described in the text, was made for a seventeenth-century edition of the Dutchman von Mandelslo's travels. The columns around the outside came from the pavilions of Pasargadae.

In the absence of recognizable details in classical authors, which might answer the questions raised by the form and images of the ruins, the Iranian culture and stories absorbed by travellers provided beguiling answers. Persepolis was commonly seen to be much older than it really was, being attributed to Cyrus the Great or the more archaic kings of distant Persian history. One interpretation written by a British Museum curator in 1819 suggested that it was over four thousand years old.[23] From the time of Thomas Herbert's visit in 1611 until the early twentieth century, visitors and scholars imagined Persepolis to be the site of an ancient new year celebration at the spring equinox. The theory grew out of their observation of the modern Persian No-Ruz or New Year festival, and perhaps also from their knowledge of the associated literary origin-myth for the ceremony – that Jamshid held the first at his palace in Istakhr.

Other perpetual debates centred on the question of whether the buildings at Persepolis were temples or secular palaces, open colonnades in form or enclosed halls. Important studies and illustrations of Persepolis and other sites were included in the travel accounts of Engelbert Kaempfer (1684–88), Cornelis de Bruijn (in Iran

7.6 Persepolis from the northern fortifications, by Cornelis de Bruijn (1711). The Dutch artist socialized extensively in the Tsar's court in Moscow before proceeding southwards to Iran. He spent three hot summer months making extraordinarily detailed drawings of Persepolis, from careful close-ups of reliefs and individual structures, to panoramic fold-out views of the entire terrace from four directions. De Bruijn even made a few hand-tinted, full colour editions of his two-volume folio memoir. His much pirated drawings were the best visual document of Persepolis so far made, and remained unsurpassed until the nineteenth century.

in 1704) and Carsten Niebuhr (travelling through Iran, 1764–65); their publications did much to disseminate more detailed and coherent views of the site and its inscriptions outside of Iran.[24] Intensifying foreign scholarly activity in the second half of the eighteenth century became merged seamlessly with increased European political involvement in Iran and Mesopotamia. Such a competitive combination sparked the revelation of historical contexts extending beyond Persepolis.

THE LANGUAGE KEY AND CULTURAL IMPERIALISM

The characters are of a strange and unusual shape … well worthy the scrutiny of some ingenious persons that delight themselves in this dark and difficult art or exercise of deciphering … I have thought fit to insert a few of these for better demonstration … Which nevertheless, whiles they cannot be read, will in all probability, like the *Mene Tekel*, without the help of a Daniel hardly be interpreted.

Tho. Herbert, 1634

The cuneiform inscriptions visible at the two known ancient sites in Fars and on Mount Bisitun increasingly became the focus of interest for academic discussion in Europe; they promised to reveal a hidden world, if only a modern prophet could be found to decipher them. In William Beckford's gothic Orientalizing novel, *Vathek* (1786), the strange, shimmering letters which appear on the satanic pillars of 'Istakar' lead his impious protagonists deeper into the city and to their doom. Although his vision is romantic and mythologizing, it was born of an atmosphere of intensified study of the Persian language that was to accelerate the understanding of the ancient language. Beckford's highly coloured vision of the Zoroastrian faith as devilish may have emerged from his study of Islamic-period Persian texts. But at around the same time, Zoroastrian religious texts in Old and New Avestan (two related archaic Iranian languages used to record hymns, prayers and Zoroastrian histories) began to be translated into European languages. The tradition of multilingualism in Persian imperial inscriptions provided the first of two important points of translation: parallel Greek texts of Shapur's achievements at Naqsh-i Rustam helped Silvestre de Sacy to unravel Sasanian Middle Persian. The deeper understanding of these languages, both closely related to Old Persian, gave scholars more guidance in their attempts to find meaning in the inscriptions of Fars.

The drive to look for an antique Persian 'key' to Old Persian is clear in some misguided and imaginative translations of the Perspolis inscriptions from the beginning of the nineteenth century. William Price, who derived his suggestions from a once-seen 'ancient manuscript' glimpsed in Shiraz, read at Persepolis the proclamations of three kings; he was perhaps influenced by the idea that the Magi came from Persia, and confused by the triple-paragraph form of the trilingual inscriptions.[25] But the extensive transcriptions of Carsten Niebuhr provided a German schoolteacher named Georg Friedrich Grotefend with sufficient material to suggest that repeated groups of symbols represented kings' names. Drawing on

7.7 The two sides of this small tablet of polished, dark limestone show three names for the Achaemenid capital Parsa: on the first side, we read 'Persepolis' in Greek (spelled here as 'Perspolis') and 'Takht-i Jamshid' in Farsi. On the other side, Ker Porter included what he considered at the time to be the site's most ancient name, 'Istakhr'. The apocryphal cuneiform word is based on Grotefend's early interpretation of Old Persian signs, and in fact reads (roughly) 'Sanataugra'. Both this and a small pale limestone plaque inscribed 'Naqsh-i Rustam' in Persian were probably chipped from the sites in question, to become unique samples for Ker Porter's cache of treasures, collected in 1821.

classical Greek and Avestan versions of these names, he suggested sounds for some of the signs, with some success.[26] His conclusions were rapidly taken up and immediately applied back in Iran by contemporary visitors; Robert Ker Porter created his own brief inscriptions (fig. 7.7).[27] Some of Grotefend's mistakes arose from using Greek and Avestan forms of royal names as his starting point, substituted for the slightly different Old Persian syllables and sounds. He and others also assumed that the signs worked alphabetically (always representing a single vowel or consonant sound rather than a combination).[28] His conclusions were slowly revised in the following decades and finally, over forty years later, further activity in Iran, and intensive scholarly work back in Europe, built the foundation for a more comprehensive understanding.

Once Old Persian began to be understood, it became conceivable that the texts in two other languages inscribed alongside could be deciphered. Since the mountain at Bisitun offered the longest parallel texts, an interested amateur, Henry Rawlinson, contrived to transcribe them while serving as the East India Company's political officer in Iran in 1836–37, first by dangling perilously from the cliff above (along with his Kurdish assistants), and later by training his telescope from a nearby ledge. At the same time, the extent of earlier Assyrian and Babylonian remains in the territory of modern Iraq was becoming clear through increased excavation.[29] By combining the information from Persepolis and Bisitun with the lengthier inscriptions emerging from the ground at contemporary digs at the neo-Assyrian palace sites of Nimrud and Nineveh, the Akkadian and, to a certain extent, Elamite languages could at last begin to be understood. The Mesopotamian finds also offered the first opportunity to glimpse the depth of imperial culture upon which the Achaemenids drew in constructing their own capitals. The heads of massive bull guardians or *lamassu* began to emerge from northern Iraqi mounds. In comparison, the beasts at the gates of Persepolis no longer looked like exotic basilisks, but clearly became a response to a tradition of monumental Eastern architecture in Assyria. Up until this point, the sculptures at Persepolis and Pasargadae had been Europe's only visual experience of the Ancient Near East. Seals and tablets from all periods of earlier history, found across Iran and Mesopotamia, bore images and cuneiform letters that had been universally and unhelpfully labelled 'Persepolitan'. With the vast expansion of the historical horizon brought by exploration in Mesopotamia, images, as well as letters, began to be deciphered.

7.8 A sensationalist newspaper reconstruction of Henry Rawlinson's derring-do in copying the trilingual inscription on the cliffside of Bisitun, 60 m above the main Khorrasan road, with a 30-m drop to the boulder-strewn foot of the mountain. The narrowness of the ledge and the precariousness of Rawlinson's situation have both been exaggerated. The copies of parallel texts in Old Persian and Babylonian Akkadian were of sufficient length that they could serve as the first key, like a Rosetta Stone in the Zagros mountains, for deciphering the more complex, older writing systems of Mesopotamia. The inscription was copied again in the mid nineteenth century, and 'squeezes', moulded impressions taken from the inscription's surface, were made in the twentieth.

7.9 Nineteenth-century casts of ancient sculpture were once seen as an important part of museums' universal collections of art. The earliest casts of Persepolis stood alone in the British Museum, as novel examples of Near Eastern art. Later these additional casts, of the royal hero in combat, were displayed with reliefs from Nineveh, just visible in the gallery above, as part of the growing context of neo-Assyrian art.

The political dimensions of these intellectual revelations were ever-present. A new wave of concentrated foreign investigations into Persepolis, Pasargadae and their inscriptions in the first two decades of the nineteenth century were undertaken by two British diplomatic missions to Persia, who seem to have spent just as much time demanding that local village headmen take them to see 'undiscovered' ancient sites as negotiating a treaty of mutual assistance with the Shah. They were driven partly by a political and cultural reaction to Napoleon's influence in Egypt, which threatened their connections and influence east of the Suez Canal. The French grand cultural enterprise of documenting ancient Egypt may have been one key influence on their activities, which included excavations around the Persepolis *apadana* (to the annoyance of the local governor) as well as cast-making of the visible reliefs there.[30] The transport of these casts and some fragmentary original reliefs back to the British Museum and private collections gave public access to Achaemenid images on an unprecedented scale, before the quantities of Assyrian reliefs transported back in the next thirty years over-shadowed them.

By the middle of the nineteenth century, scholarly exploration of Iran became more wide-ranging and the resulting publications more ambitious. In 1839, the French artist Texier realized that the reliefs at Persepolis had been coloured, and

7.10 This view of the palace of Xerxes taken by Luigi Pesce is one of the earliest extant photographs of the site. Pesce was a Neapolitan colonel who travelled to Iran as a diplomat and military adviser; he settled there in 1848. His calotype photographs, including the very first views of Persepolis, were exhibited to acclaim in the London international exposition of 1862.

reconstructed them as such in his lavishly illustrated two-volume travel account. In the following two years, the travels of Eugène Flandin and Pascal Coste produced another massive atlas filled with meticulous site drawings and reconstructions of Persepolis that drew on their experience of Islamic buildings.[31] Their plates became the main resource for authors wanting to consult or copy views of Iranian ruins for over fifty years. Neither the first calotype views of Persepolis, taken in the 1850s nor the results of an extensive photographic survey of the site in the 1880s showed enough detail to supersede Flandin and Coste's publication as an archaeological and art-historical resource.

British political involvement in Iran continued to provide opportunities for archaeological investigation. While on a mission to settle the southern border between Persian and Ottoman territory, a Colonel Williams and Sir Kennett Loftus strayed to the town of Shoush in Khuzistan province, part of the area of ancient Elam. Their surface digging there brought to light inscribed column bases which immediately identified the area of the Achaemenid palace.[32] Such activity was quickly building a critical mass of interest and excitement for investigating the emerging world of ancient Iran. The exhibited casts and artefacts, the debate over Persepolis and the discovery of Susa were combined to create visions of Achaemenid Persia in subsequent history paintings (fig. 7.11).

FOREIGN EXCAVATION AND IRANIAN POLITICS –
ACHAEMENID RUINS IN QAJAR AND PAHLAVI IRAN

When the governor of Marv Dasht halted James Morier's illegal excavations around the Persepolis *apadana* in 1812, Morier snidely commented that it was because he had not lined his pocket. This mistrustful relationship between local authorities and foreign antiquaries was not unusual. To Iranians, each ancient site was loaded with subtle local histories and sensitivities; to foreign scholars, the remains needed to be elevated from their remote locations and set into a universal network of historical connections. It was this perceived intellectual necessity that led to the transport of ancient artefacts to other countries, where

7.11 The painter Edwin Long drew upon travelogue illustrations and artefacts in the British Museum in order to produce this vision of Queen Esther in Ahasuerus' palace at Susa, exhibited at the Royal Academy in 1878. The door-jamb relief may have been copied from a drawing. *Apadana* processions are adapted for tiered wall decoration, and a rose planter. On the right-hand side, Long enlarged Darius' miniature chariot scene, as found on a cylinder seal (fig. 2.8), to a scale he was more accustomed to seeing in Assyrian reliefs. The glimpse of the textile-draped palace in the background seems to have been influenced by the colourful reconstructions of Flandin and Coste.

7.12 When Stephanoff painted his *Assemblage of Works of Art, from the earliest period to the time of Phydias* in 1845, Assyrian reliefs had yet to make an impact. Instead, reliefs from Persepolis are placed low in an overall, achronological hierarchy in which the Parthenon sculptures of fifth-century Athens were considered the culmination of world art. The miscellany of Persian images adapted from artefacts, casts and drawings include (left to right), the Pasargadae 'genius', a Sasanian rock relief from Naqsh-i Rustam, two Achaemenid seal impressions transformed into reliefs (figs 2.8, 2.9), two door-jamb reliefs from the Hundred-Columned Hall and a bull protome column capital.

they took their place in collections of antique art. The fragmentary reliefs that were acquired as a result of the British embassy's visit were not the first pieces of Persepolis to leave Iran; the travelling artist de Bruijn had transported a few small pieces back to Europe in the early eighteenth century. In European collections, the still figures of servants, soldiers and subjects that had been levered out of fill or off the parapet of the *apadana* were a required piece in the expanding jigsaw puzzle of world art, filling a somewhat undefined space between Egyptian, Assyrian and Greek sculpture.[33] In Iran, the iconography of Persepolis had a rather different role to play.

The official status of many of the foreigners escorted to Persepolis suggests that such visits were seen as an essential element of hospitable politicking on the part of governors, merchants and kings in Fars. By the late nineteenth century, Achaemenid imagery was becoming an important visual ingredient in the Iranian elite's expression of their identity and position. Motifs from Takht-i Jamshid were brought in from the open plain and incorporated in some of the elegant courtyards and *eivans*, or open-sided audience halls, in which the elite of Shiraz conducted their business. Both the complex of the regional governor, now known as the Narenjestan, and the central building of the country seat, the Afifabad garden, now west of the city centre, were adorned with faux-Persepolitan reliefs and mosaics. Images seem to have been selected and adapted with some thought; rows of bowed gift-bringers line the lower wall near the entrance of Narenjestan, guards

7.13 Achaemenidizing sculptures on the base platform of the courtyard of the Narenjestan, Shiraz, residence of the Qajar city governor. Hidden behind the curtain is a guard with a spear. By the gate, at the opposite side of the courtyard, Persepolitan gift-bearing figures process inwards. Inside, an ornamental fireplace is adorned with an audience scene.

flank the central *eivan*, and at both Afifabad and Narenjestan royal audience scenes appear in the most prominent or privileged spaces.[34]

Closely bound up with these building projects are inscriptions from the palace of Darius at Persepolis, showing that the governor of Fars, the uncle of the reigning king, undertook the first below-surface extensive excavations in the Hundred-Columned Hall there in 1878:

> For long years the country of Fars had been insecure. In a short time … perfect security was attained; the seditious were punished … His Highness came to Persepolis, and commissioned several thousand workmen to clear away the earth which had been heaped up through countless centuries on this platform, so that foreign and national travellers might view the carvings.[35]

The restoration of the site closely followed the restoration of order in Fars, an important publicity strategy that Darius I would have recognized. A second inscription, made a year later to commemorate a princely visit, makes more extravagant claims for the governor's excavations, which covered 'not only this part of the site [palace of Darius], but all the abode of Jamshid, for the glory of his justice … and the peasants became happy …'.[36] Signs of some of this earth clearance can be seen in contemporary pictures, the first published photographs of Persepolis and several other sites in Fars, produced in 1882 by Franz Stolze and his colleague Friedrich Andreas.[37]

Despite Andreas's and Stolze's interest, fifteen years later the same excavations were viewed through the lens of a negative stereotype by Herbert Weld, an aspiring British archaeologist, who flexibly used a restricted survey permit to explore remote corners of the Persepolis terrace. The Shirazi elite's efforts, he commented, had been 'conducted not for the purpose of research, but with the idea of something valuable turning up'.[38] The misunderstanding was mutual. Weld was interested in finding out more about the layout and structure of the buildings on the terrace, but popular Iranian opinion saw in such, occasionally rather underhand, foreign operations the signs of extreme skulduggery. Weld, in turn, was probably unaware of the way in which Iranian artists, intellectuals and politicians saw Persepolis and other ancient monuments as central parts of both their national and personal histories. At around the same time as Weld's sojourn at Persepolis, a printed edition of Firdowsi's *Shahnama* was published, in which the illustrator drew, for the first time, on Achaemenid and Sasanian reliefs in his visualization of poetic history.[39] In 1896, a Shirazi draughtsman and scholar named Fursat Shirazi published a historical travel memoir of Iran, complete with his illustrations of important shrines, mosques, reliefs and ruins. His panoramas of landscapes and sites follow different principles of representation to Western archaeological illustration, but his close-up drawings of reliefs and the ground-plan of Persepolis are extremely detailed. Shirazi was a polyglot who freely exchanged knowledge with foreigners. But the popular perception of European interest in Iran was far more negative and mirrored the mean suspicions of Morier and Weld.

In a number of stories circulating towards the turn of the century, thieving and unscrupulous Europeans were said to have obtained design patterns for 'revolvers,

7.14 Susa from the 'Friend of Iran', 1935. Now developing an urban sprawl, it was once a small town centred on the shrine of Daniel (bottom left). Digging close to the pilgrimage site triggered some violent opposition in 1884, when the surrounding population was largely nomadic. Marcel Dieulafoy decided to continue the dig despite this unrest, at which his wife reported, 'We all applauded this manly resolution.' The later French mission's château dominates the ancient site.

bandoliers, helmets, shoes' and the Martini Henry rifle either from their studies of the Persepolis reliefs or from plundering the contents of the royal tombs. If not finding the source of their technological wealth in Fars, foreigners at least found the traditional sort. Several of the most typical tales were later collected by an army lieutenant travelling through Iran in 1907–8:

> It is said that about twenty-five years ago two Englishmen came to Shiraz in company with a third person … a Persian … Abbas Khan, one of the leading men of the neighbourhood, was out shooting alone and happened to pass by the great platform … Whilst he was watching they produced a piece of paper, which they carefully studied … Having found a certain spot on the ground, they mixed a colourless liquid … and poured it out on the place they had ascertained … After a while the men set to work to dig at the two points where the liquid had been poured out, Abbas Khan assisting … they discovered two metal boxes of red colour presumably made of gold … Abbas Khan told the strangers that he could not allow them to carry away the boxes without due authority, whereupon they said that they had the permission of the Persian Government to do as they liked. Abbas Khan replied that they would have to obtain the sanction of the Governor of Fars at Shiraz. On this they tried to bribe him … [but finally] bound him hand and foot … they put him in one of the stone sarcophagi, placed beside him some bread and water … they departed from the neighbourhood taking off the treasures they had found. [Abbas Khan raised the alarm and an order to arrest them was sent, but] … they escaped safely out of the country with their booty.[40]

While foreigners were not averse to carrying off antique souvenirs from sites, it was perhaps lack of communication that encouraged the development of such sensational tales. In the 1880s, in relaxed conversation with a village headman, the

7.15 The use of Achaemenid motifs in decorative arts in the late nineteenth century was extensive. These glazed tiles at Kirmanshah adapt some of the same motifs used in the Narenjestan, recalling the style of Fursat Shirazi's illustrations. Achaemenidizing pieces in printed clothes and beaten metal continue to be produced for the bazaar and souvenir market to this day.

7.16 A Shirazi police officer with 'Persepolis' reliefs intercepted before sale or export in the 1930s. These fragments sold as ancient may have come from a Qajar mansion.

British doctor Edward Browne heard a complaint that, although two French savants had spent many hours making drawings and photographs of the tombs at Naqsh-i Rustam, they refused to let curious villagers see the results.[41]

The Frenchmen, unlike the British, had no reason to be surreptitious about their work; the French Archaeological Mission was one of the first permanent research institutes to be established in Iran in 1897. Until 1929, it held an agreement granting it the sole right to excavate ancient sites. This deep involvement was prompted by a substantial project at Susa. After Loftus's brief investigation, Marcel and Jane Dieulafoy began the first large-scale excavations of one of Persia's ancient cities in 1884. The excavation was revealed in two successive publications in 1893 and 1913, but it was enlivened by Madame Dieulafoy's accompanying illustrated memoirs and articles, describing, amongst other hair-raising incidents, the civic disturbances caused in this major pilgrimage centre by their excavations. Her account led Vita Sackville-West to comment, 'It was not so much she who accompanied her husband as her husband who accompanied her ... Jane was not afraid of brigands, but inclined rather to the belief that they were afraid of her.' The Dieulafoys' work opened up a far wider prospect of layered settlements than the original discovery of an *apadana* promised. The robust walls of the château built for the security of the Dieulafoy expedition embody the durable character of the archaeological activity of the French Mission in Iran.[42]

7.17 A plaque in the 1930s church of St Simeon, Shiraz, calls in the name of God for Cyrus the Great and his country to be blessed. The plaque and the church, a modern amalgam of Iranian church and mosque architecture, were designed by the Persian language scholar, the Reverend Norman Sharp.

More regular publication followed as purely academic expeditions were mounted. Sir Aurel Stein's epic journeys across Iran and Central Asia initiated the first systematic collecting of ceramic sherds for survey purposes.[43] The first comprehensive photographic survey of rock reliefs in Iran was produced by Friedrich Sarre and Ernst Herzfeld, after they commissioned the Georgian-born Tehran photographer Antoin Sevreguin to illustrate their surveys (fig. 7.1).[44] Ernst Herzfeld's taste for archaeological excavation in Iran was merely whetted and he returned again in 1923–24 and 1927 to conduct extensive surveys at Persepolis and Pasargadae. His enthusiasm for discovering new insights into the ruins crackles from the pages of the journals he kept there. Playing host to several influential Iranian visitors and staying in regular touch with local contacts such as the Shirazi historian Sayyed Muhammad Taqi Mostafavi, he pushed the case for opening up excavation opportunities to other archaeological missions as well as the French. Both he and the scholar of and dealer in Persian art Arthur Upham Pope observed closely the development of an antiquities law that would forbid the uncontrolled export of antiquities.[45] This law was passed in 1930, marking a step away from the private dealing of unprovenanced objects.

Two developments made the national and international climate more favourable to large excavations in Iran. In 1925, a colonel from the Persian Cossack brigade, Reza Khan, seized power in Tehran and was crowned king. He selected the name Pahlavi for his new dynasty, an attempt to associate his rule with the glamour of Iran's pre-Islamic history. This measure set the tone for the monarchy's use of the ancient past for the next fifty years. Public buildings in Tehran, such as the central bank and post office, were adorned with Achaemenid architectural motifs. At the same time, the profile of Achaemenid ruins was raised internationally by exhibitions of Persian art in Europe and the USA, not as a triangulation point for Greek and Egyptian remains as before but as part of an Iranian cultural continuum. American collectors, in particular, awoke to the desirability of Persian antiquities, and the museums of Chicago and the University of Philadelphia both manoeuvred to secure a prestigious dig. Chicago won Persepolis, together with Herzfeld's supervision, with the

7.18 The façade of the old central National Bank, Ferdowsi Street, Tehran, guarded by Achaemenid archers and a winged disk. Several Pahlavi-era official buildings carried Achaemenid motifs to give them the aspect of a modern *apadana*.

7.19 Persepolis, 1971:
a Persian army of all ages,
headed by the Great King's
chariot and standard (in an
array modelled on the
accounts of Xenophon and
artefacts from Persepolis)
parades past an invited,
international audience of
dignitaries. An immense
security operation was put
in place to support this
culmination of the Pahlavi
dynasty's ideological use of
Persian monarchic history.

aid of their benefactress, Ada Small Moore. The Metropolitan Museum of Art moved in nearby to work on Qasr-i Abu Nasr.[46]

Persepolis came under the supervision of the Iranian Archaeological Service in the 1940s, and over the next thirty years several other large excavation projects began. The British Institute was founded in Tehran in 1951 and the sites of Pasargadae and Nush-i Jan became its two major projects. In 1960, an Italian team began work on the large and enigmatic site of Dahan-i Guleiman in Seistan.[47] The work of Ali Sami, who became the director of the Scientific Institute of Persepolis in 1939, and the keen antiquarian Mostafavi brought to light new architectural finds in Fars and raised the exciting possibility of ongoing surveys filling in further information about other types of habitation and the system surrounding the royal palaces. The piecemeal task of comparing remains from Iran to similar artefacts or architecture of roughly the same period found within or beyond the bounds of Achaemenid rule increased along with the amount of available information.[48] The interests of research institutes and the government of the country for once met harmoniously in the promotion of Iran's rich history. This was to culminate in the ambitious plans of Reza Shah's son, Mohammed Reza Shah.

The idea of a state celebration at Persepolis had first been aired in 1960 and was later fixed as an anniversary festival marking 2,500 years of the Persian monarchy in 1971. Sixty-four world leaders and their representatives were invited to the

7.20 In keeping with the theme of countless Islamic inscriptions on the ruins of Persepolis, the glories of the 1971 celebrations have faded in turn. The air-conditioned vinyl tents that accommodated world leaders were later used by the army. Only one of the banqueting tents, where peacocks were served at dinner, today (barely) retains its cover.

extravagant festival, which attracted the criticism of the liberal press, along with the unwelcome attentions of extremist groups in Iran. A Persian imperial army of all ages, in fancy dress, paraded below the terrace, 'Persia on parade!' as Orson Welles narrated in the official film. Chefs, banqueting equipment and even hairdressers were flown from Paris to cater to the modern 'Cloth of Gold' tent city laid out in the Marv Dasht plain.[49] The Shah saluted and addressed an earnest speech to the empty tomb of Cyrus II. He made a post-banquet speech calling for a 'world free from fear' to which the Ethiopian emperor Haile Selassie gave the vote of thanks. Cyrus II, the empire's founder and ideological hinge for this idealized, promotional vision, was praised as the first advocate of human rights. The Cyrus Cylinder, a Babylonian document which had never before been east of the Zagros mountains, was loaned to Tehran for the duration of the opening ceremony and became the design mascot of the event.

SEARCHING FOR THE EMPIRE

Whatever positive public relations impact the *jaashnha* or celebrations may have had at the time, the hindsight bestowed by the Iranian revolution in 1979 sees them as gestures of doomed extravagance. Sustained unrest and protests caused the Shah to flee the country, leaving the way open for an entirely new government.

The institution of an Islamic republic with the Ayatollah Khomeini as its leader transformed both the research climate and the modern perspective from which Iran's imperial past was viewed. The close association of the Pahlavi dynasty with the promotion and study of pre-Islamic Persia subsequently created an ambivalent atmosphere for the pursuit of Achaemenid studies in Iran. The words of Ayatollah Khamenei, visiting Persepolis when serving as president of the republic, illustrate the qualified national pride surrounding a monument so clearly evoking the country's monarchic tradition.

> In my visit … I witnessed two distinct attributes lying side by side. First, the art, elegance, and the superb ability that has created … monuments which, after the lapse of tens of centuries, still remain a marvel to mankind. On the other hand, next to it lies exploitation and brute force … an individually cruel greatness … 'one has become the ruler of many.' This is the dark and bitter history of the exploited … We must recognize these monuments as a valuable treasury in which we can see history and humanity, Iran and the Iranians, together with their legacy. We must preserve them.[50]

The Ayatollah's words, although incorporating inevitable reservations about royal despotism, echo the inscriptions of past visiting rulers in their meditation on the glories of the site and its connection with Iranian history. Since the foundation of the Islamic republic, a long-term archaeological project has begun at Ecbatana, investigations have continued at Dahan-i Guleiman, while at other sites, including Bisitun and Persepolis, the emphasis has been on supporting conservation, under the regional supervision of the Iran Heritage Organization. More recently, the number of international collaborations on archaeological surveys, at sites such as Pasargadae and regions such as Khuzistan and the Persian Gulf, has increased.[51]

Aside from the issues facing researchers within Iran, the nature of Achaemenid studies continues to change and expand. The existing textual evidence for the Achaemenid period is subjected to fresh analysis, while the database of sources in Near Eastern languages increases. Establishing the archaeological reality of the Achaemenid period across the whole territory under Persian rule also remains a challenge. Fully published and documented material evidence still exists only in small, scattered patches across a vast area. The full and precise dating of phases of use at individual sites during the Achaemenid period is made difficult by lack of clarity about artefact-based chronologies. More detailed information about patterns of settlement and land use should provide a more realistic view of the Achaemenid landscape, revealing a wider context offsetting the historical prominence of royal architecture and governmental centres. The questions researchers are now asking seek to deepen our understanding of populations, cultures and settlements in Iran and across the empire.

NOTES

INTRODUCTION

1 *Parsa* or *Parsu* may originate in an Old Persian word for border. 'Parsu' occurs in Assyrian documents of the ninth to seventh centuries BCE, but the context is not extensive enough to decide whether it refers to exactly the same geographical area or ethnic group as later, rather than being a similar term in use by an Iranian speaking people.

2 There is ongoing bibliography on this issue, particularly relating to pottery parallels to styles in Iran, by Young, Kroll and Summers. The most recent detailed discussion by Rémy Bourcharlat of the lack of synthesis in the discussion of 'Achaemenid' archaeological characteristics and periodization, with a focus on Iran, is about to be published in the *BHAch* series (in French).

3 A preliminary distinction between Iron IV as the universal term for this period in Iran, with 'Achaemenid' reserved only for those sites and objects directly associated with the royal dynasty, is outlined by Bourcharlat (forthcoming).

4 Multilingualism: see Lewis 1994 for references for multilingual annotations on the Persepolis tablets, including Greek.

5 Supplemented with the (fictional) comments of Cyrus Spitama, as created by Vidal (1993), pp. 3f.

6 *Persika* and Persian tales: Ctesias and Dinon of Colophon (father of Cleitarchus) are the subject of several comments and articles from the Persian history perspective in the Achaemenid history series (Murray, Kuhrt, Griffiths, Sancisi-Weerdenburg, Stevenson). The evidence for all the writers and sources of *Persika* is discussed in the extremely readable but hard to come by book by Stevenson (1997) which includes a good bibliography for further reading on the individual authors (Heracleides etc.) who can be found also in the *Oxford Classical Dictionary*. Other interesting further discussions, touching on the identity of 'Oriental' story-telling, include Momigliano 1977, Drews 1973 and Bickerman 1967.

7 Apart from the administrative letters of the Achaemenid period, the Biblical texts also find parallels in fragments from the Dead Sea Scrolls, where glimpses are seen of a wider variety of tales set in the Persian court (White and Crawford 1996).

CHAPTER 1

1 Xenophon also lists the Sakai, Paphlagonians, Magadidae, Greeks, Cypriots and Egyptians as subject to Cyrus. Both in this list and in the whole passage on Cyrus' imperialism, Xenophon's rhetoric may be influenced by Persian concepts of the empire with which he came into contact at the turn of the fifth century.

2 Proto-Persian history in the Greek authors: Hdt. 1.95–1.109; the histories of Nicolaus of Damascus dealt with stories about early Median and Persian history sourced from Xanthus and Ctesias (*FGrHist* 90); Ctesias' *Persika* consisted of twenty-three colourful books based on his interpretation of stories heard while he worked within the Achaemenid court (although he also claimed to access ancient records, Diod. Sic. 2.32.4). Texts: *FGrHist* 3c, 688, recently translated and re-edited by Lenfant (2004) and previously translated by Auberger (1991). The stories used by Diodorus and Athenaeus as well as smaller fragments in works such as Strabo's Geography are available in English translation in their Loeb editions (e.g. Athenaeus 12, 38); see also Drews 1973.

3 Assyria: Roaf 1990, pp. 158–91; Kuhrt 1995, ch. 9.

4 Translation from Streck 1916, II 252–3, discussed in Kuhrt 1995, II p 523 (q.v. for further aspects of kingship ideology). Ashurbanipal further boasts that he can dispute the meaning of omens with scholars and solve difficult mathematics. His inscriptions reach a new level of self-justification partly because his right to the kingship was challenged by his brother.

5 Assyrian ideology and palace imagery – see Reade 1998 (palace reliefs, discovery and content), Russell 1999 (inscriptions and palaces), Oates 2001 (the city of Nimrud). See also Curtis and Reade 1995.

6 Urartu: the war with Assyria, from Assyrian sources, discussed in Lanfranchi and Parpola 1990, pp. xv–xx (introduction to the translated diplomatic texts). Archaeological evidence shows continuing use in some Urartian centres in the seventh century, but the idea of the decline and disappearance of Urartu is more of a distinct phenomenon in the historical record. The final neo-Assyrian mention dates to *c.*643, but, less than a hundred years later, neither accounts of early Median history nor the Bisitun inscription alludes to a state or system resembling Urartu, while new geographical names ('Media', 'Armenia') have cloaked their former territory. Only a later ethnic term used by Xenophon to describe a people in Armenia in the time of Cyrus II hints at a historical tradition about a warlike tribe hostile to the Armenians who made peace with the Persian conqueror and joined his army ('Chaldaea' and 'Chaldaeans' used without the later transferral to Babylonia, but derived from 'Haldi' as the ethnic name used by the Urartians, see *Cyropaedia* bk. 3.2)

7 See Tadmor 1994 for the Iran *stela*.

8 See Lanfranchi 2003 for a more comprehensive view of the involvement of the Zagros region with the Assyrian political world.

9 Kuhrt (forthcoming, ch. 2.1) compiles extracts of these references, with commentary and bibliography. The geography of these Assyrian

campaigns into Media is still disputed.

10 See extracts in Starr 1990.

11 Assyrian activities in the Zagros may have incorporated some of these rulers within army and imperial structures (see Lanfranchi 2003), resulting in later ideas that the Median attack, like that of the Babylonians, came from within the ruling power structure.

12 The name was actually a negative and generic one given to a destructive invading force, and the extent to which it always referred to the Medes in these sources is debatable.

13 Hdt. 1.96–101. The character of the entire Median history, or '*Medikos Logos*', has been discussed by Sancisi-Weerdenburg 1994. See Kuhrt on this part of the story (forthcoming, ch. 2.13).

14 Radner 2003.

15 In Ctesias, the earlier mythologized Assyrian monarchs Semiramis and Ninos rule the larger territory of the later Persian empire, from Egypt to Bactria (Diodorus 1.1–28, drawing on this source material; particularly chapters 24–8).

16 The learned Assurbanipal, for example, was transformed into the reclusive and effeminate Sardanapalus in Ctesias; see Macginnis 1988 on this transformation of the tradition of the end of the neo-Assyrian empire; compare the Median court as represented by Xenophon, *Cyropaedia* 1.3.

17 Schmitt 1991, p. 56 (II.14), p. 68.

18 Transformed royal names can be found in Herodotus' account of conflict and diplomacy between Media and Lydia, with the involvement of the king of Babylon (1.73–4). See Kuhrt forthcoming, chs 2.15–16.

19 For 'The Dream of Nabonidus' see Pritchard 1969, and the Babylonian Chronicle, Grayson 1975, nos. 104–111. Ctesias' details of Cyrus' war against Astyages preserve a more practical Persian ideological perspective, in which Cyrus honours his predecessor and marries his daughter (only briefly referred to by Herodotus), *FGrHist* 688 F9.

20 Median art: earlier influences on the culture of the Zagros mountains reach beyond the imperial trends of Assyria and Urartu to include strong local traditions, such as the cultures of Hasanlu and metal-working at Ziwiye (the latter's archaeological analysis is obscured by some problems of provenance). For a sparsely illustrated discussion of Median art as the 'missing link' see Porada 1965 (pp. 137–41) and Muscarella 1987.

21 See Sarraf 2003 for a recent summary in English.

22 Nush-i Jan: excavation reported in a series of reports in *Iran* by Stronach and Roaf (vol. 7, 1969, pp. 1f. (Stronach); vol. 11, 1973, pp. 129ff. (Stronach and Roaf); vol. 16, 1978, pp. 1f.); fuller publication is forthcoming.

23 Baba Jan: the excavations were published in successive volumes of *Iran*; in the years 1968–70, 1977–8 and 1985. Its dating is discussed in the context of the other sites by Liverani (2003, p. 3).

24 Godin Tepe, level 2: Cuyler Young and Levine 1974, pp. 29ff.

25 The organization of these centres, and their decline, has been linked (Liverani 2003, p. 9) in tandem with the involvement and collapse of Assyrian power, rather than with the successor power envisioned by Classical authors.

26 For the renovation of Babylon see Kuhrt 1995, p. 593.

27 See Grayson 1975, no. 7, and Kuhrt 1990.

28 The year of Cyrus' death is relatively reliably fixed by Babylonian documents to 530; in the absence of any absolute evidence, the twenty-nine-year reign assigned to Cyrus by Herodotus is counted back to produce the accession year 559. His defeat of Astyages in 550 is fixed by the Babylonian Chronicle while the traditional date of the conquest of Lydia is suggested by logical proximity, rather than by definite evidence.

29 Elam as the background to the rise of a Persian dynasty: for an overview of Elamite history see Kuhrt 1995, Curtis 2000, pp. 14–19 (earlier period) and Potts 1999, pp. 259–307 (on the neo-Elamite period and the roots of Cyrus' dynasty there).

30 See Henkelman in Henkelman and Kuhrt 2003 for an extensive discussion of the evidence for acculturation during this period, including a valuable survey of one of the two sites, discovered in the 1980s, recently brought into discussions of Iranian-influenced neo-Elamite culture.

31 For the Elamite invasion portrayed in Assyrian relief-form see Reade 1998, pp. 80–87; Kuhrt 1995, pp. 500f.

32 Miroschedji 1985 discusses this phenomenon.

33 Hdt. 1.107–130, Ctesias *FGrHist* 90 F66, and see Justin 1.4.10 and Athenaeus 14.633d–e.

34 On this see most recently the full discussion by Kuhrt (in Henkelman and Kuhrt 2003).

35 Grayson 1975, no. 7, col. ii, lines 3–4.

36 The association with the date 547 was established by a reference in the Babylonian Chronicle to a victory in that year (Grayson 1975, no. 7, col. ii lines 15–17), but no place or opponent is named.

37 For the account of Croesus' defeat see Hdt. 1.53–54, 73–88.

38 Grayson 1975, no. 7 col. iii lines 12–15 (layout slightly adapted).

39 Compare Alexander's paced takeover of Babylon after the victory at Gaugamela. Like Alexander, Cyrus advertised his promise to restore shrines in the city.

40 For this possible 'co-regency' see Peat 1989.

41 Cyrus in Babylon: for a discussion of Cyrus' policy in Babylon see Kuhrt 1983 and 1990 and Briant 2002, pp. 43f. The translated text of the Cyrus Cylinder is reproduced in Brosius 2000 (Lactor 16, text no. 12) and Kuhrt forthcoming, ch. 3, both with historical commentaries. A further fragment of a cylinder from Ur suggests that similar texts were formulated for each city of the region. This wider strategy is reflected its application to a third religious legitimization, in the Old Testament description of Cyrus as the chosen ruler 'the anointed' of Yahweh 'whom he has taken by the hand … "I will go before you" … ' (Isaiah 41).

42 Excerpted from lines 13-15 and 17, see Brosius 2000, p. 10.

43 Verse account: Kuhrt forthcoming, ch. 3, no. 23. There is no find-spot for the text. This view also reached the fourth-century Dynastic Prophecy (Grayson 1975) which 'predicted' that Nabonidus 'will plot evil against Akkad'.

44 Ctesias, *FGrHist* 680 F9, see Grayson 1975, pp. 32f.

45 Ezra 1.

46 Hdt. 1.177.

47 Hdt. 1.205ff. Also reflected in Ctesias' account of the Cyrus' conquests, which may well have been influenced by alliances of the late fifth century (*FGrHist* 688 F9).

48 For Cyrus' verbose departure (Xenophon *Cyropaedia* 8.7), see Sancisi-Weerdenburg 1985.

49 Xenophon *Cyropaedia* 8.6.

59 For a discussion see Briant 2002, pp. 70–76.

51 Pasargadae: the site was first surveyed in detail by Herzfeld in the 1920s (1935), subjected to further investigation by Ali Sami from 1949 (1956, available in English, 1971) and the British Institute of Persian Studies' excavations were published in Stronach 1978. For a summary of more recent geophysical surveys see Boucharlat forthcoming and, in less detail, in Nielsen 2001. A highly readable pre-revolution guide ('one can eat Persian food inexpensively at the Takht-i Tavoos restaurant') can be found in Matheson 1976, pp. 214–20.

52 Root 1979, pp. 49–58.

53 Pictured with comparisons in Boardman 2000, figs. 3.22a, b.

54 The Pasargadae 'genius' is discussed by Root (1979, pp. 46–9, 300–303).

55 See Nylander 1968a, where all possibilities are considered; inscriptions could have been added to the buildings at any time, but building chronology on some structures may extend up to *c*.510 (into the reign of Darius I).

56 Tomb of Cyrus: Stronach 1978, pp. 24–43 and Schmidt 1970, pp. 41–4; for comparable stepped and gabled monuments see Boardman's discussion (pp. 53–7).

57 Nylander 1970.

58 For Dasht-i Gohar and Takht-i Rustam, the name given to the stepped base, see Stronach 1978, pp. 300–304, Roaf 1983, p. 150 (there remains the possibility that this work also took place early in the reign of Darius I), Matheson 1976, p. 223 and Boardman 2000, p. 63.

59 Two later authors also refer to Cyrus choosing Cambyses as his successor (Hdt. 1.208 and Ctesias *FGrHist* 688 F8).

60 See Brosius 2000, 1.4, text no. 18.

61 Cambyses' madness is described by Herodotus, 3.30; Preston 1570, 'a lamentable tragedy mixed ful of pleasant mirt' (the one good deed is unclear).

62 Herodotus gives an involved origin of the war in a marriage alliance gone wrong (3.1–3) using stereotypical elements such as a wise adviser who transfers his loyalties from the Egyptians to the Persians, and a marital link which in the abstract made Cambyses ideologically a legitimate Egyptian ruler. The Polycrates alliance (3.30) is isolated, but is a symptom of the Saite dynasty's wider involvement in the affairs of the Mediterranean.

63 Suggested by Hdt. 3.34 and discussed by Briant 2002, p. 53.

64 Hdt. 3.13.

65 Lichtheim 1980, p. 37 (line 11); see Brosius 2000, no. 20.

66 Posener 1936, nos. 3 and 4; see Brosius 2000, nos. 21 and 22.

67 Hdt. 3.17–26.

68 Hdt. 3.27–33 and expanded later in Diodorus Siculus 1.46.4.

69 The turmoil in Sais is mentioned by Udjahorresnet and is usually linked to the possible dispossession of some priestly families' positions during the invasion.

70 Hdt. 3.30: the associated drama of Cambyses' courtier Prexaspes is a particularly strong fable about Cambyses' inversion of the kingship.

CHAPTER 2

1 See Brosius 2000, nos. 41–42.

2 Other primary sources include dated documents from Babylon recording the accession of the pretender, Nidintu-Bel/Nebuchadnezzar III (while documents in Uruk suggest that he was not recognized there). For discussions of this evidence, and chronological problems, see Balcer 1987 and Briant 2003, pp. 114f. and 899f.

3 According to Darius, Cambyses died 'his own death', which avoids stating whether he died of natural causes or suicide. In the Achaemenid court, it was a serious matter to be involved in the death of a king; this form of words may have been solely designed to indicate that no one else was involved in Cambyses' death.

4 Hdt. 3.66–88. For translated passages, see Brosius 2000, nos. 27–32.

5 The location of the Annubanini relief is described, with a drawing, in Matheson 1987, p. 135.

6 For a discussion of the iconography of the Bisitun relief, see Root 1979, pp. 182–226.

7 Bisitun inscription: for translations of the Old Persian, see Schmitt 1991, Kent 1953 (in English) and Lecoq 1997 (in French, annotated with textual variations in the Babylonian and Elamite versions); the Elamite version is seen as the first written text (Trümpelmann 1967).

8 The word for the Old Persian language, *ariya*, is not used here to denote a group of people (they are 'Persians', 'Armenians', 'Medes') but a language. On the debate about the formulation of Old Persian for this inscription, see Stronach 1990.

9 Seidl 1976.

10 The Aramaic text, fragmentary in places, is translated by Greenfield and Porten 1982, and an edited section of Darius' tomb inscription in the same text is discussed by Sims-Williams 1981.

11 The Pasargadae inscriptions (known as CM*x* after Morghab, the surrounding plain and the Iranian place-name) have been at the centre of the debate about the date of the creation of Old Persian, since, at face value, they appeared to suggest that Old Persian (and the genealogy of the Achaemenids) was in use by Cyrus. See Schmitt 1981 (in German) and Herrenschmidt 1989 (in French). Hdt. 1.209 illustrates an imaginative incorporation of Darius' future in Cyrus' reign, through a prophetic dream of his royal destiny.

12 For Darius' trick, see Hdt. 3.84–88.

13 For example, Darius, who condemned 'the Lie' at Bisitun, is portrayed enthusiastically arguing for a lie in order to gain access to the usurper, Hdt. 3.72.

14 The accomplices in Bisitun are named in column IV, lines 80–86, and feature throughout the relevant section, with a couple of name changes, in Herodotus.

15 The cuneiform (wedge-shaped) signs used for Old Persian differed from Babylonian and Elamite signs in being almost purely syllabic; most of the twenty-two signs are equivalent to a consonant sound combined with a vowel, for example *ya, pa, ma, mi*, while a few indicate pure vowels; in combination they produced a variety of syllable sounds. There are six ideograms, single signs standing for entire words: king, earth, people, god, Ahuramazda.

16 Lecoq 1997, pp. 247f. (DZc).

17 This blend of practicality and idealism surrounding the connection of the edges to the centre of the empire resurfaces in an expedition reported by Herodotus (4.44), in which several crews, including an Ionian informant, took thirty months to sail down the Indus to the mouth of the Nile – a direct connection between the end limits of the empire. Herodotus may have been subverting Darius' positive ideology about the Egyptian canal, since he pointedly attributes the canal to an Egyptian king, Necos, and contrasts a Persian failure to sail around Africa with an alleged Egyptian/Phoenician success on the same route (4.42–44).

18 Stronach 1974.

19 The formulation of this imagery from existing Near Eastern iconography is fully discussed by Root 1979, pp. 131–61.

20 Hdt. 3.89–92.

21 On the difficulty of isolating Darius' reforms from later reforms, see Briant 2003, pp. 137f.

22 Hdt. 8.13.

23 The story of Syloson, Hdt. 3.139–41 and 1.144–9. Later, Ctesias gave a version of a Scythian expedition in the reign of Darius I, where the satrap of Cappodocia intervened in a dispute between two royal brothers. While it may be influenced by contemporary disputes between the royal brothers Artaxerxes and Cyrus, it also fits into a general pattern whereby Achaemenid power was based on patronage of local factions or forms of government.

24 The fifth column of the Old Persian text on the cliff at Bisitun was added in the year 519 BCE. In it, Darius tells of two further campaigns against Scythians and Elamites; translations were not added. This account, one of two campaigns added only in Old Persian at the very end of the Bisitun inscription (the other was against Elam), contains several restored words. This includes parts of the words that give the visual image of an entire army balanced on one tree trunk, crossing the 'sea', but the account generally reflects the prominence given to such an epic sea-crossing.

25 Hdt. 4.118–42.

26 Aristagoras is portrayed, plausibly, as an ambitious individual attempting to use Persian power to his own ends (and to the benefit of an exiled faction from Naxos), Hdt. 5.30–35; it is this kind of local division and ambition which was often used beneficially by the Persian king and his satraps.

27 Hdt. 5.35–8, 49–51, 97–104. The rebellious insider was Histaeus, Aristagoras' cousin, who was reportedly unhappy with his prolonged stay at the Persian court in a kind of enforced guest friendship; Herodotus also airs the story that Histaeus feared that the Ionians would be resettled in Phoenicia in a common tactic for population control, 6.3.

28 Hdt. 5.105–26.

29 Briant 2002, pp. 146ff.

30 Hdt. 5.66–78. There is little corroborating evidence for the 'earth and water' demanded as symbols of submission by the Persians in Herodotus. However, the idea of physical portions of conquered territory being offered as gifts to the king fits in with the general picture of Achaemenid ideology, and may be Herodotus' shorthand for it. There are other suggestions that the source of river water was regarded as important (Hdt. 1.188, Briant 1994).

31 Hdt. 6.48–9.

32 Hdt. 6.94–102.

33 Hdt. 6.102–19.

34 Hdt. 6.117, 6.113.

35 For a collection of (mostly late) sources about customs on the death of the Persian king, see Briant 2002, p. 522.

36 Justin 2.10.1–11, Plutarch *Mor.* 173b.

37 Interestingly, in the light of Darius' ambiguous legitimacy, Herodotus airs an additional argument in favour of Xerxes' succession: that he was descended (through his mother) from Cyrus II (Hdt. 7.2), showing that Darius' direct marriage alliance with the existing royal family may have continued to have substantial unofficial currency in wider

perceptions of his and his son's royal status. On Xerxes' succession status and the decision-making process, see Kuhrt forthcoming, ch. 7, nos. 1–4.

38 For three translated inscriptions of Xerxes, see Brosius 2000, nos. 63–5.

39 Kent 1953, p. 148.

40 Referred to in Herodotus (7.4–5).

41 Kuhrt and Sherwin-White 1987.

42 Stolper 1994.

43 Herodotus can be supplemented with two more contemporary poetic responses to the wars, Aeschylus' *Persians* (produced in 472 in the Athens theatre in view of Salamis) and Simonides' *Persian War* of which new fragments have recently been discovered.

44 Hdt. 7.22–4.

45 See Hdt. 7.22, where two Persian engineers are mentioned; the project is likely to have begun earlier in the 480s. Geophysical surveys of the route began in the early 1990s and full publication of borehole, sounding and survey results were published in 2000–1, see Isserlin et al 1994. The survey of sediment in the centre of the canal suggests that its active use was very short.

46 Canal-building had a practical importance for both agriculture and communications, see Hdt. 1.194, 2.99. The *qanat* form of underground irrigation is long-established and well-known in Iran; a *qanat* system in Egypt has been recently investigated as a Persian-period phenomenon in *Persika* 2.

47 Hdt. 7.34–6 – the division between Phoenician and Egyptian work and materials sounds very similar to the ideological presentation of the building of Susa (see ch. 3).

48 Herodotus improbably claimed (7.186, depending on the manuscript reading) that there were over two million men in Xerxes' army *plus* their entourage; although it is true that there would have been a significant population of suppliers, servants, families and hangers-on with the many army divisions, this number is likely to be erroneous. Number problems are discussed in Briant 2002, p. 527.

49 Thermopylae, Hdt. 7.210–25; Artemisium, 8.8–23.

50 Hdt. 8.51–4; there is one remaining clearly Greek sculpture found in the treasury at Persepolis, a veiled woman in marble of a date later than the Persian expedition.

51 Artemisia is introduced in an audience before the battle (Hdt. 8.66–9) where she criticizes Xerxes' decision to fight at sea (and the king approves of her free speech, but goes with the majority of his advisers) (8.87–8). During the battle she narrowly escaped the attack of an Attic ship by accidentally (perhaps on purpose) ramming another Persian ally; Xerxes, observing this assault from afar, thought that she had sunk an enemy ship and later made her a central adviser (8.101–3). Some people have all the luck. The whole story is an illustration of the intense competition between peoples and states in the service of the king and the high court status to which members of regional elites

aspired.

52 Hdt. 9.17–25, 38–41, 46–70. Factors in the Persian defeat may have included a lack of battle tactics to counteract effectively the heavily armed Greek foot-soldiers. The reported dependence on the heroic single leader, Mardonius, for direction could have been more symbolic than practical, since accounts of Persian battles often highlight the heroic king or his deputy.

53 Hdt. 9.82–3.

54 Hdt. 9.90, 9.115f.

55 Hdt. 9.106; later named the Delian league and controversially used by Athens to levy forces and monetary resources from islands and cities who became near-imperial subjects (Thuc. 1.96).

56 Herodotus (9.108) suggests that Xerxes journeyed straight from Sardis to Susa, while Diodorus (11.36) used a source which instead reported that he went to Ecbatana. If both of these were generalizations or educated guesses, it is also possible that Xerxes stayed in the region to co-ordinate responses to the turmoil in the Aegean, since a later reference (Xenophon *Anab.* 1.2.9) attributes the development and fortification of the satrapal centre at Celaenae to him. The fullest sketch of the situation comes from Photius' summary of Ctesias (bk. 12, 27, Auberger 1991, pp. 74–5), who says that Xerxes returned to Babylon in order to tackle a rebellion there. This has been connected with contemporary Babylonian tablets which appear to show the rebellion of a Shamash-eriba 'king of Babylon' (Briant 2002, pp. 534f.). In both cases, the chronology is not entirely clear, and may relate to the rebellion right at the beginning of Xerxes' reign.

57 In order to fit with his picture of a declining monarchy, Herodotus places a folkloric court tale – with the ingredients of rebellion and unbalanced gift-giving – at the end of his final book, placing Xerxes in a web of intrigue involving his lusts after unsuitable court women (9.108-13). Since the story concerns the death of his brother Masistes ('Mathista', the greatest, whose real name, Ariaramnes, may be supplied by Ctesias), the inspiration may have lain at some early point in Xerxes' reign.

58 A joint Greek navy campaigned in different areas in the early 470s, at one point or another gaining control of Byzantium, parts of Cyprus (Diodorus 11.44.2) and Eion in Thrace. After a scarcity of references in the sources, an expedition is recorded in 466 to the Eurymedon river in Cilicia, where Greek forces won a victory.

59 For example, the Persepolis Treasury Tablets continue into the reign of Xerxes, illustrating the continuing intense employment of a multi-ethnic workforce around Persepolis; see Briant 2002, p. 554.

60 See Kuhrt forthcoming, ch. 7, F. 90f.; Walker 1997, p. 21 and Stolper 1988.

61 The sources for Xerxes' death are many and colourful, including Justin 3.1, Diodorus 11.69 and Ctesias 13.29–30.

62 A late source, Justin, includes a feature that puts Artabanus in a scenario similar to that applied to a king; the new king Artaxerxes has to trick him into taking off his armour before he can stab him. Other parts of Justin's version recall the Bisitun story; the imagined antics of the Persian court at different dates frequently show common features, reflecting their transmission through repeated and creative story-telling.

63 Ctesias' typically dramatic account alleges that Xerxes' death was the result of a plot between the adviser Artapanus and a powerful eunuch, Aspamitres, who then framed Darius. After Darius' execution by Artaxerxes, a new co-conspirator, Xerxes' son-in-law Megabyzus (on whom Ctesias is really concentrating in his account), spilt the beans, and Artaxerxes (who had succeeded to the throne) promptly executed both Artapanus and Aspamitres. Diodorus also points to 'Artabanus', but names a different eunuch and a more extensive plot against the king's sons. These stories could conceal a number of possible power struggles within the ruling family and aristocracy, but they all emphasize Artaxerxes' successful vengeance against the killers of his father and brother. The unspecific Babylonian report 'his son killed him' may reflect an official story which kept responsibility for the king's death within the direct line of succession. Both types of account treat Artaxerxes' succession as legitimate. The different names appearing in this and other court stories retold in later Greek authors are the result of the common habit of retrospectively highlighting (or inserting) different participants in the light of later interests.

64 Diodorus Siculus talks about Artaxerxes I's actions at the beginning of his reign at book 11.71.1–2. For possible events in the upper satrapies at the very beginning of Artaxerxes' reign, see Kuhrt forthcoming, ch. 8, nos. 1–2.

65 The process of reaffirming the crucial loyalty of the satraps may have become formalized under later kings.

66 The evidence for this revolt consists largely of short references in Thucydides (1.104, from the perspective of an Athenian force who joined in), and a rationalizing narrative constructed in retrospect by Diodorus (11.71). Xerxes' appointee as Egyptian satrap, Achaemenes, reportedly died in the first attempt to break through to a besieged Persian force in Memphis. The rebellion broke down when the Egyptian rebels lost their support from Athens (Thuc. 1.110).

CHAPTER 3

1 *The six voyages of John Baptiste Tavernier, Baron of Aubonne …*, 1677.

2 Greek authors describe the seasonal travels in general terms, but detailed evidence comes from the Persepolis Fortification Tablets; see Tuplin 1998.

3 See QCR 3.3.22f. The 'nomadism' of the Great King is examined in Briant 1988 and summarized in Briant 2002, pp. 186–92. A proverb alluding to the mobility of the Islamic

Moroccan court reinforces the idea that movement was a way of reinforcing power: 'Roam and you will confound adversaries, sit and they will confound you' (Geertz 1983, p. 134, where various mobile courts are compared).

4 These sites are summarized in Boucharlat forthcoming, with specific remains examined in Razmjou (Briant and Boucharlat forthcoming) and Mostafavi 1978.

5 See Boucharlat 1997 and 2001.

6 See Stronach 1978.

7 See papers particularly on Armenian and Georgian architecture of the Achaemenid period in Nielsen 2001.

8 Xenophon, *Anab.* 3.5.14, *Cyrop.* 8.6.22; references also in Strabo, Athenaeus and Quintus Curtius Rufus.

9 Hdt. 1.98.

10 See Auberger 1991, pp. 39–40 (Semiramis' constructions at Ecbatana connected with her carving of the Bisitun relief, Diod. 1.13.1–6), 66f. (fragment cited in Photius' summary, Astyages takes refuge from Cyrus in the palace buildings at Ecbatana – readings vary). For commentaries on these fragments, see Lenfant 2004.

11 Sarraf 2003.

12 For translations of these texts, see Brosius 2000, nos. 2 and 3, with commentary. The history of publication of these pieces is summarized in Kent 1953; Schmitt (1999) suggests that the grammatical peculiarities of these inscriptions would fit with a date of composition in the fourth century (for example, following on from Artaxerxes II's use of the entire Achaemenid genealogy in his building inscriptions).

13 On this issue, see Muscarella 1980.

14 Aristophanes, *Wasps* ll. 1143–5.

15 Travellers' reports of these sites are discussed by Knapton, Sarraf and Curtis 2001.

16 For a translation and commentary, see Brosius 2000, no. 40. Multiple copies and fragments of this inscription were found at Susa, where it was displayed in three languages in clay, stone and glazed tiles (the latter apparently displayed in a frieze, possibly in the *apadana*, Kent 1953, p. 110).

17 Strabo summarizes Susa's lost historical identity and geographical usefulness as follows: 'The Persians and Cyrus, after mastering the Medes, saw that their native land was situated rather on the extremities of their empire [*sic*], and that Susa was farther in and nearer to Babylonia and the other tribes, and therefore established the royal seat of their empire at Susa … they were pleased with the high standing of the city and with the fact that its territory bordered on Persis, and, better still, with the fact that it had never of itself achieved anything of importance, but always had been subject to others and accounted merely a part of a larger political organization, except, perhaps in ancient times, in the times of heroes', 15.3.2 (translation from the Loeb edition).

18 Susa excavated: for the early explorations, see Loftus 1857; the early Dieulafoy excavations were published in massive tomes (in which the stratigraphy of finds was not always clarified), Dieulafoy 1887ff., and continued in the publications of the Mission to Iran under de Morgan (*MDP* and *MDFP*) and later of Miroschedji, Perrot and others in the *Cahiers de la Délégation Archéologie Française en Iran*. An overview in English is provided by the excellent exhibition catalogue, Harper, Aruz and Tallon 1992.

19 The vanished '*Ayadana*', excavated in the nineteenth century, on a *tell* north of the *apadana*, was probably a Hellenistic construction, using stones from the older palaces – references summarized in Boucharlat 1997.

20 DSe para. 5. Accessible in Brosius 2000, no. 46. This inscription survives largely in Old Persian fragments, with a few fragments of the Elamite and Akkadian versions (Kent 1953, p. 110).

21 Kent 1953, pp. 142f.

22 So far only reported in summary in English, Kaboli 2000.

23 The technical term is 'siliceous brick', whereas glazed brick at earlier buildings in Babylon were made from terracotta. See technical discussions in Harper, Aruz and Tallon 1992. For the parallel between miniature inlay and monumental glazed brick decoration, see Moorey 1998.

24 The full set of this jewellery was first re-assembled and photographed for the catalogue, Harper, Aruz and Tallon 1992.

25 Harper, Aruz and Tallon 1992, nos. 158 and 159.

26 A full report is contained in Boucharlat and Labrousse 1979 and summarized in English in Boucharlat 1997.

27 An Akkadian inscription by Artaxerxes III indicates that he may have added some small structure to either palace in the later fourth century. Clear and detailed archaeological descriptions of Susa can be found in Boucharlat 1997 (and forthcoming) and Miller 1997, pp. 117–21.

28 Mostafavi 1978, translated by R. Sharp.

29 Mentions of Persepolis as *Persai* can be found in fragments of Ctesias; the adaptation is similar to the translation of *Sousa* to *Sousai* in Greek terms.

30 Persepolis excavated: the first phase of the Chicago excavations at Persepolis, under Ernst Herzfeld, was not published fully; Herzfeld's travel and excavation journals (in Washington and Chicago) preserve extensive surveys of the site in 1923 and notes on the finds in 1932–4. Herzfeld published summary findings in 1934 and 1941. His successor Schmidt published three large folio volumes (I, the palaces (1953), II, the treasury and finds (1957), III, the royal tombs and surrounding sites (1970)) with a summary volume focusing on the treasury (1939). The photographs of the expedition are now accessible online courtesy of the Oriental

Institute, Chicago. Iranian excavations and investigations involving Mostafavi (1978), Sami (1976) and Tadjvidi are only reported in summary in English publications (or news commentaries, such as Godard 1954) and work is underway to make more reports available. The restorations in the 1960s and 1970s produced the detailed publications of A. B. Tilia (1972 and 1978). Other valuable analyses include Roaf on the technique and sequence of stone carving (1983) and an excellent survey of the entire site (2004 – *RA* vol. 10, s.v. *Persepolis*).

31 Elamite and Akkadian texts which are not direct translations of Old Persian are available in fewer easily accessible translations. This text can be found in French in Lecoq 1997.

32 On a British Museum relief from the upper tier of the *apadana*, see Curtis 2000, pp. 50–53.

33 For one discussion of the significance of the Treasury, see Cahill 1985.

34 Schmidt 1957.

35 The inscriptions associated with this palace are brief: XPi, XPj and XPo (Kent 1953, pp. 112f.).

36 See Tilia 1972, pp. 241–392.

37 Sancisi-Weerdenburg (in Sancisi-Weerdenburg and Drijvers 1991).

38 Kuhrt 1987.

39 For a discussion of royal processions, and the options in this case, see Briant 2002, p. 183–6.

40 Kent 1953, p. 136f.

41 Roaf 2004, p. 406 (including a reference for the idea that these buildings may have been used, at some point during their life-span, as temples).

42 Diodorus Siculus 17.70.1–2, 71.4–8.

43 Hdt. 1.188–91, 3.150–60.

44 Kuhrt 1995, pp. 523–5. See comments in ch. 6 on the influence of omens on Alexander in Babylon.

45 Xenophon *Anab.* 1.4.10. For the Babylonian documents relating to Belesys/Belshunu, see Stolper 1987, 1994 and 1995.

46 Diodorus Siculus 2.23–8 and 2.32, *FgrHist* 90F2–3. See Murray 1987.

47 Kuhrt 1983 and 1987.

48 Dalley (2001) discusses Achaemenid-period and later stories in Aramaic literature as a legacy of Assyrian court narratives.

49 Quintus Curtius Rufus 5.1.32–5, Diodorus Siculus 2.10.1.

50 For a summary of the site excavations, see Koldewey 1914. For the context for Achaemenid remains at Babylon, see Haerinck 1973.

51 The confusion of Persepolis with Pasargadae is evident in a late source: Aelian 59.62: 'Cyrus the great, or the elder, became renowned for the famous palace which he constructed at Persepolis, of which he laid the foundations.' The local geographical connection with the unfinished palace and tomb in the Marv Dasht may have also blurred associations in popular tradition.

52 See the discussion within Tuplin 1998 on the documentation of stays at Pasargadae and Persepolis.

53 Plutarch *Artax.* III.1–2. He uses the word *telete*, which often refers to initiation into mysteries or secret rites.

54 Arrian 6.29.4–8.

55 Arrian 6.29.1–3.

CHAPTER 4

1 Plutarch *Themistocles* (a biography drawing on a century or so of elaboration of stories about Themistocles' life in Persia; for Themistocles' service to the Persian king, see Hdt. 8.112).

2 Aristophanes *Acharnians* line 74; see comments about this scene in Miller 1997, pp. 189–90.

3 An aspiring king distributes food from his table, Xenophon *Anab.* 1.9.24f. For later sources contributing to a lavish and elaborate picture of the royal table, see Briant 2002, pp. 304–10 (gift-giving, including vessels), pp. 286–94 (Greek authors on the banquet and Near Eastern comparisons) and Lewis 1987.

4 Achaemenid luxury vessels: literary sources on the prestige of vessels are collected in Briant 2002, pp. 294–7, and the context assessed by Miller 1997, ch. 6; discussions of precious metal Achaemenid vessels include Gunter and Root 1998 (the inscribed Artaxerxes bowls and the context of their discovery), Curtis 2000, pp. 55–7, Curtis, Cowell and Walker 1995 (on the British Museum Artaxerxes bowl), Nylander 1968 (on the wider desirability of inscribed bowls, based on an apocryphal letter of Themistocles). For the variety of bowls found in grave goods from the Achaemenid period cemetary of Deve Hüyük, along the route of the railway line to Baghdad, near the Syrian/Turkish border, see Moorey 1980; for bowls in grave groups from the Levant coast, see Stern 1982, ch. 5. For dissemination of the Achaemenid bowl form, see Dusinberre 2002 (based on a case study of Sardis ceramics) and Miller 1997 (a case study of Attic ceramic and culture in the fifth century BCE).

5 Fragments from fourth-century comedies by Menander, Hipparchus and Diphilus with comments playing on Persian luxury are quoted in Athenaeus, *Deipnosophistae* 11.484c.

6 Nylander 1968.

7 Further sources for Achaemenid vessel finds: Hermus valley, or *tumuli* in the Uşak region, finds are housed in the Ankara Museum of Anatolian Civilizations and the Uşak Museum, between Izmir and Afion; Georgian precious metal finds are largely from the late nineteenth and early twentieth century, partially illustrated in the elusive publications Smirnov 1934 (in Russian, but illustrated), Javakhishvili and Abramishvili 1986; recent excavations have unearthed largely metal-influenced ceramic shapes, see references in Knauss 2000 and 2001; for Oxus and Anatolia, see Dalton 1964 (second edition); a detailed commentary with comparisons between Iran and Thrace by Timothy Taylor, *CHI* IV plates, pp. 103–94. For an overview with selections from these references pictured together, see Boardman

2000, pp. 184–94.

8 Demographics and 'Iranization': inferences about the 'Iranization' of subject territories tend to be indirect and subject to disagreement. It is particularly difficult to propose ideas about any uniform phenomenon of settlement and assimilation across the empire; assessments need to be made on a case-by-case basis. See Briant (2002, p. 701) commenting on a reference to the 'barbarized' culture in late fifth-century Ephesus included by Plutarch in a biography of Lysander. Contrast Keen (1998, pp. 61ff.) on the sceptical approach to 'Iranization' in Lycia, to the south. He highlights an existing observation that new Iranian settlement in Anatolia probably continued well beyond the Achaemenid period, making it difficult to base arguments on later evidence for Iranian personal names. This is particularly relevant to areas such as Commagene and Paphlagonia, but may still (in the first place) be related to the degree of settlement and Persian estate ownership (which could be extensive) in the Achaemenid period. For detailed surveys using onomastic and historical evidence for Anatolia, see Sekunda 1988 on Hellespontine Phrygia/Daskyleium, Sekunda 1991 on Caria, Lycia and Greater Phrygia; for Egypt, see Huyse (in German) and for Cyprus Petit (in French), both in *Achaemenid History 6*.

9 If we can accept onomastic evidence alongside apparent iconographic syncresis, the stele of Djedherbes found at Saqqara seems to record a mixed marriage between a Persian and an Egyptian (Mathiesen *et al.* 1995, pictured in Boardman 2000, fig. 5.58).

10 Dusinberre 2002.

11 Miller 1997.

12 The Oxus Treasure is an assemblage of about 180 gold and silver items and other artefacts recovered in 1880 from the vicinity of Kabul (but said originally to be from the north bank of the river Oxus on the ancient border between Bactria and Sogdiana). For modern summaries and in-depth discussions, see Curtis 2000, pp. 60–65, Curtis 1997, pp. 230–49, Moorey 1988, p. 52, and the first full publication, Dalton 1964 (second edition). On recent Russian excavators of the site of Takht-i Sangin on the Oxus and attempts to link this to the nineteenth-century finds, see Pichikiyan 1981.

13 On this ornamental monumentalism, see Moorey 1998.

14 For the strong fourth-century context for the painted original of this mosaic, see Cohen 1997, ch. 2.

15 Hermitage Inv. No. 1687/93. The Pazyryk carpet was first published in the comprehensive report of the tumuli excavations by Rudenko (1970, English edition) and now features in books and catalogues of the Hermitage, St Petersburg. Dating suggestions have wavered between the fifth and fourth centuries, and possible places of manufacture have included Bactria, Iran and Mesopotamia. This sheared woollen pile was one of several carpet manufacturing techniques in use at the time.

16 Jidejian 1971, pls. 192–5.

17 Daskyleion gravestones are illustrated in Boardman 2000, figs 5.61 and 62, see also Nollé 1992 (in German); for other western Anatolian sites with iconographic parallels, see pp. 503–5.

18 See discussions for all these sites in Nielsen 2001.

19 A summary of Georgian sites in the Achaemenid period will be available in Knauss (in Briant and Boucharlat forthcoming). A summary of the Gumbati excavation is included in Nielsen 2001.

20 The fullest discussion of the audience scene and its use in Achaemenid-period iconography is Gabelmann 1984 (in German).

21 On the Nereid and other Xanthian monuments, see Demargne and Childs 1989 (in French), Demargne 1983 and Shahbazi 1975 (in English).

22 For the royal banquet as a theme in Greek historiography with discussions, see Lewis 1987, Briant 1989, pp. 35–44, and Sancisi-Weerdenburg 1995, Brosius 1996, pp. 94–7.

23 Plutarch's Life of Artaxerxes, chs. 15–16, available in an English Loeb translation (vol. 11).

24 See a discussion of the theme of decadence in these sources, Sancisi-Weerdenburg 1987.

25 See Brosius 1996, pp. 46–7 and 66–8.

26 Women within the court: see Brosius 1996 for a comprehensive and detailed discussion of the Greek perspective and the Elamite evidence; also, Wiesehöfer 1996, pp. 83–5 and Briant 2002.

27 Oppenheim 1973. The Akkadian term means 'he who is stationed at the head of the king': we have little guidance for an equivalent in languages other than Greek or Aramaic in the Achaemenid period.

28 *Eunoukhos* for *oinokhoos*, a switch most famously applied to Nehemiah in the Septuagint.

29 For a survey of eunuch stories, see Briant 2002, pp. 268–77.

30 See Quintus Curtius Rufus 8.1.1–2, 19 (Sogdiana), Xenophon *Anabasis* 1.2.7 (Celaenae, Daskyleium). Herodotus makes a characteristically pointed link between Persians as hunters and the conquest and punishment of Chios, Lesbos and Tenedos after the Ionian revolt, where the population was 'netted' (6.31). For comments on the royal hunt, see Briant 2002, pp. 297–9.

31 A good example is provided by tales of Megabyzus, general of Xerxes I, which are contained in fragments of Ctesias (14, 40, derived from Photius, see Auberger 1991, p. 79). The king's kinsman killed a lion before Xerxes could, and only narrowly escaped a death sentence. A narrow boundary stood between assistance (rewarded) and interference (punished).

32 Plutarch, *Artaxerxes* 10.3.

33 See for example Herodotus' (slightly cutting) description of Xerxes' vigilance for good performances during the battle of Salamis, 8.88–90.

34 Duel episodes recur in Diodorus Siculus 17.6.1f. (Darius III), QCR 7.4.33 (Satibarzanes).

35 Most information for these actions comes from brief references in Thucydides, whose account may not give a realistic assessment of their impact. Athenians ships join Inarus, Thuc. 1.104.2; a defeat for the Persians at the Eurymedon river, Pisidia (Asia Minor), Thuc. 1.100; events on Cyprus are known in far too vague terms to make any assumptions about whether Athens's forces caused long-term disruption there (Thuc. 1.94).

36 Lewis 1977, p. 50. Thuc. I.109.2–3, but see Diodorus Siculus 11.74.5–6.

37 According to Diodorus, the ships for this expedition came from Cilicia, Phoenicia and Cyprus.

38 For a discussion of whether all or only some of the Greek forces here were destroyed or taken prisoner, see Miller 1997, pp. 18f.

39 Thuc. 1.110.2 suggests that rebellion continued locally under a king called Amyrtaeus. Other references highlight the warlike nature of the Delta population, see Hdt. 2.164–5 (although on this kind of characterization see below, ch. 4); on the suggestion that these kings were maintained as client dynasts, see Briant 2002, pp. 576f.

40 Posener 1936, no. 31.

41 The reference to Sarsamas is Ctesias': *FGrHist* 688 F14.38. For Arsames' letters, see Cowley 1923.

42 Ctesias *FGrHist* 688 F14.35, see Brosius 2000, no. 83.

43 Bactria, despite being far beyond the orbit of the Assyrian empire, is integrated in both Xenophon's and Ctesias' accounts of early Assyro-Babylonian empire-building (Xen. *Cyrop.* I.5.2), and Bactrians are seen as an influential part.

44 Ctesias *FGrHist* 688 F14.40–42. The dispute was over a point of honour and at one point allegedly involved a battle with the king's brother, the satrap of Babylon. Megabyzus himself was highly connected, being a noble descendant of one of Darius's co-conspirators.

45 The suggestion of appointments made and revised comes in a very generalized statement in Diodorus Siculus 11.71.1–2.

46 For collected sources for the reign of Artaxerxes I, see Kuhrt forthcoming, ch. 8.

47 A Persian embassy turns back on news of the king's death, Thuc. 4.50; a Babylonian contract dated to the forty-first year of Artaxerxes' reign is drawn up in late February 423 (Brosius 2000, no. 91) while others turn to Darius II at around the same time.

48 Darius II's accession: Ctesias – *FGrHist* 688 F14.46 and F15.47 – suggests that the only legitimate son was Xerxes, who was the first to claim the throne. Unfortunately neither Xerxes nor Sogdianus is known to have been acknowledged as king in Babylonia through dated documents, and the relative status of each brother is unknown; Xerxes did hold the throne name of his grandfather, which might indicate that he had been designated crown prince. His brother Ochus instead chose 'Darius'. What is clear from contemporary documents of the

Murašu business is that estates in the vicinity of Nippur passed into the control of royal relatives who had supported Darius, rather than his brothers (Stolper 1985).

49 Arsites apparently rebelled with the support of the son of Megabyzus, Artyphios (Ctesias *FGrHist* 688 F15.52); both are killed, although Ctesias alleges that the king was reluctant to kill his brother.

50 Ctesias relates the further adventures of the family of Hydarnes, who must have had a significant hand in preserving Darius' claim on the kingship (*FGrHist* 688 F15.51). Their eventual misfortunes may have arisen from this fact.

51 Ctesias *FGrHist* F15.53. A date at the beginning of Darius' reign is only suggested by the sequence in which Ctesias reports these events.

52 Athens sent money to Amorges (Thuc. 8.53) despite the fact that a later fourth-century source (Andocides, *Pace*) claimed that the city concluded a new peace agreement with Persia at the beginning of Darius II's reign. Athens' weakness after it lost its fleet in a misadventure to Sicily led to increasing aggression against its allies in Asia Minor too.

53 See Thuc. 8.58 and 8.81 for events surrounding these Persian–Spartan alliances *c.*412–411.

54 This seems to have been the result of a lack of unity between the satraps about how to control disputed territory, combined with revived Athenian force in the area (*c.*411–407): Xen. *Hellenika* 1.3.9.

55 See, for example, the discussion in Briant 2002, pp. 593–5. Divining the satraps' motives from our remaining Greek sources (Thucydides and Xenophon) is a tricky matter, since they are only selectively reported or hypothesized.

56 Cyrus arrives in Anatolia, Xen. *Hellenika* 1.5.8f. The precise meaning of Cyrus' title of *karanos* as reported by Xenophon is unknown, but it has been connected to the Persian word for army or people (*kara*). See Xen. *Anabasis* 1.9.7.

57 On the mechanisms of army drafting and indebtedness continuing during this period, see Cardascia 1978 and Stolper 1985, pp. 104–24; on the business of the Murašu family see Stolper 1985 and 1994, and on the governor of Babylon, Belshunu, see Stolper 1994.

58 'Median revolt', Xenophon *Hellenika* 1.2.19. Possible signs of unrest are discernible only in the briefest references. For discussion of a Babylonian tablet (Nov. 407) that may refer to a blockade at Uruk and a reference in a letter of Arsames to a rebellious Egyptian fortress (411–408), see Briant 2002, pp. 596–7.

59 Darius II happens to be campaigning in Cadusia: Xen. *Hellenika* 2.1.13.

60 Hornblower 1994, p. 64.

61 Artaxerxes in the Cadusian landscape, Plutarch *Artaxerxes* 24.2–5; the future Darius III slays a Cadusian in a heroic duel, Diodorus 17.6.1–2; for Cadusians incorporated

anachronistically in proto-imperial history, see also Xen. *Cyropaedia* 5.4.13–23.

62 A phrase sometimes quoted to illustrate this, Xenophon's claim (*Anabasis* 3.5.15–16) that 'a king's army . . . had once invaded their [Carduchian] country and not a man of them had got back' because of the hard terrain, is of the most generic and traditional kind. Rather than referring to a historical event, Xenophon's poignant reference echoes a general legendary stereotype of heroic or hubristic kings (Cambyses in Egypt) and refers to a king of unknown nationality in an area traditionally invaded in exploratory neo-Assyrian expeditions.

63 See Alexander's rhetorical counter-offensive, in which he tells his troops not to fear merely the names of Scythians and Cadusians (QCR 4.14.3), by this point possibly quite a stereotypical pre-battle assertion.

64 A rental receipt recording a payment covering both the nineteenth year of Darius and the first year of Artaxerxes is cited by Stolper 1994, p. 238. Ctesias somewhat overestimated the length of this reign (*FGrHist* 688 F16.57).

65 Plutarch *Artaxerxes* 3.1–2 (assigned to a 'little while' after Darius' death). On the relative positions of Arses and his brother Cyrus, we have only the evidence of Ctesias, sourced by Plutarch (*Artaxerxes* 2.3–5).

66 Plutarch *Artaxerxes* 6.3.

67 Xen. *Anab.* 3.1.9 and 1.9.14–15.

68 Plutarch *Artaxerxes* 8–13 and Xen. *Anab.* 1.8.

69 Xen. *Anabasis* 1.9, to be compared to Darius' tomb inscription DNb (Kent 1953, p. 140, Brosius 2000, no. 103).

70 Plutarch *Artaxerxes* 1.14f.

71 Briant 2002, p. 630.

72 Kent 1953, p. 154.

73 A2Hc, A2Sa, Kent 1953, pp. 154f.

74 In Artaxerxes' inscriptions at Susa and Hamadan, A2Sa, Sb and Ha.

75 Artaxerxes II's inscription formula including Anahita and Mithras is traditionally connected to a fragment of Berossus, cited by Clement of Alexandria (*FGrHist* 680 F11), where Artaxerxes II is reported as having issued an edict providing statues for worship in the heartland capitals and the far-flung centres of Sardis, Damascus and Bactria. This could be linked to the religious practice of an Iranian population, but the nuances of the report may have been lost through its quotation.

76 The success of Amyrtaeus' rebellion is indicated by a document dated to his fourth year at Elephantine (autumn 400): Cowley 1923, no. 35. In the previous year, Artaxerxes' regnal year was still being used.

77 See Lloyd 1994, p. 337 and n. 6, for the demise of Amyrtaeus. For Nepherites' succession as apparently documented in a damaged Aramaic papyrus (Brooklyn), see Lloyd 1994, p. 338 n. 9.

78 For the excerpted chronology of Manetho forming the basis for this chronology, see Lloyd 1994, p. 356.

79 For the identity of this dynasty, as recorded in the Demotic Chronicle, see Johnson 1974.

80 Diodorus Siculus 15.92.5 and see Xenophon *Agesilaus* 2.30 and Athenaeus IV.150b–c, where Tachos becomes, like other deposed kings, the honoured courtier of the Great King.

81 Lloyd 1994, pp. 349–55.

82 Isocrates *Panegyricus* 140.

83 Diodorus Siculus 15.29.

84 According to the inscribed labels to supporting subjects depicted on a fourth-century tomb at Persepolis, A?P, Kent 1953, pp. 155f.

85 This story is told in somewhat idealized and general form in Isocrates' posthumous *Evagoras*, designed to help the legitimacy of the rule of Nicocles, Evagoras' son.

86 Diodorus also suggests that Evagoras had secret alliances with others in the Mediterranean, including Hecatomnus of Caria (15.2.3) and Achoris (15.4.3) but the effects of these arrangements are difficult to trace.

87 This was after a force was gathered under Orontes and Tiribazus and Salamis besieged (Diodorus Siculus 15.2, 15.3–6).

88 Agesilaus' campaigns are historically better known from the eulogistic accounts of Xenophon (*Agesilaus*, and see *Hellenica* 4.1) while the fourth-century history *Oxyrhynchus Hellenica* (21–22.4) indicates that Agesilaus failed to take significant towns and expended much energy obtaining booty and supplies by ravaging satrapal lands. However, Agesilaus did temporarily win alliances with an ambitious dynast in Paphlagonia and a Persian noble named Spithridates (Xenophon *Hellenica* 4.1).

89 Tissaphernes was executed by his successor, by some reports (Diodorus Siculus 14.80.8).

90 His activities were limited by the Spartans, who failed to see the profit in his activities when they were threatened at home.

91 The picture is strengthened by links made by contemporary authors between satrapal activities and the aggression of Evagoras in Cyprus and Achoris in Egypt.

92 Diodorus Siculus 15.90.2–4.

93 It is notable that Diodorus does not link Datames with the result until he reports him taking part in one engagement (15.91). For other sources about Datames, see Briant 2002, p. 657.

94 Nepos *Datames* 5.

95 Nepos *Datames* 7.

96 Additional 'evidence' of Datames' revolt is his striking and over-striking coinage in Anatolia. It is entirely likely that this was a measure to pay a mobilized army, but to read political intention into minting is difficult for this period. There is little to show that Datames was more rebellious than Evagoras, merely that he was in intense competition with his peers. Stories about Datames were not selected by Plutarch for his biography of Artaxerxes II.

97 Ariobarzanes is listed as a rebel by Pompeius Trogus alongside Datames.

98 See Demosthenes, *Sym.* 31.

99 Pompeius Trogus reports that Artaxerxes II defeated Orontes in Syria, but we have no specific context or confirmation of this.

100 Unfortunately the city and satrapal coinage of this period, although a rich resource, cannot be used to decide whether a participant was in revolt or not (especially during a period when forces were raised to settle affairs in Cyprus and to pressure Egypt). Coining silver was a mechanism for raising and maintaining forces, whether in defence or in attack.

101 Contrary to the suggestion of disloyalty in Diodorus, Mausolus always appears to be mentioned fighting on the side of the king (Xenophon *Agesilaus* 2.26.2). For the addition of Lycia to his sphere of authority, see the Xanthos trilingual inscription (*SEG* xxvii 942).

102 Hornblower 1982, ch. 9.

103 Scholiast on Demosthenes 4.19.

104 Plutarch *Artaxerxes* 30.

105 Plutarch *Artaxerxes* 24–9.

106 Diodorus Siculus 16.41–2. The Sidonian unrest appears to be related to interference from Nectanebo II directed at obstructing an imminent invasion of Egypt.

107 Grayson 1975, no. 9.

108 Diodorus Siculus 16.51.

109 Official biography: Lichtheim 1980, pp. 41–4. For negative retrospectives on this phase of Persian rule, see the inscription of Petosiris, Lichtheim 1980, p. 44. See Lloyd 1994, pp. 343–5, on additional problems of evidence during and following the reconquest.

110 Diodorus Siculus 16.75.1–2, see Arrian 2.14.5, *Demotic Chronicle* 4, 22f. Kuhrt forthcoming, ch. 9, no. 79.

111 Brosius 2004.

112 Diodorus 17.5.

113 Stolper 1994, p. 240; van der Spek 1993, p. 86.

114 Darius III: on this interesting personality and problematic source material, see Briant 2002, pp. 569–783, Nylander 1993 and Briant 2003.

CHAPTER 5

1 Peoples: the precise meaning of the Old Persian word *dahyu*, which in origin seems to refer collectively to people, is flexible and the following regional names are often the same as the singular or plural ethnic term for the inhabitants (Kent 1953, p. 56; on the meaning of the word see Lecoq 1990). Darius' Bisitun inscription lists a limited number of twenty-five subject areas, moving from the centre to the west, north and then east, clockwise (Schmitt 1991, p. 49, DB I lines 12–17). The more developed lists of peoples in inscriptions of Xerxes (XPh) and Artaxerxes II or III (A?P) move from Persia and Media northwards and eastwards to Arachosia, Bactria etc., then return to the centre with Babylonia and Assyria, and move west to Scythians, Ionians and Libyans, etc. The only countries 'out of place' here are India and Gandara, which are listed with the western

and southern (i.e. North African) provinces. This is possibly due to a conception of them as part of the southern sector along with Ethiopia and Egypt, or may be related to an idea that the Indus and the Nile rivers were connected in the far south, a theory aired in the Alexander historians. For the provinces listed with subdivided districts see Kent 1953, pp. 55f.: see also Wiesehöfer 1996, pp. 60 and 265. The great rivers of the Danube, Jaxartes, Nile and Indus appear to have been conceived of as frontiers to the king's power (Plutarch *Alex.* 36.4).

2 Two or three separate classes of evidence are usually brought to bear on the numbers of distinct peoples seen as ruled over by the Persian king: reliefs, inscriptions and Herodotus. The reliefs of the Persepolis *apadana* appear to show twenty-three distinct groups; the identification of some remains uncertain. The lists in the royal inscriptions of Darius (with varying numbers) are tabulated in Briant 2002, p. 173, and compared with the reliefs, pp. 175ff. Herodotus (3.89) gave a list of twenty satrapies set up by Darius (and their tribute), which suggests that he was responding to a dissemination of Darius' earlier or simpler subject country list.

3 For discussions of this evidence see Wiesehöfer 1996, p. 61, and Briant 2002, pp. 62ff.

4 Satraps: Bisitun 3.13, 56 (Schmitt 1991, pp. 63–4); these men are Darius' *bandaka*, a word commonly translated as slave (in Greek) and subject or servant (in modern English), but with a flexible meaning conveying individual loyalty and obligation; a related modern Persian word conveys both servitude and devotion. Herodotus calls the regional Persian governors under all the Persian kings 'hyparchs'. For a commentary on Darius' country lists see Brosius 2000, no. 135.

5 The Old Persian word transliterates most simply as *khsachapava* (the first two syllables meaning kingship or kingdom, the last two meaning protector). Herodotus first uses the term *satrapeia*, implying that the Persians themselves used it as a term for the province (3.89). The sound of the Persian word came through more accurately in Xenophon's adaptation of the original title as *xatrapes* (*Anabasis* 3.4.31). Our use of 'satrapy' uniformly to designate all provinces officially subject to the Persian king does not necessarily echo a consistent use in ancient times.

6 See a summary in Wiesehöfer 1996, pp. 61f. In Egypt, the satrap's immediate subordinate was the *frataraka*, who dealt with local affairs on his behalf. For a summary definition and references (in Aramaic correspondence), s.v. FRATARAKA, see *Encyclopaedia Iranica* (Wiesehöfer).

7 The story of Pythias is one example of a benefaction to the campaigning king; unfortunately, according to Herodotus' formulation, it turns out badly (7.29, 39).

8 Xenophon attributes a Persian title, *Karanos*, to Cyrus the Younger, as an indication of a supervisory role assigned him by the king over all military and diplomatic activity in Asia Minor: *Hellenica* 1.4.3. It is possible that the evidence for the hierarchy within the court employs a more specific set of titles indicating degree of closeness to the king (spearbearer,

cupbearer, friend and table-fellow); for an example see Xenophon *Cyropaedia* 8.4.2.

9 The two major archives for the Achaemenid period which combine known texts (on tablets) with plentiful seal images are the Persepolis and Babylonian Murašu archives (below) published without the texts in Garrison and Root 2001 and Bregstein 1996 respectively.

10 The excavators' focus was on extracting and preserving the texts, and our knowledge of the archaeological context is limited. See discussion in Garrison and Root 2002 and for an outline of the texts and their study see Hallock 1969, pp. 1–10. Only just over two thousand are published and over four thousand more were studied by Hallock before his death. Most are in Elamite, with approximately five hundred in Aramaic, and one in Akkadian.

11 Published by George Cameron (1948, *Oriental Institute Publication*, vol. 65). See also his articles in the *Journal of Near Eastern Studies* in 1958 and 1965, and Hallock 1960. Their number stands at one hundred and twenty-nine, in striking contrast to the Fortification archive.

12 References to texts outside the normal range of orders and letters are scattered and difficult to interpret. The book of Esther referred to a 'book of memorable deeds' (6) brought out to entertain the insomniac king like a substitute Sheherazad; both this and notes referred to by Herodotus as made on Xerxes' behalf at the battle of Salamis record benefactions to the king for the sake of administering and remembering rewards (8.85, 90). This kind of document may be regarded as an extension of the kind of archived letter document that granted privileges to communities (e.g. the Jerusalem Temple). More controversial is a famous citation of Ctesias' alleged usage of court records for his Persian history (Diodorus Siculus 2.32) implying more extensive historical texts. Wax-covered boards were in use for shorter and less permanent documents (Hdt. 7.239). Briant (2002, p. 423) observes that surviving texts are even restricted as to the commodities to which they refer.

13 Two examples of Aramaic letter groups from satrapal administration are so far known, one of which is from Egypt, the other from Afghanistan. Archives: (1) *Bullae* – a full publication of the Daskyleion *bullae* is available (Kaptan 2002); in this case, several hundred of the *bullae* bear the impression of papyrus and string on their backs (p. 14), smoother examples may have sealed leather. An extensive Ur sealing cache seems unrelated to active use in transactions (Collon 1996) and may be an image archive. The Aršam letters were accompanied by *bullae*. Other examples from Lebanon and Iran are largely unprovenanced and isolated. (2) Published document groups (in Aramaic): Shaked 2004 (preliminary), Cowley 1923 and Driver 1957. (3) Archives of the Achaemenid period: see Greenfield 1986 and Brosius 2003; Shaked (2004, pp. 24–5) suggests the existence of scribal schools teaching a uniform Aramaic epistolary and chancellory style. See also Lewis 1994.

14 For a discussion of the tablets' evidence see Briant 2003, pp. 447f. and bibliography, pp. 938f.

15 See Stolper 1985, 1994.

16 See the fable at Herodotus 3.128; comments in Steiner 1994, pp. 152f.

17 The inscription portrayed Darius reprimanding Gadatas for exploiting the labour of gardeners dedicated to a sanctuary of Apollo. This text, like other claims on the authority of past kings, may have passed into apocryphal territory, and its historical reality is uncertain. Meiggs and Lewis 1988, no. 12; Brosius 2000, no. 198.

18 This theme is developed in Steiner 1994, ch. 4; compare incidents of subterfuge in communication collected by Briant 2003, p. 369.

19 Driver 1957, no. 6; see Brosius 2000, no. 184.

20 Roads and stations surveyed in Fars: Schmidt 1957, pp. 20f., Kleiss 1981 and Sumner 1986.

21 Classified as 'Q' texts by their translator Hallock (1969, pp. 40–45); see also Briant 2003, p. 448.

22 Elamite tablet from Old Kandahar (Arachosia) in Afghanistan, Helms 1982.

23 Graf 1993.

24 Hallock notes the high number of variant tablet formats, which suggests a wider number of locations.

25 For a brief selection of travel texts see Brosius 2000, p. 88.

26 See Graf 1994. Hallock compares the system with the US postal service, whose motto, engraved on the old NYC headquarters, 'neither snow nor rain nor heat nor gloom of night stays these couriers the swift completion of their appointed rounds', uses Herodotus' description of the Persian express courier system (8.98). Records of rations to post horses covered their long-term maintenance, noting their daily consumption over periods of months (Hallock 1969, 459ff.).

27 The tablets do not give the essentials of rank ('wife of Mardonius'), ration amount ('360 quarts of flour') or place or origin of the ration. PFa 5, translated in Brosius 2000, no. 168. The ration recipient's purpose in travelling is occasionally summarized, for example: 'Mannuya the treasurer took silver from Susa, and went to Matezziš' (a centre usually identified with Shiraz). Mannuya's task appears in PF 1342 (Hallock 1969, p. 379).

28 PF Q 1809 published in Lewis 1980, Brosius no. 56. Security and supervision: indications of security or laxness of provincial monitoring of official travellers vary according to the tone of the travel account. Official monitoring, perhaps through the king's reputed 'eyes and ears' spies, may have been less important than the individual strictness of station or garrison commanders along the way. See Briant's discussion of assorted evidence for route security and surveillance: 2003. pp. 367ff.

29 For a detailed survey see Tuplin 1998.

30 Herodotus 5.52–4. Communications: many Greek accounts focus on the movement of diplomatic messages via individual social contacts, linked by ethnic or familial interest. More scattered reports indicate the occasional use of communication that could move faster than a galloping horse. Over short distances, armies on campaign could apparently use criers whose voices could reach across strategic gaps. Chains of beacons reaching across the empire are also mentioned (de Mundo), although it is not clear how much these were geared to transmit limited, pre-agreed signals.

31 For a digest of evidence on the Royal Road, the route of which is debated, see Miller 1997, pp. 114–17.

32 Referred to in Photius' condensed Library, 72.45 a 1–2.

33 Chariot/cart track, hamaxitos: Xenophon Anabasis 1.2.21.

34 Xenophon Anabasis 1.5.7f.

35 Xenophon Cyropaedia 6.2.36, Herodotus 7.131.

36 Because most detailed logistical knowledge comes from campaign accounts of fordings, they are adapted to show the king's heroic leadership in taming a river. On bridges, the most commonly mentioned are pontoon bridges, being able to support such unusually large traffic.

37 On navigability and coastal routes see references in Briant 2002, pp. 378–81.

38 Hdt. 5.54.

39 Xenophon Cyropaedia 1.5.

40 There also are traces of numerous levels of agricultural and customs taxes administered throughout the empire, and documented in Aramaic, cuneiform or Demotic. See Briant 2002, p. 385, on one case study, an Aramaic tally from an Achaemenid customs post of the reign of Xerxes I.

41 Baji, usual English translation 'tribute' with overtones of 'the king's portion' used in DB 1.19, DPe line 9, DNa line 19, DSe line 18 and one inscription of Xerxes, XPh line 17. The Elamite translation bajiš is usually translated simply as 'tax' within documents recording payments in kind to the central authority.

42 The word is fully analysed in its Old Persian context by Sancisi-Weerdenburg (1998), who emphasizes the differences in meaning that different contexts may have given to the word.

43 Parsa did not appear in official inscriptions as bearing 'tribute' to the king. Sancisi-Weerdenburg (1993, pp. 29f.) suggests that the 'banquet-servants' carrying animals and containers in reliefs of the smaller palaces of the southern terrace at Persepolis represent the Persians bringing tithes.

44 PF 267–73, C4 texts, Hallock 1969, p. 16; Briant argues that this produce may be from crown lands. Sancisi-Weerdenburg suggests that the whole of Parsa could be seen in some way as royal land.

45 That Parsa's difference in status may have been communicated ideologically is suggested by the fact that it does not appear in lists of the nations subject to the king in all texts after the Bisitun inscription, nor are a Persian delegation present on the apadana (rather, they are the courtiers and army). On the distinctions of their different status see Sancisi-Weerdenburg 1998, pp. 27–9; Herodotus' statement, 3.97. The difference may merely have been one of definition and ideology; the farmers and herders of Parsa contributed piecemeal to Achaemenid coffers through local tax mechanisms which accommodated exchanges and payments in kind, rather than building towards a single assessed amount of tribute covering the entire province. Such contributions in turn underpinned a complex system of disbursed rations, supporting a range of skilled male and female workers in the region of Persepolis.

46 Briant 2002, pp. 452–4.

47 Herodotus 3.90–97; see Briant 2002, pp. 390–94, a discussion of parallel evidence. These sources suggest that tribute-giving could be presented diplomatically as almost an act of generous free will, with several districts defined as giving gifts (dorai) rather than formal tribute (phoroi). Individual, compulsory gift-giving is attested only as anecdotal stories in Classical authors, yet the exchange of benefit that often ensues (with the king's overwhelming reward) parallels the ideological tone of Achaemenid inscriptions. Gifts presented to the travelling king: Plutarch, Artaxerxes 4.5.1, and described as a Persian practice, with striking parallels to DNb, by Aelian Varia Historia 1.31. Semi-obligatory 'gift-giving' is attributed to individuals encountered by the travelling king and several peoples on the edges of Persian control, such as the Arabs, whose nomadic lifestyle and beneficent relationship with the king required distinctive treatment.

48 Documents from the Murašu family firm archives continuing to function as an emergency source of armed manpower in the late fifth century, at a time when Darius II mustered his army there. It is quite possible that similar systems lay behind a large proportion of the king's army, mustered as they were by people or region. If the land-holder was unable to fulfil his military obligation, he could pay another to do so, and even pay for their equipment. The hatru system of land-grants is examined in detail within the Murašu archive by Stolper (1985, pp. 103–24); the system is further attested in smaller private archives of the reign of Artaxerxes II: see Briant 2002, p. 599, for quotation and discussion.

49 See Gunter and Root 1998 for a survey of precise weighting of silver vessels (using research by Vickers); a set of three silver phialai are seen carried towards a Persian treasurer reckoning sacks of payments on the sophisticated 'Vase of the Persians' by the Darius Painter, from the second half of the fourth century (Naples).

50 Exchange texts: Hallock 1969, pp. 16–17. Weights: see Bivar 1985; the shekel was a weight historically used in the Levant and Babylonia and is found most commonly referred to in Egyptian Aramaic documents of silver transactions; inscribed weights from Susa were tailored to reach one karš (= ten shekels), or many times that; in dry goods transactions, the irtiba (attested in both Egyptian and Elamite documents, as irtaba, and at Herodotus as artaba

1.192) also spread across the empire. The Persepolis Fortification Tablets introduce smaller measures, the *BAR* (= one third of an *irtaba*) and a *bauiš* (= one tenth of an *irtaba*) used for dry goods such as grain. A liquid measure from the Persepolis administration was the *marriš* (Hallock 1969, pp. 72f.). While Achaemenid documentation shows widespread application of official measures, conversions to other systems could still vary, and local measures continued to be used.

51 Silver *siglos* coins carried a half-figure of an archer. The silver *siglos* coin in fact corresponded to half a shekel; see Tuplin (in Carradice 1987); the early coin hoard at Persepolis is analysed by Root (1988).

52 Herodotus' fable of the otherwise elusive Aryandes, who challenges Darius' hold on coinage, is one striking allegation of the policial use of minting (4.166); discussed by Tuplin 1989.

53 For an overview of imagery see Babelon 1893; a silver coin inscribed for Baal of Tarsus was discovered at Susa. The Achaemenid influence on these and similar issues from Samaria can be seen in two examples shown by Boardman 2000, p. 178.

54 Such images could be combined with reverse generic images of horsemen or archers recalling the elite hunting genre found on contemporary stamp seals. For a selection see Boardman 2000, pp. 176f. The portrait character of western satrapal coinage is debatable; the images are perhaps also influenced by a generalized 'Persian man' image related to more anonymous seal images of heroic Persians. Individual characteristics moved coinage images further away from the stereotyped and unchanging visual identity of the Great King.

55 On Artaxerxes III's Egyptian coin issue see Mørkholm 1974 and Shore 1997.

56 BM 13249, see Stolper 1994, p. 250.

57 Murašu: discussions primarily accessible through the surveys and studies of Stolper (see particularly 1980 and 1994, pp. 245ff.).

58 Stolper 1994, pp. 249f.

59 Belesys/Belshunu: his career has a number of interesting interconnections with sources of this period. In particular the appearance of his name given to a historical character in archaic Persian histories written by Ctesias (and Xenophon) may illustrate one of the common manipulations of the past through political lenses: back-projected genealogy for influential individuals of later times (Xenophon *Anabasis* 1.4.10, Agathias *Histories* 2.25.3, Diodorus Siculus 2.23–8, Ctesias *FGrHist* 688, F1).

60 DNb, Kent 1953, pp. 139–40, Brosius 2000, no. 103.

61 This appears to be reflected in the iconography of the winged disk, which visually mirrors the king. On the interpretation of the winged disk as the king's 'charisma' rather than as the god Ahuramazda see Shahbazi 1980. The idea of the king's *farnah* or *khwarnah* and the enabling royal patron Ahuramazda may in fact be connected in the development of Iranian

kingship tradition (for the range of meaning associated with the word – *Xwarenah* – see Malandra 1983, pp. 88f.).

62 Ahuramazda emerged from an Indo-Iranian religious context, and became central to the later monotheistic focus of the Zoroastrian religion. Most modern works on Zoroastrianism analyse his role in the Achaemenid empire as if it were set in an existing Zoroastrian belief system (for example, a useful discussion of the god's context within Indo-Iranian traditions, Malandra 1983, pp. 44–7).

63 For example, Ahuramazda is 'greatest of the gods' in Darius' inscription on the wall of Persepolis (DPd, Brosius 2000, no. 104) and Xerxes' inscription at Mount Elvand (XE, Brosius 2000, no. 65); Darius' Persepolis inscription (DPd) also appeals for protection for his country of Pars, 'May Ahuramazda bring me aid, together with all the gods …', suggesting that where the ambits of other gods were involved (i.e. the landscape, in addition to Darius' Ahuramazda-protected royal house) they were invoked in an inclusive way.

64 Mithra is associated in Avestan texts with both oath-giving and enforcement, and the irrigation of land (Malandra 1983, pp. 55f.) and in other pre-Islamic material with the sun; Anahita was more strongly associated with water (Malandra 1983, pp. 117ff.). Some practical and long-term syncretism with the Babylonian goddess Ishtar (Artaxerxes II at the sanctuary of a 'warlike goddess', Plut. *Artax.* 3.1) may have influenced an emerging iconographic tradition depicting her.

65 Clement of Alexandria citing Berossus for evidence that the Persians began to worship statues during the Achaemenid period, *FGrHist* 680 F11; Anahita referred to as Aphrodite Anaitis.

66 Xenophon appends a lengthy speech on Cyrus' deathbed that includes meditations on the nature of the spirit and death (*Cyropaedia* 8.7.21ff.) but this is particularly difficult to relate to sixth-century Iranian religion.

67 This includes persecutors of the Jews in the book of Esther, and the Branchideans of Central Asia, massacred by Alexander's army, who had betrayed their sanctuary to Xerxes I.

68 Stronach 1978, pp. 117ff.; on the possible context of royal initiation ceremonies see Sancisi-Weerdenburg 1983 and, in summary, Kuhrt 1995, pp. 685–6.

69 Hdt. 1.131–2, excerpted with commentary in Brosius 2000, no. 199. Herodotus denies that a fire was involved, however, a statement which is apparently undermined by the ubiquity of fire altars in Persian worship scenes. It is possible, however, that some rituals did not require the lighting of a fire.

70 See Arrian 6.29.4–7.

71 For a sample of the documentary evidence for official rations disbursed to priests see Brosius 2000, nos. 192–4, with commentary.

72 See an extensive discussion by Henkelman (2003).

73 Ctesias *FGrHist* 688 F14.

74 Ahuramazda, when named, receives sacrifices from the *šatins*, while the objects of ceremonies enacted by magi, when named, are rivers and mountains (Brosius 2000, p. 90). The scope of the *lan* ceremony is still a matter for debate, since no documents referring to it specify particular divinities as recipients (Handley-Schachler in Brosius 1998).

75 For example, there are no specific documents demonstrating that a horse was donated for sacrifice to a god. Yet several references or hints in Greek authors suggest that horse sacrifice may have been an important but rare practice reserved for particular royal rituals: Arrian 6.29.7, Xenophon *Cyrop.* 8.3.14, Hdt. 1.189–90. Mismatches like this are a reminder that the Greek evidence also needs to be scrutinized before being accepted.

76 Hdt. 1.131.2.

77 Brosius 2000, no. 195.

78 The survival of actual letters from the Elephantine community enables us to compare constructively the edited officialese attached to the later accounts of administrative missions on behalf of the Jerusalem temple.

79 Boyce 1984, pp. 39f.

80 Boyce 1984, pp. 30–38.

81 Boyce 1984, pp. 3–4, and see discussion and images in Moorey 1988, pp. 45–50.

CHAPTER 6

1 Arrian 3.18–19; QCR 5.7.1.

2 Arrian 1.11; Diod. 17.17.3–4.

3 Arrian 1.13; see Bosworth 1988, pp. 40–44. The Persian strategy is unclear from the Greek sources.

4 Arrian 1.17f.

5 Miletus' initial diplomatic gambit was the interesting solution of being an 'open city' to both Macedonians and Persians, showing that while such cities saw it as better to demonstrate loyalty to the Great King, practical civic concerns made it acceptable to accommodate what might be seen as temporary political difficulties.

6 Arrian 1.20–24.

7 See a discussion of the Persian reaction, see Briant 2002, pp. 866f.

8 2.1–2 (after Memnon's premature death, the campaigning was continued by Persian commanders).

9 Arrian 2.4, and see Briant 2002, p. 831, on continuing resistance here.

10 For a description of the entourage, see Plutarch *Alex.* 20.11–13.

11 See Brosius 1996, p. 78; Arrian 1.12–13. Barsine had been the wife of the general Memnon: she and her son by Alexander, Heracles, were murdered in 309.

12 QCR 4.3.4 and Arrian 2.16.

13 Tyre: Arrian 2.16–25 and QCR 4.2.1ff. It is suggested that the commanders of Tyre persisted in the hope that the siege would buy time for Darius' preparations.

14 Arrian 2.26–7; for the Homeric punishment see QCR 4.6.29 (an episode regarded sceptically by some ancient and modern historians).

15 Mazaces was a recent replacement for the previous Egyptian satrap, who had been killed fighting at Issus.

16 QCR 4.7.1–4.

17 Arrian 3.3–5, QCR 4.7.5–31.

18 The marriage proposal in particular suggests that this report of diplomacy (the third approach by Darius suggested in various authors) may have been a later fabrication designed to herald Alexander's impending acceptance. See Diod. 17.14.2, Plut. *Alex.* 29.7 (for Alexander at Tyre) and for a discussion of these diplomatic overtures, Briant 2002, pp. 832–9.

19 Gathering of the troops: Diod. 17.39.104, QCR 4.6.1–2.

20 Gaugamela: Arrian 3.9–15, QCR 4.13.1, 4.16.15.

21 On the phantom, perhaps Graeco-Persian source behind this material, see Pearson 1960, pp. 78–82.

22 QCR 4.16.15.

23 See documents discussed in van der Spek 2003.

24 Briant (2003) argues that Darius did not intend these capitals to surrender and that it was a surprise that Mazaeus 'defected' (see his discussion, pp. 841–3). Possible reasons behind Alexander's destruction of Persepolis (below) suggest that royal capitals were still more useful intact to Darius and loyal nobles rather than in ruins.

25 QCR 5.1.17–35, Arrian 3.16. For the fragmentary guarantees, see van der Spek's comprehensive survey and commentary, 2003, pp. 297–8.

26 The extensive wrecking of the lower palaces and citadel gateway at Susa, possibly in the course of a siege, might well date to later rebellion and conflict in the area. But since Cyrus II's account of a welcome pageant at Babylon may have screened a violent stage in its seizure (ch. 1), it is not totally impossible that the preliminary 'negotiation' with Abulites before Alexander set out for Susa included some demolition. In the accounts of Alexander's entries into these cities, ideology is foremost, not reality.

27 QCR 5.3.16, Diod. 17.67.4–5, Arrian 3.17.1–6.

28 The Uxians claimed to Alexander that they were utterly independent of the Persian king. Sometimes taken seriously as an illustration of weakness in the heart of the empire, this claim should in fact be examined for signs of diplomacy, oblique neutrality or simple opportunism on the part of these strategically crucial settlements. They were well-connected enough to benefit, according to one account, from the special pleading of the king's mother. To claim that the Persian king could not control chaotic elements in the heart of his territory was a significant piece of negative ideology, the natural counterpart of the 'liberation'

experienced by the Babylonians; the new king burned villages and imposed tribute, neutralizing the chaos. From the harsh treatment meted out to the Uxians, it is likely that Alexander did not believe the assertion that 'the Persian king usually pays us to pass this way'. For a discussion of the Uxians in context, see Briant 2002, pp. 731–2.

29 Approaching Persepolis: the capitulation of Tiridates is again presented ideologically as an opportunity for Alexander to preserve property against anarchy but may have been due to disagreement among the Persian commanders about the best policy: QCR 5.4.2, Arrian 3.18.11. The incoming army was met this time not by a soothing property parade but instead by a troop of mutilated Greek expatriate workers whose extensive disfigurement by the Persians inflamed the Macedonians' righteous thirst for destruction (actually a misinterpreted or exaggerated diplomatic party? See Briant 2002, p. 735).

30 Persepolis destroyed: for the fullest discussion of the ideological power of Persepolis as the reason behind Alexander's destruction, see Sancisi-Weerdenburg (1993). She suggests that the foreigner's angry realization that he could not be fully accommodated as a new legitimate king in the Persian setting was also a factor.

31 For these events, see QCR 5.13.19–25.

32 For Bessus' throne name, Artaxerxes, see Diod. 17.25.43, QCR 6.6.13, and independently confirmed by the dating of Aramaic documents in Bactra to his accession year, Shaked 2004, p. 16 (incidentally, confirming an acceptance, if only local, of Bessus' legitimacy as a new Achaemenid king).

33 QCR 6.4.23.

34 QCR 6.5.1–10, 5.22–3.

35 QCR 6. 6.18–22, Arrian 3.25–6.

36 QCR 7.3.1–2, Arrian 3.28.

37 The story of the duel (QCR 7.4.33–40) may be a stereotypical interpretation of a battle involving the Persian aristocracy, since duel-like confrontations occur at Gaugamela, the Granicus (Diod. 17.20.2–3) and Cunaxa (ch. 4); see also Briant 2002, p. 822.

38 QCR 7.5.19–27, Arrian 3.28–30.

39 Bessus' banquet: one of the most interesting accounts of the last days of Bessus is that of Curtius Rufus (QCR 7.4.1–19) describing an episode characteristic of the failing king in Persian court tales. A Mede, Cobares, foretells his downfall at a banquet and deserts to Alexander, his successor (compare with the book of Daniel and a fragment attributed to the fourth-century historian Dinon and retold in Athenaeus, in which a Median bard, Angares, displeases King Astyages with a sung prophecy of Cyrus' rise (*FGrHist* 690 F9, Athen. 14.33p.633c–e). For Bessus' end, see QCR 7.5.36–43 (an alternative place for his execution was Rhagae, the scene of his crime).

40 One of the many folkoric episodes in the later books of Quintus Curtius Rufus, this story (QCR 7.5.28–35) has parallels to the inter-ethnic enmities authorized by the king alluded to in both the book of Esther (a climactic purge

of enemies of the Jews) and Herodotus (an annually commemorated massacre of the *magoi* in commemoration of their usurpation of the kingship, attested nowhere else, Hdt. 3.79). This savage genre appears to be related to the Achaemenid king's role as arbiter of ethnic competition between peoples of the empire, but its relationship to real events is mysterious.

41 Arrian 4.7.

42 Arrian 4.16–18, QCR 8.3.10–17.

43 QCR 8.4.21–30 and Arrian 4.21.

44 QCR 8.10.1–3.

45 Arrian 4.22–5.18.

46 Arrian 5.18–19, QCR 8.14.1–43.

47 Arrian 6.18–20.

48 QCR 9.10.8–18.

49 QCR 9.10.19–21, Arrian 6.21.

50 Arrian 6.29.3, QCR 9.10.21, Diod. 17.111.1 and see Bosworth 1988, pp. 156f.

51 Macedonian rule in Parsa: Orxines' replacement, Peucestas, had been a saviour of Alexander when he was injured in the siege against the Malli in India. In Parsa, he acquired an equivalent aura of royal power by being granted permission to wear the Persian robe by Alexander (Diod. 19.14.5 and see Bosworth 1988, p. 155); his privileged orientalism perhaps preserved an illusion of the special status of the province for a while.

52 For the royal weddings at Susa, see Diod. 17.38.1, Arrian 7.4.1–8, Plut. *Alex.*70.3, Athen. 538b (a description attributed to Chares). See the discussions of Bosworth 1980.

53 See Arrian 7.8.1, 7.22, Diod. 7.77.4–7, Plut. *Alex.* 45.1–2.

54 Arrian 17.14f.

55 Arrian 17.16–18, 7.22–3.

56 The vision of the peoples of the world seeking audience with the new conqueror in Babylon is in fact conventional in descriptions of conquest in the Near East – it is found in accounts of the campaigns of Sargon II (late eighth century) and Cyrus II (see the Cyrus Cylinder, lines 18–19, 28–30).

57 Alexander's death: Arrian 7.25–8, Diod. 17.118.3; see the discussion in Bosworth 1993, pp. 171f. Curtius' report of Persian grief (10.5.15–25) is a particularly interesting additional tale.

58 See Pearson 1960 on the lost primary sources.

59 Court tales and Chares of Mytilene: see the discussion and translated excerpts in Pearson's 'Lost Histories' (1960). Chares may have written in a kind of Eastern court tale tradition in which the intrigues and symbols surrounding the king and his advisers were a central preoccupation; his status, as the *eisangeleus* or 'introducer' for Alexander, was relatively high in the court mechanism; it was comparable to the kind of position close to the Great King aspired to by people such as Ctesias, but in fact held by close deputies with an investment in their monarch's power. Chares' incidental folktale 'Odatis and Zariadres', quoted by Athenaeus, is worthy of

Sheherazad's thousand-and-second night (Pearson 1960, pp. 58–9).

60 Documents C1 and C4, Shaked 2004, pp. 16–17, figs 1 and 2; full publication of these texts is awaited as part of the *Corpus Inscriptionum Iranicarum*.

61 Walker 1997, p. 24.

62 Dynastic Prophecy: English translations of the Dynastic Prophecy are available in Grayson 1975 and van der Spek 2003. Certain lines are usually cited as showing a will to resist the Macedonian invasion, invoking a new Persian leader who will overthrow the occupiers. Van der Spek's recent discussion shows exactly how difficult it is either to match the laconic prophecies with events or to distinguish exactly where retrospective prophecy ends and 'real' prophecy begins. The text is usually dated to the late fourth century BCE (hence the accuracy of predicted reigns) but the colophon names as author one Munnabtum, a historical adviser in the Assyrian court of the seventh century BCE. The prophecies of the book of Daniel, which covered events into the Hellenistic period, are a close parallel for this kind of dynastic account attributed to a past sage. Stories of archaic prophets foretelling the latest change of monarch or dynasty are also common in Greek texts dealing with Near Eastern and specifically Persian history.

63 Because of a lack of documentation, it is unclear how the ritual of substitute kingship may have changed or influenced other areas of royal ritual during the Achaemenid period. A tale from Herodotus uses some of the ingredients of the ritual for a vision experienced by the king's uncle (7.16–18).

64 Substitute kingship: Arrian 71.24.3; Diodorus 116.2–3. Curtius Rufus (5.2.13 and 8.4.16–17) reports two kinds of parodied substitute kingship reflecting positively on Alexander. The importance of donning the king's clothes in order to take on his identity shows how important it had been within the empire for Alexander to adopt some of the Persian king's dress. For a discussion of these incidents see Briant 2002, p. 863. Labat (1946) is a more detailed discussion of the substitute kingship tradition. Evidence for the Persian period is scanty but aspects of Darius III's confinement and collective murder are perhaps influenced by this ritual more than the Greek reports suggest. The use of astrologers and sages continued in later pre-Islamic and Islamic period courts; a substitute kingship ceremony prompted by exceptional cosmic omens is recorded as late as the Safavid period, when, in 1591, a non-Muslim called Yusefa was crowned king for three days and then executed, in order to protect Shah Abbas I. The substitute king ritual finds its way into the Arabian Nights genre of stories in the form of 'The Tale of the Sleeper Wakened' or Abu al-Hasan ('the fool'). Abu al-Hasan entertains the disguised Caliph Harun al-Rashid; in return the Caliph plays a joke on his subject: he drugs him and has him woken up in his own bed, dressed in royal clothing, to be treated as ruler of Baghdad in his place. Having become convinced that he was Harun al-

Rashid, Prince of the Faithful, Abu al-Hasan is returned home and treated as a madman. For the entire story, including a connected 'death' of the protagonist, see Mardrus and Mathers 1993, III, pp. 230–67.

65 Bosworth 1988, p. 157.

66 Plutarch *Alex.* 34.

67 Episodes of heroic conquest occur at QCR 5.6.13, 6.5.11–20 (Mardians), 6.5.24–32, 7.3.6–18 (the Parapamisadae). Semiramis is used as a comparison at Arrian 6.24, QCR 9.6.23, with Cyrus at QCR 7.6.20 and QCR 7.3.1. A traditional heroic lion hunt occurs at QCR 8.1.11–18.

68 The parallels do not lie just in military accounts. Several anecdotes suggest that the manipulation of rivalries for honour, on both a personal and an ethnic level, seems to have continued as a way of interpreting status (or perhaps even as a real management tool). The advisers and scholars Callisthenes and Anaxarchus vied for position at Maracanda like Babylonians, Egyptians and Greeks in the Persian court. The peculiar story of the massacre of the Branchidae, descendants of deported Greeks in a city of their own in Sogdiana, apparently to avenge an ancestral wrong at the sanctuary of Didyma, Miletus, echoes Herodotus' belief that errant Magi could be massacred on the anniversary of the evil Smerdis' death, or King Ahasuerus' guarantee of the Jewish right to avenge themselves in the book of Esther. All three stories are usually smoothed over in the search for historical conclusions, but the strangest features of the sources present some of the most interesting unsolved questions.

69 Diod. 18.26–8.

70 For a discussion of (mainly) the western Alexander Romance tradition, see Stoneman 1994. See Briant 2003 for an interesting discussion of the eastern tradition with a particular emphasis on Darius' character.

71 For a summary of the dissemination and variations, see the entry for ESKANDAR-NAÚMA in the *Encyclopaedia Iranica*. For an early, burlesque version, see Southgate 1978.

72 For the Gilgamesh story, see George 2003.

73 The *Shahnama* is a little easier to find in translation than Nizami. Excerpts were published in a translation by Levy 1967 (the Dārā and 'Sekandar' story is in chapters XVIII–XX). Nizami's *Iskandernama* is available in German translation and partial English translation (Nizami 1881).

CHAPTER 7

1 The chapter epigraph is printed in Mostafavi 1978, p. 219. The author of the poem, on signing his work, boasted that he had composed and inscribed it at the age of nine. The genre of lamentations about past ages is a long-lived and extensive one; for comparable examples from both the third millennium and the Roman period, see van der Spek 2003, p. 326. The lamentation genre, or *sic transit gloria mundi*, is a significant one in the graffiti written in Arabic and Persian on Eastern monuments; see Crone

and Moreh 2000.

2 Solomon in Fars: there are explanations for the local associations with the biblical king and Quranic prophet. Muhammad Mirza Fursat suggested the reason was that Fars was once ruled by a governor called Solomon. This Solomon was the son of Ja'afar and the brother of the famous Abbasid Caliph Harun al-Rashid (Shirazi 1896). Archaeologist Ali Sami cites the association of the original Solomon with magic and the control of djinns, who, it was believed, could have been the only beings capable of raising the structures at Persepolis and Pasargadae (Sami 1971, p. 19).

3 The reception of Classical history: for elaboration and transformation of early Near Eastern and archaic Persian histories in late fifth to fourth century BCE authors see the Persian tales retold by Nicolaus of Damascus and Diodorus Siculus (Diod. 2.24, Nicolaus, Jacoby *FGrHist* 90, and see also the early books of Xenophon's *Cyropaedia*). Historical traditions derived from the Akkadian tradition continued; the third-century BCE multi-lingual historian Berossus drew on chronological sources to reconstruct his Babylon-centric history. His work was little used by later anthologists and survives only in fragments and summaries. The Greek fragments are collected in Jacoby's *FGrHist* 680, translated into English by Burstein 1978.

4 E.g. Cyrus in medieval and early modern literature: see Sancisi-Weerdenburg 1990 and Nadon 2001, pp. 13–25 ('Machiavelli's Cyrus').

5 Persian literature from the early medieval period onwards uses the pre-Islamic Persian past as one of its central reservoirs of material and settings. The earliest Arabic and poetic Persian compendia purported to use pre-Islamic texts as their source material. Some of these claims can be attributed to a rhetoric of authenticity. See Meisami 1999. The history of the ancient dynasties of Persia embedded in Tabari's Islamic universal history is contained in vol. IV of the recent translation by Moshe Perlmann (1987). On the lost 'Book of Lords' or *Khwaday-namag*, a universal history composed in the late Sasanian period, see *CHI* IV, ch. 10(b), and Daryaee 2001–2. For debates about the remembrance of Achaemenid culture, see Roaf 1998 (architecture) and Yarshater 1971 (historical traditions). Firdowsi's *Shahnama*: stories from the *Shahnama* are adapted in V. S. Curtis (1996) and extracts are translated in Levy (1967). For later literary works based on the legendary kings, see the twelfth-century poet Nizami's *Iskandernama* and the *Haft Paykar* or 'Seven Domes', the latter available in a recent Oxford Classics translation (Nizami 1995). Translations of Zoroastrian texts from Avestan Persian vary in their accessibility, styles of translation and even in their original edited source text. For stories of Zoroaster in the archaic court of Vishtasp, see excerpts from the Denkard. For a brief summary on King Jamshid, see Meisami 1999, pp. 167–8. For a summary of the early dynasties in general, see *CHI*, pp. 366–7.

6 For the Donjon at Susa, see the summary in Boucharlat 1997; for Persepolis reuse, see Tilia 1978, vol. 2, and *Archaeological Reports, Iran* 1974. The palace building at Babylon, a neo-

Babylonian foundation with Achaemenid additions, continued to be used and altered in the Hellenistic period.

7 For coin design of the second century BCE, see Wiesehöfer 1996, pl. XVa. Discussions of Achaemenid architectural, artistic and occasionally linguistic influence in the Hellenistic and Parthian periods have included monarchies and centres in Anatolia (Nemrud Dagh, Turkey), Bactria (Ai Khanoum, Bernard 1976), India (Wheeler 1974) and Central Asia and the Caucasus (where there was no distinct break in material culture with the invasion of Alexander).

8 These *frataraka* are discussed briefly in Wiesehöfer 1996, pp. 109–10. For details of the building, see *Iran* 1974, vol. 12.

9 I owe my knowledge of these inscriptions to Shahrokh Razmjou, who kindly showed me his transcription of the Aramaic. I am very grateful to Mark Geller for his preliminary suggestions about the content based on a brief look at this transcription.

10 Wiesehöfer 1996, pp. 159–62, 223–5.

11 Istakhr: earlier writers, including Herzfeld (1935), assumed that the mosque was founded directly on top of a pre-Islamic religious building, possibly a fire temple. Whitcomb (1979), pointing out that the Sasanian grid lay west of the Islamic town, connects the mosque with the building activities of Ziyad ibn Abihi, governor 659–62 CE, who incorporated ancient columns in at least one of his other foundations in Basra. See in particular Whitcomb 1979, p. 347, comparing accounts of the Basra mosque and Persepolis.

12 Qasr-i Abu Nasr: the site was subjected to large-scale excavations in the early 1930s by a Metropolitan Museum of Art team led by C. K. Wilkinson (*Metropolitan Museum of Art Bulletin* 1933–4). Apart from the doorways, they found a few objects that appear to be approximately Achaemenid in date, suggesting possible Achaemenid-period use, or later transferral.

13 These inscriptions are published alongside translations of the Pahlavi in the appendix to the hard-to-find but invaluable *Land of Pars* by Mostafavi, published in English translation in 1978 (pp. 217–19). Arabic texts of the Buyid rulers at Persepolis are discussed in the accessible Blair 1998, pp. 46–9 and fig. 4.18.

14 See Melikian-Chirvani 1971 (historical memories of Fars involving Solomon) and Crone and Morch 2000 (nostalgic graffiti in Arabic, compiled as a literary *florilegium*).

15 For the legendary King Jamshid, see Meisami 1999, pp. 167–8. Shahbazi (1980) argues for an annual ceremony for a different, Mithraic festival at Persepolis.

16 *CHI*, pp. 366–7. Much of the good/evil opposition of this history draws on beliefs related to Zoroastrian cosmology and can be compared to the Achaemenid use of the 'Lie' as an abstract evil.

17 Ibn al-Balkhi: the name ('Son of the Balkhi') was assigned by the author's twentieth-century British editor, Guy Le Strange, on the basis of a

comment in the text that the author's father was from Balkh. Le Strange translated geographical sections in his early journal article (1912); both Mostafavi (1978, pp. 21–2) and Shahbazi (1980) quote from the section describing Persepolis. Meisami (1999, pp. 162ff.) gives a historiographical summary and some context.

18 Underground breezes are referred to nine hundred years later by Captain C. M. Gibbon, who was told that underground passages at Persepolis went some distance and ended in the Charkh-i-Almas or the Diamond Wheel, which was set in motion by Rustam. Its 'strong head wind' and a burning light in mythological literature perhaps also influenced William Beckford's description of the underworld beneath Istakhr.

19 Persian histories in the West: G. T. Minadoi (1587) dealt with the wars between the Turks and the Persians. European powers, perceiving the religious difference of the Shi'a Safavids from the Ottomans, hoped the Persian king could be converted to Catholicism and therefore become an ideological ally against the 'heathen'. Milestones in the critical isolation of ancient sources on Persia, and the desire to discover the reality behind them, were Petrus Bizarus' *Rerum Persicarum Historia* (1583) and the more focused *De Region Persarum Principatu Libri Tres* of Barnabe Brissonius (1590, followed by Livelie 1597). See Lewis 1990 on Brissonius. A later comprehensive work was Hyde 1700.

20 Early modern orientalist dramas: drawing inspiration from accounts of ancient Persia were Thomas Preston for his 'Lamentable tragedy … [of] Cambises king of Persia' (1570) and, in 1595, R. Farrant for his confusing 'Warres of Cyrus King of Persia, against Antiochus king of Assyria'.

21 Sources on the first identification of Achaemenid ruins: the debate about the source of the identification has seesawed between seeing the connection made as a result of the scholarship of missionary monks in Shiraz and attributing it to research back in Europe (see Sancisi-Weerdenburg 1991, pp. 4–6), but a constantly developing dialogue between travellers and Persian sources in Iran is also important. The earliest alleged identification is attributed to Geoffrey Ducket in Hakluyt's compendium of voyages, 1598, vol. 1, pp. 394–401 (first published in 1589). The origin of Ducket's account is mysterious; the printed version is third-hand and a manuscript of his travel account in the British Library (BL MSS 48151b., ff. 169–174b) does not mention Chilminar or Persepolis. He seems to have travelled only between north-west and central Iran. The printed version may have been edited competitively by Hakluyt in order to promote the Muscovy Company. For John Cartwright, see an edited extract in Parker 1999, pp. 106–27 (which also includes extracts from the important first diplomatic mission of the Sherley brothers). Cartwright's account shows only an evangelistic Classicist's determination to locate (prematurely) the sites of Babylon, Ecbatana and Susa. His account, published 1611 but originating from the years 1600–1604, echoes features of Ducket's, but is more extensive and clearly related to Iranian ideas about the history of

Shiraz. An Iranian, 'Uruch' Beg a.k.a. 'Don Juan of Persia', who travelled back to Europe in 1599–1602 with the remains of the Sherley expedition, published a book identifying Persepolis with modern Shiraz, with no mention of Chilminar (Valladolid 1605; English translation, G. Le Strange in 1926) – Uruch Beg was actually from Tabriz. The same identification of Persepolis with modern Shiraz appeared in an account of the travels of Philip II's emissaries by the Goan Augustinian priest de Gouvea between 1602 and 1608, even though he also included a detailed description of the ruins of 'Chilminara', which he connected with Ahasuerus from the biblical book of Esther (see Booth 1902, pp. 13–17); he still significantly influenced Figueroa (below). Ahasuerus was brought to visitors' minds because in the sixteenth century some reports mention 'Ardashir' (a later royal name derived from Artaxerxes). See also discussions (in German) in the excellent Arndt 1984, p. 97.

22 Silva y Figueroa 1620 (reprinted in English in Purchas' *Pilgrimes* five years later). The speed of dissemination of the ideas in Figueroa's letter is clear from an account written by Sir Thomas Herbert, member of the embassy to Persia under Sir Dodmore Cotton in 1627–30, which closely echoes some of the themes and problems of Figueroa. His illustrated *Relation of Some Yeares Travaile … into Afrique and the greater Asia* went into several expanded editions in the eighteenth century and was reprinted (with simplified spellings) in the 1920s (see Vickers 1991 and Ferrier 1977).

23 Maurice 1816.

24 Kaempfer 1712; de Bruijn 1711; Niebuhr 1778.

25 Price 1825, and see Ouseley 1819–23.

26 Heeren 1815, and see discussions by Booth 1902 and Larsen 1996.

27 BM 1821-1-20-14; see Ker Porter 1821 and, on his drawings, Vasileva 1994.

28 Heeren 1815; see Adkins 2003, p. 62.

29 Layard 1849, Larsen 1996.

30 British diplomacy and scholarship: the tomes of Ouseley (3 vols, 1819–21), Kinneir (1813), Malcom (1815), Morier (1818) and Price (1825) formally published the intellectual efforts of the successive missions of Sir John Malcom and Sir Gore Ouseley. William Ouseley (the ambassador's brother, acting as his secretary) wrote his travel memoir as an intensely footnoted culmination of several decades of orientalist studies, not quite constituting a 'Description of Persia' but reaching very close. Morier gives the fullest account of the digging on the Persepolis terrace, which he supervised. For detailed accounts of the routes by which reliefs and casts reached collections in the nineteenth century, see Barnett 1957, with Mitchell 2000 and Curtis 1998; Simpson 2000 describes the cast-making during the nineteenth century.

31 Texier 1842–52; Flandin and Coste 1851; Fergusson (1851) architecturally compared Nineveh and Persepolis.

32 Loftus (1857) also explored southern Iraq: see Larsen 1996, pp. 280–83.

33 On the diaspora of Persepolis reliefs, see Barnett 1957, Roaf 1987, Curtis 1998, Curtis 2000 (BM reliefs pictured) and Mitchell 2000.

34 Qajar Achaemenidizing: the buildings of the Afifabad garden were begun in 1867 by Mirza 'Ali Mohammad Khan. The Narenjestan complex was constructed between 1879 and 1886: the first was the country seat of the Qavam ol-Molk, the second their townhouse. Photos from the archive of Mansour Sane, published in *Be-yad-e Shiraz* 'In Memory of Shiraz' (2001–2/1380) show gatherings in these courts. Lerner (1980) gives a fascinating history of similar Qajar sculptures in the Brooklyn Museum that had been later stained to look more ancient and sold abroad in 1898 as genuine antiquities.

35 Inscribed on one of the northern doorways of the Palace of Darius, translation by Sharp in Mostafavi 1978, p. 228.

36 Mostafavi 1978, p. 229.

37 Stolze, Andreas and Nöldeke 1882. The two volumes are now rare, but accessible in older research libraries; many of the plates were reproduced despite having faded, or being from overexposed and often shattered glass negatives. The expedition got off to a shaky start: a telegram from Stolze in Shiraz in February 1875 demanded to know the whereabouts of Andreas, who had gone AWOL in London. Nudged on to a steamer from Southampton by his German professor Hoffmann and an English contact, Andreas nevertheless took the time between boats to lecture the Bombay branch of the Royal Asiatic Society on the massive range of his projected research project. It is possible that Andreas and Stolze took some part in the governor's excavations. Some letters and documents relating to this early research trip now form part of the Herzfeld Papers in the archives of the Freer Gallery of Art, Washington (N-130); Ernst Herzfeld perhaps used them as research pointers for his own trips.

38 Blundell 1893, pp. 537–8. Weld's story about the consequences (the governor was about to be removed from office) is remarkably similar to tales told about governors' misdeeds at the ruins, repeated since two early French travellers (Daulier-Deslandes and Thevenot) visited in the 1660s and understood from what they were told that the governor had destroyed sculptures in order to be relieved of the trouble of escorting visitors there; de Bruijn made exactly the same allegations in 1711, as did Morier a century later. The theme has more to do with the attitude of the denizens of Marv Dasht to the city authorities than with an official policy of vandalism.

39 Robinson 1982, p. 295.

40 Gibbon 1909: while this tale is an amalgam of folktale and political anxiety over foreign interference, one cannot help noting that the incident is dated (roughly) between the activities of Stolze and Weld at the site. Another tale has some Greeks plundering a tomb, perhaps generated by hostile feelings older than by the advent of Englishmen.

41 Browne 1893, p. 250.

42 The French Mission to Iran: the link was concrete – when requesting permission to build the 'Château' (which stood on land belonging to the nearby shrine of Daniel), the local sheikh 'granted the desired authority, on condition that when there were no more French at Susa to live in it, the house should be placed at the disposal of the administrators of the domain of Daniel' (Dieulafoy 1887b, p. 16). It is disconcerting to recognize in the Dieulafoys' affable and popular assistants, Messrs Babin and Houssay, the two 'very unsociable and reticent' scholars of Browne's anecdote. For Sackville-West's arch account (1926), see ch. 8. Original publications: Marcel Dieulafoy, 1893 and 1913; J. Dieulafoy, 1887 and 1888; Madame Dieulafoy wrote an English-language summary article for *Harper's New Monthly Magazine* (June 1887, vol. 75, no. 445). Morgan summarized the early excavations in *La délégation en Perse*; modern surveys of the subsequent work under J. de Morgan are available from the Réunion des musées nationaux (Chevalier 1997) and Harper, Aruz and Tallon 1992, pp. 16–24.

43 Stein 1940; see Wang 1999.

44 Bohrer 1999.

45 Herzfeld and Upham Pope: for the early rock relief survey, see Sarre and Herzfeld 1910. Herzfeld's diaries and papers are kept in the archives of the Arthur M. Sackler Gallery and the Freer Gallery of Art, Washington, DC, with some in the Metropolitan Museum of Art, New York (see Hennessey 1992 and Root 1976). On the ambiguities of his position at Persepolis, see an excellent discussion by Gunter and Root (1998) and Gunter and Hauser 2004. On Arthur Upham Pope, the most famous scholar of Persian art of the time, who was very involved in the export of Iranian artefacts of all periods, see select papers in Gluck and Siver 1996 and comments in Muscarella 1999.

46 Sarre's 1923 publication is an example of the desire to survey all pre-Islamic art (and reproduces some of Stolze and Andreas' pictures). Exhibitions of Persian art were held in 1926 in Philadelphia, in 1930 in Detroit, and in 1931 at the Royal Academy at Burlington House, London, in response to which the British Museum casts were redisplayed. Letters relating to competition over sites can be found in Gluck and Siver 1996. For Ada Small Moore's support of the Persepolis excavation, see Sensabaugh and Matheson 2002 and Breasted 1943. The Metropolitan Museum's excavations at Qasr-i Abu Nasr were published in the museum's bulletin in 1932–3 and 1933–4.

47 Dahan-i Guleiman: unfortunately not fully published but dated to the first half of the Achaemenid period (sixth to fifth centuries BCE), see Scerrato 1966 and a summary in Boucharlat forthcoming.

48 In English, Sylvia Matheson's *Persia: An Archaeological Guide* (second edition 1976) is still a good survey of the early archaeological work undertaken almost until the Islamic revolution in 1979; only now is a project under way to revise it. For Fars, see Mostafavi 1978, which is

also a good guide to the many relevant publications in Persian. Sami's guides to Fars, Shiraz and Persepolis were published in 1956 and 1958.

49 The Shahbanou Farah's discomfort at the event is recorded in Blanch 1978, pp. 133–5; almost an entire issue of *Kayan International*, 5 October 1971 (Mehr 23, 1350), was dedicated to the event: 'Congratulations to the World's Most Experienced Monarchy' (see Nemazee 1971).

50 Khamanaei 1988.

51 For a survey of the state of knowledge for Iron age and Achaemenid sites, see Boucharlat forthcoming.

BIBLIOGRAPHY

ABBREVIATIONS AND SOURCES

Achaemenid History 1–9 (conference proceedings). Leiden, Nederlands Instituut voor Het Nabije Oosten.

AMI Archäologischer Mitteilungen aus Iran

CAH Cambridge Ancient History

CHI Cambridge History of Iran

FGrHist Jacoby, F. (1923–). *Fragmente der griechischen Historiker*

Agathias *Histories*

Arrian *Anabasis*

Athenaeus *Deipnosophistae*

Quintus Curtius Rufus *History of Alexander*

Diodorus Siculus *Library of History*

Herodotus *Histories*

Photius *Library*

Plutarch *Lives of Artaxerxes, Alexander*

(Plutarch) *De Mundo*

Thucydides *Histories*

Anonymous, ed. (1998). *Regards sur la perse antique: exposition, eglise saint-cyran du blanc et musee d'argentomagus a saint-marcel, 21 juin–20 septembre 1998*, Le Blanc / Argentomagus.

Adkins, L. (2003). *Empires of the Plain*. London, HarperCollins.

Arndt, H. (1984). *Persepolis – Entdeckungs-reisen in die Vergangenheit*. Stuttgart, Edition Erdmann in K. Thienemanns Verlag.

Auberger, J. (1991). *Ctésias Histoires de L'Orient*. Paris, Les Belles Lettres.

Babelon, M. E. (1893). *Les Perses Achéménides, les satrapes et les dynastes tributaires de leur empire, Chypre et Phénicie*. Paris.

Balcer, J. M. (1987). *Herodotus and Bisitun: Problems in Ancient Persian Historiography*. Stuttgart, Steiner Verlag Wiesbaden.

Barbaro, J. and Ambrogie, C. (1873). *Travels to Tania and Persia*. London.

Barnett, R. D. (1957). 'Persepolis'. *Iran* 19: 55–77.

Beckford, W. (1796). *An Arabian Tale (The History of the Caliph Vathek), from an Unpublished Manuscript*. London, J. Johnson.

Beg, U., trans. G. Le Strange (1926). *Don Juan of Persia, A Shi'ah Catholic*. London, Broadway Traveller.

Bernard, P. (1976). 'Les traditions orientales dans l'architecture bactrienne'. *Journal Asiatique*: 245-55.

Bickerman, E. J. (1967). *Four Strange Books of the Bible*. New York.

Bivar, A. D. H. (1985). 'Achaemenid Coins, Weights and Measures'. *CHI* 2: 610–29.

Bizarus, P. (1583). *Rerum Persicarum Historia*. Antwerp, C. Plantinius.

Blair, S. S. (1998). *Islamic Inscriptions*. New York, New York University Press.

Blanch, L. (1978). *Farah Shahbanou of Iran*. London, Collins.

Blundell, H. Weld (1893). 'Persepolis'. In E. Delmar Morgan, ed., *Transactions of the Ninth International Congress of Orientalists II*. London, International Congress of Orientalists: **II** 537–59.

Boardman, J., ed. (1988). *CAH: Plates to Volume IV – Persia, Greece and the Western Mediterranean c.525 to 479 B.C.* Cambridge, Cambridge University Press.

Boardman, J. (2000). *Persia and the West: An Archaeological Investigation of the Genesis of Achaemenid Art*. London, Thames and Hudson.

Bohrer, F. N., ed. (1999). *Sevruguin and the Persian Image – Photographs of Iran, 1870–1930*. Washington, Seattle and London, Arthur M. Sackler Gallery and University of Washington Press.

Booth, A. J. (1902). *The Discovery and Decipherment of the Trilingual Cuneiform Inscriptions*. London, Longman.

Bosworth, A. B. (1980). 'Alexander and the Iranians'. *Journal of Hellenic Studies* 100: 1–21.

Bosworth, A. B. (1988). *Conquest and Empire: The Reign of Alexander the Great*. Cambridge, Cambridge University Press.

Boucharlat, R. (1997). 'Susa under Achaemenid Rule'. In J. Curtis, ed., *Mesopotamia and Iran in the Persian Period*. London, British Museum Press: 54–67.

Boucharlat, R. (forthcoming). 'La période achéménide en Iran: Données archéologiques'. In P. Briant, ed., *L'archéologie de l'empire Achéménide*. Paris.

Boucharlat, R. and Labrousse. (1979). 'Le palais d'Artaxerxes II sur la rive droite du Chaour à Suse'. *Cahiers de la DAFI* 10: 19–136.

Boyce, M. (1984). *Zoroastrians: Their Religious Beliefs and Practices*. New York, Routledge and Kegan Paul.

Breasted, C. (1943). *Pioneer to the Past: The Story of James Henry Breasted, Archaeologist*. Chicago, University of Chicago Press.

Bregstein, L. (1996). 'Sealing Practices in the Fifth Century B.C. Murašu Archive from Nippur, Iraq'. *Bulletin de Correspondance Hellénique Supplement* 29: 53–63.

Briant, P. (1989). 'Table du roi, tribut et redistribution chez les Achéménides'. In P. Briant and C. Herrenschmidt, eds, *Le Tribut dans l'Empire Perse – Actes de la Table ronde de Paris 12–13 Décembre 1986*. Paris and Louvain, Peeters: 35–44.

Briant, P. (1994). 'L'eau du Grand Roi'. In L. Milano, ed., *Drinking in Ancient Societies: History and Culture of Drinks in the Ancient Near East*. Padua.

Briant, P. (2001). *Bulletin d'histoire achéménide II 1997–2000*. Paris, Thotm-Editions.

Briant, P. (2002). *From Cyrus to Alexander: A History of the Persian Empire*. Winona Lake, Ind., Eisenbrauns.

Briant, P. (2003). *Darius sous l'ombre d'Alexandre*. Paris, Fayard.

Briant, P. and Boucharlat, R., eds. (forthcoming). *L'archéologie de l'empire achéménide: Actes du colloque international*. Paris.

Brissonius, B. (1583). *De Regione Persarum Prinicipatu Libri Tres*. Strasburg, Joh. Frid Spoor.

Brosius, M. (1996). *Women in Ancient Persia 559–331 BC*. Oxford, Clarendon Press.

Brosius, M. (2000). *The Persian Empire from Cyrus II to Artaxerxes I*. London, London Association of Classical Teachers.

Brosius, M., ed. (2003). *Ancient Archives and Archival Traditions: Concepts of Record-keeping in the Ancient World*. Oxford and New York, Oxford University Press.

Brosius, M. and Kuhrt, A., eds. (1998). *Achaemenid History* 11: *Studies in Persian History: Essays in Memory of David M. Lewis*.

Browne, E.G. (1893). *A Year Amongst the Persians: Impressions as to the Life, Character and Thought of the People of Persia*. London, A. and C. Black.

Bruijn, C. de (1711). *Reizen over Moskovie, door Persie en Indie . . .* Amsterdam.

Burstein, S. M. (1978). *The Babyloniaca of Berossus*. Malibu, Undena.

Cahill, N. (1985). 'The Treasury at Persepolis: Gift-Giving at the City of the Persians'. *American Journal of Archaeology* 89: 373–89.

Cameron, G. G. (1948). *Persepolis Treasury Tablets*. Chicago, The Oriental Institute of Chicago.

Cardascia, G. (1977). 'Armée et fiscalité dans le monde antique'. *Colloques Nationaux du Centre National de la Recherche Scientifique*. Paris. 936: 1–11.

Carradice, I. (1987). 'The "Regal Coinage" of the Persian Empire'. In I. Carradice, ed., *Coinage and Administration in the Athenian and Persian Empires*. London, British Archaeological Reports International Series 343.

Chevalier, N., ed. (1997). *Une mission en Perse 1897–1912*. Les dossiers du musée du Louvre. Paris, Réunion des musées nationaux.

Cohen, A. (1997). *The Alexander Mosaic: Stories of Victory and Defeat*. Cambridge, Cambridge University Press.

Collon, D. (1987). *First Impressions: Cylinder Seals in the Ancient Near East*. London, British Museum Press.

Collon, D. (1996). 'A Hoard of Sealings from Ur'. *Bulletin de Correspondance Hellénique Supplement, Archives et Sceaux du Monde Hellénistique* (Athens, Ecole française d'Athènes) 29: 65–84.

Cowley, A. (1923). *Aramaic Papyri of the Fifth Century B.C.* Oxford, Clarendon Press.

Crone, P. and Moreh, S. (2000). *The Book of Strangers, Medieval Arabic Graffiti on the Theme of Nostalgia – Attributed to Abu'l-Faraj al-Isfahani*. Princeton, Markus Wiener Publishers.

Curtis, J., Cowell, M. and Walker, C. (1995). 'A Silver Bowl of Artaxerxes I'. *Iran* 33: 149–52.

Curtis, J. (1997). 'A. W. Franks and the Oxus Treasure'. In J. Cherry and M. Caygill, eds, *A. W. Franks: Nineteenth-century Collecting and the British Museum*. London, British Museum Press.

Curtis, J. (1998). 'A Chariot Scene from Persepolis'. *Iran* 36: 45–9.

Curtis, J. (2000). *Ancient Persia*. London, British Museum Press.

Curtis, J. and Finkel, I. (1999). 'Game Boards and Other Incised Graffiti at Persepolis'. *Iran* 37: 45–8.

Curtis, J. and Kruszyñski, M. (2002). *Ancient Caucasian and Related Material in the British Museum*. London, British Museum Research Paper.

Curtis, J. E. and Reade, J. E., eds (1995). *Art and Empire: Treasures from Assyria in the British Museum*. London, British Museum Press.

Curtis, V. S. (1996). *Persian Myths*. London, British Museum Press.

Cuyler Young, T. and Levine, L. D. (1974). *Excavations of the Godin Project: Second Progress Report*. Toronto, Royal Ontario Museum.

Dalley, S. (2001). 'Assyrian Court Narratives in Aramaic and Egyptian Historical Fiction'. In Aburd et al, eds, *Historiography in the Cuneiform World*. Bethesda, MD: 149–61.

Dalton, O. M. (1964). *The Treasure of the Oxus*. London, British Museum.

Demargne, P. (1983). 'Serviteurs orientaux sur deux monuments funéraires de Xanthos'. In *Festschrift K. Bittel*. Mainz.

Daryaee (2000–1). 'Memory and History: The Construction of the Past in Late Antique Persia'. *Name-ye Iran-e Bastan* 1 (2): 1–14.

Demargne, P. (1983). 'Serviteurs orientaux sur deux monuments funéraires de Xanthos'. In *Festschrift K. Bittel*. Mainz.

Demargne, P. and Childs, W. A. P. (1989). *Le monument des néréides: le décor sculpté*. Paris, Klinckriech.

Dieulafoy, J. (1887a). *La Perse, la Chaldée, et la Susiane*. Paris.

Dieulafoy, J. (1887b). 'The Excavations at Susa'. *Harper's New Monthly Magazine* 75: 3–23.

Dieulafoy, J. (1888). *A Suse, Journal des fouilles*.

Drews, R. (1973). *The Greek Accounts of Eastern History*.

Driver, G. R. (1957). *Aramaic Papyri of the Fifth Century B.C.* Oxford, Clarendon Press.

Dusinberre, E. (2002). *Aspects of Empire in Achaemenid Sardis*. Cambridge and New York, Cambridge University Press.

Fergusson, J. (1851). *The Palaces of Nineveh and Persepolis Restored: An Essay on Ancient Assyrian and Persian Architecture*. London.

Ferrier, R. W. (1977). 'The First English Guide Book to Persia: A Description of the Persian Monarchy'. *Iran* 15: 75–88.

Flandin, E. and Coste, P. (1851). *Voyage en Perse de M. E. Flandin et P. Coste pendant les années 1840 et 1841. Relation du voyage par M. E. Flandin Perse ancienne Planches*. Paris.

Fukai, trans. E. B. Crawford. (1977). *Persian Glass*. New York.

Gabelmann, H. (1984). *Antike Audienz- und Tribunalszenen*. Darmstadt, Wiss. Buchges.

Garrison, M. and Root, M.C. (2001). *Seals on the Persepolis Fortification Tablets: Images of Heroic Encounter*. Chicago, The Oriental Institute of Chicago.

Geertz, C. (1983). *Local Knowledge: Further Essays in Interpretive Anthropology*. New York, Basic Books.

George, A. (2003). *The Epic of Gilgamesh: The Babylonian Epic Poem and Other Texts in Akkadian and Sumerian*. London, Penguin.

Gibbon, C. M. (1909). 'Some Persian Folklore Stories concerning the Ruins of Persepolis'. *Journal and Proceedings of the Asiatic Society of Bengal* N.S. 5: 279–97.

Gluck, J. and Siver, N., eds (1996). *Surveyors of Persian Art: A Documentary Biography of Arthur Upham Pope and Phyllis Ackerman*. Costa Mesa, California, Mazda.

Godard, A. (1954). 'The Newly Found Palace of Prince Xerxes at Persepolis and the Sculptures which the Architects Rejected'. London, *Illustrated London News*: 2 January.

Graf, D. F. (1993). 'The Persian Royal Road System in Syria–Palestine'. *Transeuphratène* 6: 149–68.

Graf, D. F. (1994). 'The Persian royal road system'. In H. Sancisi-Weerdenburg, A. Kuhrt and M. C. Root, eds, *Achaemenid History* 8: *Continuity and Change*: 167–89.

Grayson, A. K. (1975). *Assyrian and Babylonian Chronicles*. New York, J. J. Augustin.

Greenfield, J. C. (1986). 'Aspects of Archives in the Achaemenid Period'. In K. Veenhof, ed., *Cuneiform Archives and Libraries*. Istanbul and Leiden: 289–95.

Greenfield, J. C. and Porten, B. (1982). *The Bisitun Inscription of Darius the Great: Aramaic Version*. London, SOAS for the Corpus Inscriptionum Iranicarum.

Gunter, A. and Hauser, S., eds (2004). *Ernst Herzfeld and the Development of Near Eastern Studies 1900–1950*. Leiden, E. J. Brill.

Gunter, A. and Root, M. C. (1998). 'Replicating, Inscribing, Giving: Ernst Herzfeld and the Artaxerxes' Silver Phiale in the Freer Gallery of Art'. *Ars Orientalis* 28: 3–38.

Haerinck, E. (1973). 'Le Palais Achéménide de Babylone'. *Iranica Antiqua* 10: 108–32.

Hakluyt, R. (1598). *The Principall Navigations, Voiages, and Discoveries of the English Nation*. London.

Hallock, R. T. (1960). 'A New Look at the Persepolis Treasury Tablets'. *Journal of Near Eastern Studies* 19: 90–100.

Hallock, R. T. (1969). *Persepolis Fortification Tablets*. Chicago, University of Chicago Press.

Harper, P. O., Aruz, J. and Tallon, F., eds (1992). *The Royal City of Susa – Ancient Near Eastern Treasures in the Louvre*. New York, Metropolitan Museum of Art.

Heeren. (1815). *Ideen über die Politik, den Vehrkehr und den Handel der vornehousten Völker der alter Welt*. Göttingen.

Helms, S.W. (1982). 'Excavations at the "city and the famous fortress of Kandahar"'. *Afghan Studies* 3–4: 1–24.

Henkelman, W. (2003). 'Persians, Medes and Elamites: Acculturation in the Neo-Elamite period'. In G. B. Lanfranchi, M. Roaf and R. Rollinger, eds, *Continuity of Empire (?) Assyria, Media, Persia*. Padua: S.a.r.go.n., Editrice e Libreria: 181–232.

Henkelman, W. and Kuhrt, A., eds (2003). *Achaemenid History* 13: *A Persian Perspective: Essays in Memory of Helene Sancisi-Weerdenburg*.

Hennessey, C. (1992). 'The Ernst Herzfeld Papers at the Freer Gallery of Art and Arthur M. Sackler Gallery Archives'. *Bulletin of the Asia Institute* 6: 131–41.

Herbert, S.T. (1665). *A Relation of Some Yeares Travaile Begunne Anno 1626 Into Afrique and the Greater Asia, especially the Territories of the Persian Monarchie . . .* London, I.B. for Andrew Crooke at the Green Dragon in St Paul's Churchyard.

Herrenschmidt, C. (1989). 'Le paragraphe 70 de l'inscription de Bisotun'. In *Études irano-aryennes offertes à Gilbert Lazard*, 7. Paris, Association pour l'Avancement des Études Iraniennes.

Herzfeld, E. (1935). *Ancient Iran*.

Hornblower, S. (1982). *Mausolus*. Oxford and New York, Oxford University Press.

Hornblower, S. (1994). 'Persia'. In *CAH* **VI**: 45–96. Cambridge.

Hyde, T. (1700). *Historia religionis veterum Persarum, eorumque Magorum . . .* Oxford, Clarendon Press.

Isserlin, B. S. J., Jones, R. E., Papamarinopoulos, S. and Uren, J. (1994). 'The Canal of Xerxes: Preliminary Investigations in 1991 and 1992'. *Annual of the British School at Athens* **89**: 277–84.

Javakhishvili, A. and Abramishvili, G., eds (1986). *Jewellery and Metalwork in the Museums of Georgia*. Leningrad, Aurora Art Publishers.

Jidejian, N. (1971). *Sidon Through the Ages*. Beirut, Dar El-Machreq.

Johnson, J. H. (1974). 'The Demotic Chronicle as an Historical Source'. *Enchoria* **4**: 1–17.

Kaboli, M. A. (2000). 'The Apadana Gateway at Shurh'. *Iran* **38**: 161–2.

Kaempfer, E. (1712). *Amoenitatum Exoticarum Politico-Physico-Medicarum Fasciuli V. Quibus Continentur Variae Relationes, Observationes & Descriptiones Rerum Persicarum & Ulterioris Asiae*. Lengoriae, Henrici Wilhelmi Meyeri.

Kaptan, D. (2002). *Achaemenid History* **12**: *The Daskyleion Bullae: Seal Images from the Western Periphery of the Achaemenid Empire*.

Keen, A. G. (1998). *Dynastic Lycia: A Political History of the Lycians and Their Relations with Foreign Powers, c. 545–362 B.C.* Leiden, Brill.

Kent, R. G. (1953). *Old Persian: Grammar, Texts, Lexicon*. New Haven, American Oriental Society.

Ker Porter, R. (1821). *Travels in Georgia, Persia, Armenia, Ancient Babylonia*.

Khamanaei, S. A. (1988). *Takhte-Jamshid (Persepolis)*, Iranian Cultural Heritage Organization: 1-2.

Kinneir, J. M. (1813). *A Geographical Memoir of the Persian Empire, Accompanied by a Map*. London, John Murray.

Kleiss (1981). 'Ein Abschnitt der achaemenidischen Königstrasse von Pasargadae und Persepolis nach Susa, bei Naqsh-i Rustam'. *Archäologische Mitteilungen aus Iran* **14**: 45–53.

Knapton, Sarraf, M. R. and Curtis, J. (2001). 'Inscribed Column Bases from Hamadan'. *Iran* **39**: 99–117.

Knauss, F. (2000). 'Der "Palast" von Gumbati und die Rolle der Achaimeniden im transkaukasischen Iberien'. *Archäologische Mitteilungen aus Iran* **32**: 119–30.

Knauss, F. (2001). 'Persian Rule in the North Achaemenid Palaces on the Periphery of the Empire'. In I. Nielsen, ed., *The Royal Palace Institution in the First Millennium BC, Regional Development and Cultural Exchange between East and West*. Aarhus, Danish Institute at Athens: 125–43.

Koldewey, R., trans. A. Johns. (1914). *The Excavations at Babylon*. London.

Krefter, F. (1971). *Persepolis Rekonstruktioner*. Berlin.

Kuhrt, A. (1983). 'The Cyrus Cylinder and Achaemenid imperial policy'. In *Journal of Studies in the Old Testament* **25**: 83–97.

Kuhrt, A. (1987). 'Usurpation, conquest and ceremonial: from Babylon to Persia'. In D. Cannadine and Price, eds, *Rituals of Royalty, Power and Ceremonial in Traditional Societies*. Cambridge University Press.

Kuhrt, A. (1990). 'Achaemenid Babylonia: sources and problems'. In *Achaemenid History* **4**: *Centre and Periphery*: 177–94.

Kuhrt, A. (1995). *The Ancient Near East c. 3000–330 BC*. London and New York, Routledge.

Kuhrt, A. (forthcoming). *Sourcebook for Achaemenid History*. London and New York, Routledge.

Kuhrt, A. and Sherwin-White, S. (1987). 'Xerxes' Destruction of Babylonian Temples'. In H. Sancisi-Weerdenburg and A. Kuhrt, eds, *Achaemenid History* **2**: *The Greek Sources*: 9–78.

Labat, R. (1946). 'Le sort des substituts royaux en Assyrie au temps des Sargonides'. *Revue Assyriologique* **40**: 123–42.

Lanfranchi, G., Roaf, M. and Rollinger, R., eds (2003). *Continuity of Empire (?) Assyria, Media, Persia*. History of the Ancient Near East / Monographs. Padua, S.a.r.g.o.n. Editrice e Libreria.

Lanfranchi, G. B. and Parpola, S. (1990). *The Correspondence of Sargon II Part II – Letters from the Northern and Northeastern Provinces*. Helsinki, Helsinki University Press.

Larsen, M. T. (1996). *The Conquest of Assyria: Excavations in an Antique Land, 1840–1860*. London and New York, Routledge.

Layard, R. (1849). *Nineveh and Its Remains*. London, John Murray.

Le Strange, G. (1912). 'Description of the Province of Fars in Persia, at the Beginning of the Twelfth Century A.D'. *Journal of the Royal Asiatic Society*: 1–30, 311–39, 865–89.

Le Strange, G. and Nicholson, R. A. (1962). *The Farsnama of Ibn u'l- Balkhi*. Cambridge, Cambridge University Press.

Lecoq, P. (1990). 'Observations sur le sens du mot dahyu dans les inscriptions achéménides'. *Transeuphratène* **3**: 131–40.

Lecoq, P. (1997). *Les inscriptions de la Perse achéménide*. Paris, Gallimard.

Lenfant, D. (2004). *Ctesias de Cnide, La Perse, L'Inde, Autre fragments*. Paris, Les Belles Lettres.

Lerner, J. A. (1973). 'A Painted Relief from Persepolis'. *Archaeology* **26/2** (April): 116–22.

Lerner, J. A. (1980). 'Three Achaemenid "Fakes"'. *Expedition*: 5–6.

Levy, R. (1967). *The Epic of the Kings, Shah-nama: The National Epic of Persia by Ferdowsi*. London, Routledge and Kegan Paul.

Lewis, D. (1987). 'The King's Dinner (Polyaen. IV 3, 32)'. In H. Sancisi-Weerdenburg and A. Kuhrt, eds, *Achaemenid History* **2**: *The Greek Sources*: 79–87.

Lewis, D. M. (1977). *Sparta and Persia: Lectures Delivered at the University of Cincinnati, Autumn 1976 in Memory of Donald W. Bradeen*. Leiden, Brill.

Lewis, D. M. (1980). 'Datis the Mede'. *Journal of Hellenic Studies* **100**: 194–5.

Lewis, D. M. (1990). 'Brissonius: De Regio Persarum Principatu Libri Tres'. In H. Sancisi-Weerdenburg and J. W. Drijvers, eds, *Achaemenid History* **5**: *The Roots of the European Tradition*: 67–78.

Lewis, D. M. (1994). 'The Persepolis Tablets: Speech, Seal and Script'. In A. K. Bowman and G. Woolf, eds, *Literacy and Power in the Ancient World*. Cambridge, Cambridge University Press: 17–32.

Lichtheim, M. (1980). *Ancient Egyptian Literature: A Book of Readings*. Berkeley, Los Angeles and London, University of California Press.

Livelie, E. (1597). *True Chronologie of the Times of the Persian Monarchie . . .* London.

Liverani, M. (2003). 'The Rise and Fall of Media'. In G. Lanfranchi, M. Roaf and R. Rollinger, eds. *Continuity of Empire (?) Assyria, Media, Persia*. Padua, S.a.r.g.o.n. Editrice et Libreria: 1–12.

Lloyd, A. B. (1994). 'Egypt, 404–332 B.C'. In D. M. Lewis, J. Boardman, S. Hornblower and M. Ostwald, eds, *The Fourth Century B.C.* Cambridge, Cambridge University Press: **VI**: 337–60.

Loftus, W. K. (1857). *Travels and Researches in Chaldaea and Susiana with an Account of Excavations at Warka, the 'Erech' of Nimrod, and Shush, 'Shushan the Palace' of Esther in 1849–52*. London, James Nisbet.

Malandra, W. W. (1983). *An Introduction to Ancient Iranian Religion, Readings from the Avesta and Achaemenid Inscriptions*. Minneapolis, University of Minnesota Press.

Malcom, J. (1815). *The History of Persia: From the Most Early Period to the Present Time*. London, John Murray.

Mardrus, J. C. (revised by P. Mathers) (1993). *The Book of the Thousand Nights and One Night*. London and New York, Routledge.

Matheson, S. A. (1976). *Persia: An Archaeological Guide*. London, Faber and Faber.

Matheson, S. A. (1987). *Persia: An Archaeological Guide (illustrated)*. Tehran, Yassavoli.

Mathieson, I., Bettles, E., Davies, S. and Smith, H. S. (1995). 'A Stela of the Persian Period from Saqqara'. *Journal of Egyptian Archaeology* **81**: 23–42.

Maurice, T. (1816). *Observations on the Ruins of Babylon as Recently Visited and Described by Claudius James Rich, Esq. Resident for the East India Company at Bagdad*. London, John Murray.

Meiggs, R. and Lewis, D. (1988). *A Selection of Greek Historical Inscriptions*. Oxford, Oxford University Press.

Meisami, J. (1999). *Persian Historiography*. Edinburgh, Edinburgh University Press.

Melikian-Chirvani, A. S. (1971). 'Le royaume de Salomon, les inscriptions Persanes de Sites Achéménides'. In *Le monde iranien et l' Islam, sociétés et cultures.* Geneva and Paris: **1**: 1–41.

Miller, M. C. (1997). *Athens and Persia in the Fifth Century BC.* Cambridge, Cambridge University Press.

Minadoi, G. T. (1587). *The History of the Warres betweene the Turkes and the Persians.* London.

Miroschedji, P. de. (1985). 'La fin du royaume d'Anšan et la naissance de l'Empire perse'. In *Zeitschrift für Assyriologie* **75**: 265-306.

Mitchell, T. (2000). 'The Persepolis Sculptures in the British Museum'. *Iran* **38**: 49–56.

Momigliano. (1977). 'Eastern Elements in Post-Exilic Jewish and Greek Historiography'. In *Essays in Ancient and Modern Historiography.* Oxford, Clarendon Press.

Moorey, P. R. S. (1980). *Cemeteries of the First Millennium B.C. at Deve Hüyük, near Carchemish, Salvaged by T. E. Lawrence and C. L. Woolley in 1913.* Oxford, British Archaeological Reports.

Moorey, P. R. S. (1988). 'The Persian Empire'. In J. Boardman, ed., *Cambridge Ancient History Plates to Volume IV – Persia, Greece and the Western Mediterranean c.525 to 479 B.C.* Cambridge, Cambridge University Press.

Moorey, P. R. S. (1998). 'Material Aspects of Achaemenid Polychrome Decoration and Jewellery'. *Iranica Antiqua* **33**: 155–71.

Morgan, J. de (1905). 'Découverte d'une sépulture d'époque achéménide à Suse'. *Memoirs de le Délégation en Perse* **8**: 29–58.

Morier, J. (1818). *A Second Journey through Persia, Armenia and Asia Minor to Constantinople between the years 1810 and 1816; together with an account of the proceedings of His Majesty's Embassy under Sir Gore Ouseley, Bart.* London.

Mørkholm, O. (1974). 'A Coin of Artaxerxes III'. *Numismatic Chronicle* **14**: 1–4.

Mostafavi, S. M. T. (1978). *The Land of Pars – The Historical Monuments and the Archaeological Sites of the Province of Fars.* Chippenham, Wilts, Picton Publishing.

Murray, O. (1987). 'Herodotus and Oral History'. In H. Sancisi-Weerdenburg and A. Kuhrt, eds, *Achaemenid History 2: The Greek Sources.*

Muscarella, O. W. (1980). 'Excavated and unexcavated Achaemenian art'. In Schmandt-Benerat, ed., *Ancient Persia: The Art of an Empire.* Malibu: 23–42.

Muscarella, O. W. (1987). 'Median art and Medizing Scholarship'. *Journal of Near Eastern Studies* **46**: 109–27.

Nadon, C. (2001). *Xenophon's Prince, Republic and Empire in the Cyropaedia.* Berkeley, Los Angeles and London, University of California Press.

Nemazee, S. (1971). 'Monarch Calls for World Free from Fear'. *Kayhan International Edition.* Tehran, 15 Oct: 1f.

Niebuhr, C. (1778). *Reisebeschreibung nach Arabien und anderen umliegenden Ländern.* Copenhagen.

Nielsen, I., ed. (2001). *The Royal Palace Institution in the First Millennium BC: Regional Development and Cultural Exchange between East and West.* Aarhus, Danish Institute at Athens.

Nizami Ganjavi, trans. W. H. Clarke (1881). *The Sikandar nama e bara, or, Book of Alexander the Great.* London, W. H. Allen.

Nizami Ganjavi, trans. J. Scott Meisami (1995). *Haft Paykar, a Medieval Persian Romance.* Oxford and New York, Oxford University Press.

Nollé, M. (1992). *Denkmäler von Satrapensitz Dashyleion: Studien zur graeco-persisches Kunst.* Berlin, Akademie Verlag.

Nylander, C. (1968a). 'Assyria Grammata: Remarks on the 21st Letter of Themistocles'. *Opuscula Atheniensia* **8**: 119–36.

Nylander, C. (1968b). 'Who Wrote the Inscriptions at Pasargadae?' *Orientalia Suecana* **16**: 135–78.

Nylander, C. (1970). *Ionians in Pasargadae: Studies in Old Persian Architecture.* Uppsala, Acta Universitatis Upsaliensis.

Nylander, C. (1993). 'Darius III – the Coward King, Point and Counterpoint'. In Carlsen et al, eds, *Alexander the Great, Reality and Myth.* Rome.

Oates, J. and Oates, D. (2001). *Nimrud: An Assyrian Imperial City Revealed.* London, British School of Archaeology in Iraq.

Oppenheim, A. L. (1973). 'A note on ša rēši'. *Journal of Ancient Near Eastern Studies* **5**: 325–34.

Ouseley, Sir W. (1819–23). *Travels in Various Countries of the East: More Particularly Persia.* London, Rodwell and Martin.

Parker, K., ed. (1999). *Early Modern Tales of Orient: A Critical Anthology.* London and New York, Routledge.

Pearson, L. (1960). *The Lost Histories of Alexander the Great.* Oxford and New York, The American Philological Association.

Peat, J. (1989). 'Cyrus "King of Lands", Cambyses "King of Babylon": The disputed co-regency'. *Journal of Classical Studies* **31**: 199–216.

Perlmann, M. (1987). *The History of al-Tabari – The Ancient Kingdoms.* Albany, State University of New York Press.

Pichikiyan, I. R. (1981). 'The Temple of the Oxus'. *Journal of the Royal Asiatic Society*: 133–67.

Pitiscus, J. (1693). *Q. Curtii Rufi Alexander Magnus, et in ilum commentarius Samuelis Pitisci . . . figurae ex veterum monumentis ad historiam Alexandri illustrandam depromptae, illarumque exegesis.* Utrecht.

Porada, E. (1965). *Ancient Iran – The Art of Pre-Islamic Times.* London, Methuen.

Posener, G. (1936). *La première domination perse en Egypte: recueil d'inscriptions hiéroglyphiques.* Cairo, Institut français d'archéologie orientale.

Potts, D. T. (1999). *The Archaeology of Elam – Formation and Transformation of an Ancient Iranian State.* Cambridge, Cambridge University Press.

Preston, T. (1570). *A Lamentable Tragedy Mixed ful of Pleasant Mirth, Conteyning the Life of Cambises King of Persia.* London, John Allde.

Price, W. (1825). *Journal of the British Embassy to Persia: Embellished with Numerous Views Taken in India and Persia.* London, Kingsbury, Parbury and Allen.

Pritchard, J. (1969). *Ancient Near Eastern Texts relating to the Old Testament.* Princeton University Press.

Radner, K. (2003). 'An Assyrian View on the Medes'. In G. Lanfranchi, M. Roaf and R. Rollinger, eds, *Continuity of Empire (?) Assyria, Media, Persia,* Padua, S.a.r.g.o.n., Editrice e Libreria: 119–30.

Reade, J. (1998). *Assyrian Sculpture.* London, British Museum Press.

Roaf, M. (1983). *Iran* **21**: *Sculptures and Sculptors at Persepolis.* London, British Institute of Persian Studies.

Roaf, M. (1987). 'Checklist of Persepolis Reliefs Not at the Site'. *Iran* **25**: 155–8.

Roaf, M. (1990). *Cultural Atlas of Mesopotamia and the Ancient Near East.* New York and Oxford, Facts on File.

Roaf, M. (1998). 'Persepolitan Echoes in Sasanian Architecture: Did the Sasanians Attempt to Re-create the Achaemenid Empire?' In V. S. Curtis, R. Hillenbrand and J. M. Rogers, eds, *The Art and Archaeology of Ancient Persia: New Light on the Parthian and Sasanian Empires.* London and New York, I. B. Tauris: 1–7.

Roaf, M. (2004). 'Persepolis'. *Reallexikon der Assyiologie und Vorderasiatischen Archäologie Fascicle* **10**: 5–6.

Robinson, B. W. (1982). 'Persian Painting and the National Epic'. *Proceedings of the British Academy* **68**: 275–97.

Root, M. C. (1976). 'The Herzfeld Archive of the Metropolitan Museum of Art'. *Metropolitan Museum Journal* **11**: 119–24.

Root, M. C. (1979). *The King and Kingship in Achaemenid Art: Essays on the Creation of an Iconography of Empire.* Leiden, E. J. Brill.

Root, M. C. (1988). 'Evidence from Persepolis for the dating of Persian and Archaic Greek Coinage'. *Numismatic Chronicle*: 1–12.

Rudenko, S. I., trans. M. W. Thompson. (1970). *Frozen Tombs of Siberia.* London: J. M. Dent.

Russell, J. M. (1999). *The Writing on the Wall – Studies in the Architectural Context of Late Assyrian Palace Inscriptions.* Winona Lake, Eisenbrauns.

Sackville-West, V. (1926). *Passenger to Teheran.* London, Hogarth Press.

Sami, A. (1971). *Pasargadae – The Oldest Imperial Capital of Iran*. Shiraz, Musavi Printing Office.

Sancisi-Weerdenburg, H. (1983). 'Zendan and Ka'bah'. In H.-M. Koch and D. N. Mackenzie, eds, *Kunst, Kultur und Geschichte der Achämenidenzeit und ihr Fortleben* 10. Berlin.

Sancisi-Weerdenburg, H. (1985). 'The Death of Cyrus: Xenophon's Cyropaedia as a Source for Iranian History'. In *Papers in Honour of Mary Boyce*. Leiden, Brill. **24–5**: 459–71.

Sancisi-Weerdenburg, H. (1990). 'Cyrus in Italy: Dante to Machiavelli'. In H. Sancisi-Weerdenburg, ed., *Achaemenid History* 5: *The Roots of the European Tradition*.

Sancisi-Weerdenburg, H. (1993). 'Alexander at Persepolis'. In *Alexander the Great: Myth and Reality*. **21**: 177–88.

Sancisi-Weerdenburg, H. (1994). 'The Orality of Herodotus' *Medikos Logos* or: the Median empire revisited'. In H. Sancisi-Weerdenburg, A. Kuhrt and M. C. Root, eds, *Achaemenid History* 8: *Continuity and Change*.

Sancisi-Weerdenburg, H. (1995). 'Persian Food: Stereotypes and Political Identity'. In J. Wilkins, D. Harvey and M. Dobson, eds, *Food in Antiquity*. Exeter: University of Exeter Press.

Sancisi-Weerdenburg, H. (1998). 'Bâji'. In M. Brosius and A. Kuhrt, eds, *Achaemenid History* 11: *Studies in Persian History: Essays in Memory of David M. Lewis*: 23–34.

Sancisi-Weerdenburg, H. D. and Drijvers, J. W., eds (1991) *Achaemenid History* 7: *Through Travellers' Eyes: European Travellers on the Iranian Monuments*.

Sane, M., ed. (2001/2). *B'iad-e Shiraz*. Shiraz.

Sarraf, M. R. (2003). 'Archaeological Excavations in Tepe Ekbatana (Hamadan) by the Iranian Archaeological Mission between 1983 and 1999'. In G. Lanfranchi, M. Roaf and R. Rollinger, eds, *Continuity of Empire (?) Assyria, Media, Persia*. Padua, s.a.r.g.o.n. Editrice e Libreria: 269–80.

Sarre, F. and Herzfeld, E. (1910). *Iranische Felsreliefs*. Berlin, Ernst Wasmuth.

Sarre, F. and Herzfeld, E. (1923). *Die Kunst des alten Persien*. Berlin, Bruno Cassirer.

Scerrato, U. (1966). 'Excavations at Dahan-i Ghulaman (Seistan Iran) – First Preliminary Report (1962–63).' *East and West* N.S. **16**: 1–2.

Schmidt, E. F. (1953). *Persepolis*. Oriental Institute Publication 68. University of Chicago.

Schmidt, E. F. (1957). *Persepolis II: Contents of the Treasury and Other Discoveries*. University of Chicago.

Schmidt, E. F. (1970). *Persepolis III: The Royal Tombs and Other Discoveries*. University of Chicago.

Schmitt, R. (1981). *Altpersische Siegel-Inschriften*. Vienna, Verlag der Österreichischen Akademie der Wissenschaften.

Schmitt, R. (1991). *The Bisitun inscriptions of Darius the Great: Old Persian Text*. London, SOAS for the Corpus Inscriptionum Iranicarum.

Schmitt, R. (1999). *Beiträge zu Alt persischen Inschriften*. Wiesbaden.

Seidl, U. (1976). 'Ein Relief Dareios I. in Babylon'. *Archäologische Mitteilungen aus Iran* **9**: 125–30.

Sekunda, N. (1988). 'Persian Settlement in Hellespontine Phrygia.' In *Achaemenid History* 3: *Method and Theory*: 175–96.

Sekunda, N. (1991). 'Achaemenid Settlement in Caria, Lycia and Greater Phrygia'. In *Achaemenid History* 6: *Asia Minor and Egypt: Old Cultures in a New Empire*: 83–143.

Sensabaugh, D. A. and Matheson, S. B. (2002). 'Ada Small Moore: Collector and Patron'. *Yale University Art Gallery Bulletin*: 30–49.

Shahbazi, A. S. (1975). *The Irano-Lycian Monuments*. Tehran, Insititute of Achaemenid Research Publications 2.

Shahbazi, S. (1977). 'From Parsa to Taxt-e Jamshid'. *Archäologische Mitteilungen aus Iran* **10**: 197–207.

Shahbazi, S. (1980). 'An Achaemenid Symbol: Farnah (God gives fortune symbolised)'. *Archäologische Mitteilungen aus Iran* **13**: 111–47.

Shahbazi, S. (1999). 'The Oldest Description of Persepolis in Persian'. *Iranian Journal of Archaeology and History* **12**: 1, 2.

Shaked, S. (2004). *Le satrape de Bactriane et son gouverneur – Documents araméens du IVe s. avant notre ère provenant de Bactriane*. Paris, De Boccard.

Shirazi, F., Muhammad Mirza (1896). *Asar-e-'Ajam (Monuments of Persia)*. Bombay.

Shore, A. F. (1997). 'The Demotic Inscription on a Coin of Artaxerxes'. *Numismatic Chronicle* **14**: 5–8.

Silva y Figueroa, G. de (1620). *De Rebus Persarum epistola . . . Spehani exarata ad Antwerp*. Antwerp, Marchionem Bedmari.

Simpson, St J. (2000). 'Rediscovering Past Splendours from Iran: Nineteenth-century Plaster Casts of Sculptures from Persepolis'. *British Museum Magazine* **36**: 28–9.

Sims-Williams, N. (1981). 'The Final Paragraph of the Tomb Inscription of Darius I (DNb, 50–60): The Old Persian Text in the Light of an Aramaic Version'. *Bulletin of the School of Oriental and African Studies* **44**: 1–7.

Smirnov, Y. (1934). *The Akhalgori Treasure*. Tbilisi.

Southgate, M. S. (1978). *Iskendarnamah: A Persian Medieval Alexander-Romance*. New York.

Starr, I. (1990). *Queries to the Sungod: Divination and Politics in Sargonid Assyria*. Helsinki: *State Archives of Assyria* IV.

Stein, M. A. (1940). *Old Routes of Western Iran*. London, John Murray.

Steiner, D. (1994). *The Tyrant's Writ – Myth and Images of Writing in Ancient Greece*. Princeton, Princeton University Press.

Stern, E. (1982). *Material Culture of the Land of the Bible in the Persian Period 538–332 B.C.* Jerusalem and Warminster, Aris and Phillips / Israel Exploration Society.

Stevenson, R. B. (1997). *Persica: Greek Writing about Persia in the Fourth Century BC*. Edinburgh, Scottish Academic Press.

Stolper, M. (1985). *Entrepreneurs and Empire: The Murašu Archive, the Murašu Firm, and Persian Rule in Babylonia*. Istanbul, Nederlands Historisch-Archaeologisch Instituut te Istanbul.

Stolper, M. (1987). 'Belšuru the satrap'. In Rochberg-Halton, ed., *Language, Literature and History: Philological and Historical Studies presented to Erica Reiner*. New Haven: 389–402.

Stolper, M. (1988). 'Some Ghost Facts from Achaemenid Babylonian Texts'. *Journal of Hellenic Studies* **108**: 197–8.

Stolper, M. (1994). 'Mesopotamia, 482–330 B.C.' In D. M. Lewis, J. Boardman, S. Hornblower and M. Ostwald, eds, *CAH* VI: *The Fourth Century B.C.*: 234–60.

Stolper, M. (1995). 'The Babylonian enterprise of Belerys'. In P. Briant, ed., *Dans les pas des Dix-Mille. Peuples et pays du Proche-Orient vus par un Grec. Pallas* **43**: 217–38.

Stolze, F., Andreas, F. C. and Nöldeke, T. (1882). *Persepolis: Die achaemenidischen und sasanidischen Denkmäler und Inschriften von Persepolis, Istakhr, Pasargadae . . .* Berlin, Verlag von A. Asher and Co.

Stoneman, R. (1994). *Legends of Alexander the Great*. London, J. M. Dent.

Streck (1916). *Assurbanipal und die letzten assyrischen Könige bis zum Untergange Ninivehs*. Leipzig, J. C. Hinrichs.

Stronach, D. (1974). 'La statue de Darius découverte à Suse'. *Cahiers de la Délégation Archéologique Française en Iran* **4**: 61–72.

Stronach, D. (1978). *Pasargadae*. Oxford, Clarendon Press.

Stronach, D. (1990). 'On the Genesis of the Old Persian Cuneiform Script'. In F. Vallat, ed., *Contribution à l'histoire de l'Iran: Mélanges offerts à Jean Perrot*. Paris, Éditions Recherches sur les civilisations.

Sumner, W. M. (1986). 'Achaemenid Settlement in the Persepolis Plain'. *American Journal of Archaeology* **90**: 3–31.

Sumner, W. M. (1988). 'Maljan, Tall-e (Anšan)'. *Reallexikon der Assyriologie* **7**: 306–20.

Sumner, W. M. (1994). 'Archaeological Measures of Cultural Continuity and the Arrival of the Persians in Fars'. In H. Sancisi-Weerdenburg, A. Kuhrt and M. C. Root, eds, *Achaemenid History* 8: *Continuity and Change*: 97–105.

Tadmor, H. (1994). *The Inscriptions of Tiglath-Pileser III, King of Assyria*. Jerusalem, Israel Academy of Sciences and Humanities.

Texier, C. (1842–52). *Description de l'Arménie, la Perse et la Mesopotamie*. Paris, Ministre de l'interieur et de l'instruction publique.

Tilia, A. B. (1972). *Studies and Restorations at Persepolis and Other Sites of Fars:* I. Rome.

Tilia, A. B. (1978). *Studies and Restorations at Persepolis and Sites of Fars:* II. Rome.

Toker, A. and Öztürk, J. (1992). *Museum of Anatolian Civilizations, Metal Vessels*. Ankara, Turkish Republic Ministry of Culture General Directorate of Monuments and Museums.

Trümpelmann, L. (1967). 'Zur Entstehungsgeschichte des Monumentes Darius I von Bisitun und zur Datierung der Einführung des altpersischen Schrift.' *Archäologischer Anzeiger* **82**: 281–98.

Tuplin, C. (1989). 'The Coinage of Aryandes'.

Tuplin, C. (1998). 'The Seasonal Migration of Achaemenid Kings: A Report on Old and New Evidence'. In M. Brosius and A. Kuhrt, eds, *Achaemenid History* 11: *Studies in Persian History: Essays in Memory of David M. Lewis*.

van der Spek, R. (2003). 'Alexander in Babylon'. In W. Henkelman and A. Kuhrt, eds, *Achaemenid History* 13: *A Persian Perspective: Essays in Memory of Helene Sancisi-Weerdenburg*.

Vasileva, N. E. (1994). 'About the History of Sir Robert Ker Porter's Album with His Sketches of Achaemenid and Sassanian Monuments'. *Archäologische Mitteilungen aus Iran* 7: 339–48.

Vickers, M. (1991). 'The Views of Persepolis by William Marshall and Wenceslaus Hollar in Sir Thomas Herbert's Travels'. In H. Sancisi-Weerdenburg and J. W. Drijvers, eds, *Achaemenid History* 7: *Through Travellers' Eyes: European Travellers on the Iranian Monuments*: 59–69.

Vidal, G. (1993). *Creation*. London, Abacus.

Walker, C. B. F. (1997). 'Achaemenid Chronology and the Babylonian Sources'. In J. Curtis, ed., *Mesopotamia and Iran in the Persian Period: Conquest and Imperialism 539–331 BC*. London, British Museum Press.

Wang, H. (1999). *Handbook to the Stein Collections in the UK*. London, British Museum Occasional Papers.

Whitcomb, D. (1979). 'The City of Istakhr and the Marvdasht Plain'. *Archäologische Mitteilungen aus Iran, Ergänzungsband*: 363–70.

Whitcomb, D. (1985). *Before the Roses and Nightingales: Excavations at Qasr-i Abu Nasr, Old Shiraz*. New York, Metropolitan Museum of Art.

White and Crawford, S. (1996). 'Has *Esther* been found at Qumran? *4Q Proto-Esther* and the *Esther* corpus'. In *Revue de Qumran* 17: 307-25.

Wiesehöfer, J. (1996). *Ancient Persia from 550 BC to 650 AD*. London and New York, I. B. Tauris.

Yarshater, E. (1971). 'Were the Sasanians Heirs to the Achaemenids?' In *La Persia nel Medioevo*. Rome, Accademia Nazionale dei Lincei; Quaderno **160**: 517–33.

PICTURE CREDITS

INDEX